D1799835

Joel Rathus
JAPAN, CHINA AND NETWORKED REGIONALISM IN EAST ASIA

Claudia Tazreiter and Siew Yean Tham (*editors*)
GLOBALIZATION AND SOCIAL TRANSFORMATION IN THE ASIA-PACIFIC
The Australian and Malaysian Experience

Sow Keat Tok
MANAGING CHINA'S SOVEREIGNTY IN HONG KONG AND TAIWAN

William Tow and Rikki Kersten (*editors*)
BILATERAL PERSPECTIVES ON REGIONAL SECURITY
Australia, Japan and the Asia-Pacific Region

Barry Wain
MALAYSIAN MAVERICK
Mahathir Mohamad in Turbulent Times

Mikael Weissmann
THE EAST ASIAN PEACE
Conflict Prevention and Informal Peacebuilding

Robert G. Wirsing and Ehsan Ahrari (*editors*)
FIXING FRACTURED NATIONS
The Challenge of Ethnic Separatism in the Asia-Pacific

Robert G. Wirsing, Christopher Jasparro and Daniel C. Stoll
INTERNATIONAL CONFLICT OVER WATER RESOURCES IN HIMALAYAN ASIA

Critical Studies of the Asia Pacific Series
Series Standing Order ISBN 978–0–230–22896–2 (Hardback)
978–0–230–22897–9 (Paperback)
(*outside North America only*)

You can receive future titles in this series as they are published by placing a standing order. Please contact your bookseller or, in case of difficulty, write to us at the address below with your name and address, the title of the series and the ISBNs quoted above.

Customer Services Department, Macmillan Distribution Ltd, Houndmills, Basingstoke, Hampshire RG21 6XS, England

---

The Protection and Promotion of Human Security in East Asia

Brendan Howe
Department Chair and Professor, Ewha Womans University, South Korea

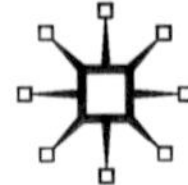

First published 2013 by
PALGRAVE MACMILLAN

Palgrave Macmillan in the UK is an imprint of Macmillan Publishers Limited, registered in England, company number 785998, of Houndmills, Basingstoke, Hampshire RG21 6XS.

Palgrave Macmillan in the US is a division of St Martin's Press LLC, 175 Fifth Avenue, New York, NY10010.

Palgrave Macmillan is the global academic imprint of the above companies and has companies and representatives throughout the world.

Palgrave® and Macmillan® are registered trademarks in the United States, the United Kingdom, Europe and other countries.

ISBN 978–1–137–29364–0

This book is printed on paper suitable for recycling and made from fully managed and sustained forest sources. Logging, pulping and manufacturing processes are expected to conform to the environmental regulations of the country of origin.

A catalogue record for this book is available from the British Library.

A catalog record for this book is available from the Library of Congress.

Typeset by MPS Limited, Chennai, India.

For my dear wife, Duckhee Sung

Contents

List of Figures

List of Tables

Acknowledgments

Research for this volume was supported by the World Class University (WCU) program through the National Research Foundation (NRF) of Korea funded by the Ministry of Education, Science and Technology (MEST Grant Number: R32-20077) and by an NRF grant on Human Security (MEST No. B00017). The author is very grateful for the support provided by his research assistant, Suyoun Jang, and for the editorial and proof-reading assistance provided by Hana Lee and Jason Park.

Part I
Operationalizing Human Security in East Asia

1

Human Security: Challenges and Opportunities in East Asia

Introduction

East Asia is an extremely successful region of development in terms of both economic growth, and stable and secure governance. A 2011 study by the Asian Development Bank (ADB), on realizing the Asian Century, found that if Asia continues to follow its recent trajectory, by 2050 its per capita income could rise six-fold in purchasing power parity (PPP) terms to reach contemporary European levels, making some 3 billion additional Asians affluent by current standards. 'By nearly doubling its share of global gross domestic product (GDP) to 52 per cent by 2050, Asia would regain the dominant economic position it held some 300 years ago, before the industrial revolution' (ADB, 2011, p. 3). Although many countries in East Asia still fall short of the democratic ideal and concerns persist regarding human rights, nevertheless, the idea that the 21st century will be one of Asian dominance and leadership owes much to the success stories of the Northeast and Southeast Asian sub-regions. Indeed under President Barack Obama, the United States, the current global leader, has paid tribute to the rise of the region. In 2009, the first Obama administration dispatched Secretary of State Hillary Clinton to East Asia as her first official foreign policy tour, and in 2012, on the cusp of the second administration, a 'pivot' toward the region was announced (later the emphasis was placed on the concept of a 'strategic rebalancing' toward East Asia).

Yet although at an aggregate or national level many of the states of East Asia have achieved startling success and, by the same measurements, even the less successful appear to be making remarkable progress, not all have benefited from the region's development. Many of the most vulnerable

---

This volume will use the terminology East Asia to refer to the sub-regions of Northeast Asia and Southeast Asia, including the states and territories of China, Korea, Japan, Hong Kong, Taiwan, Brunei, Cambodia, Indonesia, Laos, Malaysia, Myanmar, the Philippines, Singapore, Thailand, Timor-Leste, and Vietnam.

sections of East Asian populations still face tremendous challenges in their daily lives, have yet to enjoy many of the rewards of the Asian Century, and may even be further imperiled as a result of the forces of development. This volume critically assesses measurements of success in East Asian development and governance from a human-centered perspective. This involves a major re-evaluation of accepted accounts of domestic governance and international relations in East Asia from both a comparative and interdisciplinary viewpoint.

For the past two decades, the concept of human security has been promoted as a significant extension of traditional security studies as well as a field of development and governance prescription. While human security has been present and visible in academic and practitioner discourse, it is yet, however, truly to capture the imagination of specialists. Partly this is a result of the belligerent direction global politics has taken in the new millennium. Partly, however, it results from conceptual inadequacies internal to the notion itself. This book addresses the disconnect between human security as a problem-solving, policy framework and the epistemological, ontological and methodological debates favored by critical security scholars (Newman, 2010, p. 77). It does so by combining a rigorous epistemological analysis of the existing discourse with detailed analysis of challenging case studies and rational policy prescription.

The rise of East Asia and development limitations

The three largest economies of East Asia, Japan, the People's Republic of China (PRC), and South Korea, have all experienced growth of such magnitude and under such difficult conditions as not only to have attracted the tag of East Asian economic 'miracles', but also to be seen as development models to be emulated. Japan was the lead goose of the 'flying geese model' of development; China has generated interest in a Beijing consensus rather than the Washington consensus so severely undermined by the global financial crisis of 2007–08; and even South Korea, a medium-ranked power surrounded by giants, has provided leadership through the soft power of the *Hallyu* or Korean Wave, as well as its post-conflict 'miracle on the Han river' development success story. The other Asian 'tiger economies', Hong Kong, Taiwan, and Singapore, have contributed to this global perception of East Asian success, and despite the Asian financial crisis of 1997, the Southeast Asian 'tiger cubs', Indonesia, Malaysia, Thailand, and the Philippines, are also, on the whole, now making economic headlines for the right reasons, as is Vietnam.

In terms of national security, although as a result of territorial disputes and the flashpoints of the Korean Peninsula and the Taiwan Straits, the region is sometimes viewed as the most dangerous or conflictual on the planet (Calder, 2001, p. 106), again, remarkable progress has been made.

A security regime that is able to deal with so many conflictual forces, face countless skirmishes and instances of saber-rattling, and yet for more than three decades (since the 1978 Vietnamese invasion of Cambodia) prevent the outbreak of serious hostilities between social and political entities harboring historical grudges toward one another may be considered durable indeed. With the possible exception of the two Chinas, and the two Koreas, states in the region no longer pose an existential threat to each other. All are relatively secure in the knowledge that the geopolitical codes (the practical output of geopolitical reasoning) of states in the region reflect a rational imperative to come to some sort of accommodation with one another in order to best deal with the shared challenges they face. States in Northeast Asia (where there has been no instance of major interstate war for 60 years since the armistice suspending the Korean War in 1953) appear to have reached a rational, socially constructed peace based on mutual benefit, while those in Southeast Asia have evolved into an Association of Southeast Asian Nations (ASEAN) community where non-intervention, tolerance, and mutual respect have formed international governance norms. In both sub-regions, the primacy of economic development is felt over the pressing need to arm for self-defense.

These development and security success stories do not, however, tell the whole story of the region. First, although East Asia as a whole has experienced the largest aggregate growth of any region, some states in East Asia and in particular certain regions within some of these states have far less positive stories to tell. Burma/Myanmar, Lao People's Democratic Republic (Lao PDR), Timor-Leste, and North Korea rank among the worst states in the world in terms of both development performance and the measurements of human security. Cambodia fares only slightly better. Indonesia, the Philippines, and Thailand all have significant ongoing sub-state internal conflicts (Aceh and West Papua, Muslim Mindanao, and the southern provinces, respectively). The ADB notes that Asia's leaders will have to manage multiple risks and challenges, particularly increasing inequality within countries, which could undermine social cohesion and stability; rising income disparities across countries, which could destabilize the region; and poor governance and weak institutional capacity (ADB, 2011, p. 4).

The predominant regional foci on the primacy of the state in both domestic and international governance, and the prioritization of national economic growth and national security over other considerations of human development and human security, overlook some of the negative impacts of related policies, and open regional governments to internal and external criticism and pressures. Furthermore, the failure of domestic and international governance to provide safe havens free from fear and want could have spillover consequences for regional security. Indeed contemporary security considerations are best viewed as a broad spectrum or continuum of interrelated issues and actors. Insecure individuals and groups can turn to illegitimate endeavors as transnational criminals, pirates, or terrorists. Governments can turn to aggressive foreign policies and wars of diversion in order to unite their fractious populations, and unscrupulous demagogues can whip up nationalist sentiment and xenophobia.

Research framework

The research project deals primarily with areas closely related to the central concepts of human security and human development in East Asia. In particular, it focuses on case studies where governance challenges to the two disciplines overlap and policy prescription for international actors when engaging with these challenging case studies. This volume considers the threats to human security in East Asian states, but also the roles that East Asian actors can play and have been playing in protecting and promoting human security in post-conflict, conflictual, or pre-conflict (fragile or failing) states in the region. While taking into account ways in which Asian concepts of governance at both the internal and international levels can differ from Western models, it assumes that, nevertheless, Asia is not untouched by the growing international normative consensus that more needs to be done to protect individuals and groups beyond the realm of traditional state-centric security considerations.

The primary unifying theme, therefore, is a concept of near-universal principles that have coalesced in support of 'objective' but at the same time non-traditional measurements of governance and development success. The book explores the responsibilities owed by those who govern to the most vulnerable of those who are governed, even among East Asian states traditionally resistant to such perspectives – a responsibility to provide for (or at least to provide the conditions that allow for/facilitate human security), not just to protect, regardless of nationality. A secondary, closely related theme considers the intricate relationships between human security and the national security, development, and human rights spheres of discourse, as well as addressing challenges and policy prescriptions. The complexities of these relationships are explored through the detailed analysis of East Asian case studies wherein significant obstacles toward the protection and promotion of human security persist.

Finally, this volume considers whether, under certain conditions, Asian actors and approaches may be able to secure, in terms of human security, better results than could be achieved through extra-regional intervention. As a growing area of prioritization in development and security theory and practice, human security is an avenue through which the impact of the newly emerging actors and donors in rising Asia can be particularly beneficial. New actors and donors have greater theoretical and practical flexibility in terms of resource allocation prioritization. The limitations of these actors and the East Asian operating environment are readily acknowledged, and in some cases rising Asia could contribute to greater human security challenges, but there are also, at the very least, additional opportunities. The tertiary theme, therefore, is analysis of how 'same same but different' not only best describes East Asian international development assistance practices but also how these may hold a comparative advantage or additional benefit for dealing with the challenges of governance and development in the region. In sum, this research provides an overview of the threats to human security in Asia, but from a uniquely Asian perspective.

Chapter outline

The first part of the book expands on the interaction between the theory and practice of human security as it impacts on the East Asian region. Chapter 2 examines the emergence of human security within the wider security studies literature, homes in on debates about human security, and draws important parallels between development and human security. It applies a rigorous theoretical analysis of human security, situating it firmly within the paradigmatic debates and traditions of security, development, and human rights studies. It identifies how, logically, governance policy prescription flowing from a consideration of human security priorities should be reflected not only in the current international preoccupation with a responsibility to protect (R2P) but also in a responsibility to provide/facilitate. In doing so, it moves beyond the 'freedom from fear' area, which has flourished with the revival of ideas of 'just war' intervention, toward the relatively neglected 'freedom from want' (Chandler, 2008, p. 433). While adopting a normative approach, the emphasis is on entitlement rights centered on human survival rather than on the political rights of human empowerment. It is argued that such an approach is demanded by both logical and pragmatic considerations. This conceptualization generates a fresh way forward for human security studies and good governance policy prescription.

Although perhaps no other region on earth is as culturally and socio-economically diverse, opposition to Western liberal or universal cosmopolitan values emanating from East Asia has tended to be identified collectively as the challenge of 'Asian' values' (Khong, 1997). Chapter 3 explores internal and external pressures to conform to international good governance norms in the region, noting that although Asian exceptionalism survives in the constitutive documents of regional international organizations, and in many of the foreign policy priorities of Asian states, there is something like a global overlapping consensus emerging regarding the concept of individual human entitlement rights. These foundational rights are best summed up by the concepts of freedom from want and freedom from fear. As these may be seen as universal entitlement rights, they impose concurrent obligations on all national and local governments. The growing acceptance within the region of these principles is supported not only by normative convergence but also by a realization that practicing good governance, from the perspective of maximizing the well-being of the most vulnerable of those who are governed, is the rational course to follow from a national security perspective.

The second part of the book explores challenging case studies of East Asian governance. Four of the case studies involve those states in the region which consistently rank lowest according to measurements of human security and development. North Korea, the People's Democratic Republic of Laos (Lao PDR), Burma/Myanmar, and East Timor are among the most challenged in these categories not only in regional terms but even in global league tables. The fifth case study concerns Muslim Mindanao in the Philippines, site of the region's oldest conflict, and one of the most intractable on earth. Each of these case studies, however, also serves to highlight particular conceptual or procedural obstacles to the protection of and provision for human security, and expands on the complexities of the relationships between human security and the national security, development, and human rights spheres.

Chapter 4 examines the causes and consequences of domestic and international policy failures in the Democratic People's Republic of Korea (DPRK) through the lens of human security. Herein the international security continuum introduced above is brought sharply into focus, as on the Korean Peninsula 'new' human-centered approaches are intimately related to 'old' state-centric considerations, non-traditional security (NTS) issues have the potential to become traditional security threats, and issues of human security can morph into ones of pressing concern for the survival of states themselves or the peace and security of the region, or even the globe. The North Korean challenging case study represents the most striking example of the relationship between traditional and NTS considerations. Normative obligations and rational imperatives highlight the necessity of the national government, aid agencies, donor states, and the international community (strategic partners and competitors) to address the insecurity of the citizens of North Korea, and the chapter concludes with a number of possible policy prescriptions.

Chapter 5 continues the evaluation of spillover between the realms of traditional and NTS analysis and practice in the conflict between the Government of the Republic of the Philippines (GRP) and various armed groups claiming to represent the Muslim population of the southern island grouping of Mindanao. This chapter, however, further deconstructs the negative and counterproductive impact of state-centric security and development foci while also broadening the analysis of human security contributions to include conflict drivers from the arena of human development. In other words, analysis of the spillover between traditional and NTS perspectives is expanded along both the vertical and horizontal axes. The findings of the case study are that a focus on zero-sum games and positional negotiations by both sides, combined with a top-down aggregate approach toward what are seen as unitary rational entities, rather than concentrating on basic human needs (BHN) and improving the lot of the least well off, are substantially to blame for the impasse. There is hope, however, that the latest peace process has learned the lessons of previous failures and is looking to establish a holistic transformational program.

Laos faces the classic post-conflict society double jeopardy of insecurity and underdevelopment. This challenging case study is perhaps the clearest example of the negative impact conflict and its aftermath can have upon development and also the horrific toll underdevelopment can exact on the lives of the most vulnerable. It demonstrates not only the shortcomings of national and international institutions when providing good governance but also the perils of focusing on top-down governance, aggregate development measurements, and focusing on efficiency rather than providing safe havens. Chapter 6 thus demonstrates the necessity of a combined focus on freedom from fear (protection of persons) and freedom from want (provision of human needs) in a structured format, prescribing policies that prioritize the provision of safe havens for the most vulnerable sections of society (Krause, 2004). This chapter, however, further challenges the simplistic assumption of human development and human security as mutually reinforcing processes. Human security in the Lao PDR is additionally threatened by the forces of development. Consequently, a purely development-focused approach is unlikely to bolster human security, whereas focusing exclusively on protecting the population of around 6.5 million will do little to fulfill human needs.

In Chapter 7 Burma/Myanmar is described as the 'pre-eminent example of a post-colonial state subsumed in what development analysis describes as a "conflict trap"' (Smith, 2007, p. 3). Facing diverse challenges, including ethnic insurgencies and remnants of colonial experience, successive governments have adopted state-centric national security policies with an emphasis on national sovereignty, territorial integrity, and the national unity of diverse ethnic nationalities (Tin, 1998, p. 392). Alternative conceptions of security have been rejected or viewed as a threat by the government. Moreover, because the country has primarily been ruled by a military junta seeking regime survival, the distinction between the security interests of state, regime, and military have been blurred. Consequently, the human security of the most vulnerable sections of society in Myanmar has been ignored, sacrificed, or directly threatened. This policy has not, however, paid dividends for the government. Hence, in order to secure transformation of the conflictual relationship between those who govern and those who are governed, rather than just conflict management or resolution, this case study advocates a shift in focus to providing safe havens for the most vulnerable sections of society. In addition, while contrasting the impact of the human security policies of Canada and Japan upon the case study, the chapter concludes that this conflict may finally be ripe for resolution, supported by international assistance applying a combined approach.

The final challenging case study considers, in Chapter 8, international humanitarian state-building efforts in Timor-Leste. When the international community finally came to the assistance of the people of Timor-Leste, it was with a mandate to provide havens safe from fear for a traumatized population in a devastated land. Starting almost from scratch, the UN embarked on its most radical state-building exercise to date (Benzing, 2005, p. 297). Timor-Leste is widely regarded as a benchmark for UN peacekeeping efforts, and for progress along narrow human security dimensions, but Timor-Leste continues to suffer from serious challenges in the field of freedom from want. In part these ongoing problems are similar to those found in many conflict-affected states. Other problematic legacies, however, are not conflict-related but apply rather to colonial overhangs from periods of Portuguese and Indonesian governance, and even from the UN administration period, including linguistic, economic, and demographic structural impediments, food insecurity, inflationary pressures, and local market distortion. Even if a narrow human security focus was initially dictated by pragmatism, this case study concludes that it is time to refocus efforts on the broader aspects of human security and also on the distribution of development benefits to the most vulnerable sections of society.

The third part of the book looks at East Asian contributions to human security in theory and in practice. The first two chapters of this part evaluate the contributions of Asia's only two members of the Organisation for Economic Co-operation and Development, Development Assistance Committee (OECD DAC): Japan and South Korea. The final and concluding chapter briefly addresses implications of the emergence of new regional actors in the field of human security with an emphasis on China and ASEAN. At the same time it acknowledges limitations and even additional challenges posed by the rising actors. This section brings into practical focus, therefore, the tertiary theme of East Asian international development assistance practices and the potential for a comparative advantage or additional benefit when dealing with the challenges of governance and development in the region.

Japan has followed a mixture of proactive and reactive policies toward partners in East Asia. Constrained by its pacifist constitution and lingering animosity in the region over Japan's historic role, planners have looked to NTS policies to further Japanese interests. Although widely criticized for its tied aid policies, Chapter 9 contends that nevertheless significant collateral benefit in terms of regional development and human security has accrued as a by-product of Japanese strategic positioning. Japan has been at the forefront of regional official development assistance (ODA) missions, has given considerable impetus to the comprehensive and human security agendas, and has served as a major contributor to international aid and relief organizations. Japanese aid and human security initiatives may well be in part motivated by national interest, but, nevertheless, other peoples in the region have benefited significantly from their pursuance, and in particular from Japanese commitment to them precisely because of the national interest involved.

Chapter 10 examines how, through the 'miracle on the Han river', South Korea grew from a devastated shell of a state, one of the poorest in the world, let alone the region, and heavily dependent itself on ODA for 50 years (1945–95), to become the newest member of the OECD DAC, and host of both the G20 and the High Level Forum on Aid Effectiveness. In accordance with its new DAC responsibilities, South Korea is looking to expand dramatically its ODA budget and also hosts many fact-finding missions and students from small and medium-sized regional economies who see in the Republic of Korea a role model more closely analogous to their own conditions and experiences. South Korea has been criticized not only for its relatively low level of ODA as a proportion of GDP but also for high levels of tied aid. Nevertheless, as a new emerging donor of ODA, South Korea symbolizes three things: (1) a rapid rise from one of the poorest countries in the world to the 13th largest economy – a message of hope to other developing countries; (2) rapid economic development accompanied by democratization; and (3) these milestones were achieved in the context of insecurity. Furthermore, South Korea is unique among donors in not suffering from any neo-imperial baggage.

Chapter 11 briefly explores the impact and potential of China and ASEAN's newly emerging and non-traditional approaches to governance and human security in the region. It also concludes the project with consideration of the future for the protection and promotion of human security in East Asia. China has been increasingly active in the field of ODA, particularly in Africa and Southeast Asia. In the latter region Beijing's responsible policies during the Asian financial crisis were lauded, and have in turn been followed by what amounts to a 'charm offensive' toward countries in Southeast Asia. China has been criticized for assistance policies often seen as targeted to secure access to resources or to shore up diplomatic support against Taiwan. The rise of China also poses some additional regional human security challenges. China is in a unique position, however, of being trusted by regimes labeled as 'rogue' by the West (such as Myanmar and North Korea), and thus its humanitarian assistance is less likely to be viewed as external interference in sovereign states.

Meanwhile, although the 'ASEAN Way' involves mutual respect for the right of every state to lead its national existence free from external interference, subversion, or coercion, in reaction to international normative developments supportive of the provision of safe havens, ASEAN has begun to shift its focus. The new ASEAN 'political and security community' addresses the unique role that could be played by a regional organization in the provision of multilateral or collective human security. As all states in the region internalize the norms of the overlapping consensus on human security, and begin to recognize the contributions good human-centered governance can make to traditional security considerations, it is hoped that safe havens can be provided for all the region's vulnerable populations.

Conclusion

This book aims to bridge divides between theoretical and practical considerations of human security and good governance, between human- and state-centered concepts of security and development, and between East Asian and cosmopolitan perspectives. It does so through a detailed epistemological evaluation of the contemporary discourse and logical and rational implications for good governance practices. It is strongly grounded in the empirical evaluation of the region's five most serious challenging case studies. It also, however, takes a uniquely East Asian perspective when it comes to policy prescription and prediction, analyzing not only the extent to which regional actors are coming to conform to an overlapping consensus on human security and good governance norms but also what additional contributions they can make in furthering the protection and promotion of human security in the region.

References

Asian Development Bank (ADB) (2011) *Asia 2050: Realizing the Asian Century,* http://www.adb.org/sites/default/files/asia2050-executive-summary.pdf.

Benzing, M. (2005) 'Midwifing a New State: The United Nations in East Timor' in A. Bogdandy and R. Wolfrum (eds), *Max Planck Yearbook of United Nations Law*, 9, 295–372 (Leiden: Brill).

Calder, K. (2001) 'The New Face of Northeast Asia', *Foreign Affairs*, 80(1), 106–22.

Chandler, D. (2008) 'Review Essay: Human Security: The Dog that Didn't Bark', *Security Dialogue*, 39(4), 427–38.

Khong, C. O. (1997) 'Asian Values: The Debate Revisited', in T. Inoguchi and E. Newman (eds), *'Asian Values' and Democracy in Asia: Proceedings of the First Shizuoka Asia-Pacific Forum* (Tokyo: UN University Press) archive.unu.edu/unupress/asian-values.html.

Krause, K. (2004) 'The Key to a Powerful Agenda, if Properly Delimited', *Security Dialogue*, 35(3), 367–8.

Newman, E. (2010) 'Critical Human Security Studies', *Review of International Studies*, 36(1), 77–94.

Smith, M. (2007) 'State of Strife: The Dynamics of Ethnic Conflict in Burma', *Policy Studies*, 36 (Washington: East-West Center).

Tin, M. M. T. (1998) 'Myanmar: Preoccupation with Regime Survival, National Unity, and Stability' in M. Alagappa (ed.), *Asian Security Practice: Material and Ideational Influences* (Stanford: Stanford University Press).

2
Human Security and Good Governance

Introduction

We expect those who govern to do so in the interests of the governed, usefully providing services that can best or perhaps only be achieved through collective action. According to the Report of the Commission on Global Governance, 'governance is the sum of the many ways individuals and institutions, public and private, manage their common affairs' (CGG, 1995, p. 2). It is an ongoing and evolutionary process which looks to reconcile conflicting interests in order to protect the weak, through the rule of law, from unjust exploitation, and introduce security for all. Governance is also a process through which collective good and goods (including security) are generated, or their production facilitated, so that all are better off than they would be acting individually. Thus, governance implies a concern by those who govern with both the security and development, or provision/facilitation of BHN, of those who are governed. In the contemporary, academic and professional discourse steps to eradicate poverty, particularly in conflict affected areas, have assumed an increasing prominence.

Domestically, governance is primarily carried out by instruments of the state – that is to say the government and related institutions. Internationally, governance implies not only global attempts to govern in the absence of world government, dealing with those issues which transcend national boundaries, but also a concern with what can be done by international actors when domestic governance fails. Not only are some states unwilling or unable to provide the degree of governance necessary to protect their people and/or to provide collective goods for them, but at times either through neglect or intent states can be sources of insecurity and underdevelopment

---

This chapter draws on previous work with Ian Holliday (2011) published as 'Human Security: A Global Responsibility to Protect and Provide', *Korean Journal of Defense Analysis*, 23(1), 73–92.

for their citizens. The question then becomes what can be done on the international stage to provide for, or provide the conditions that facilitate the supply of, BHN, as well as protect individual human beings? 'One World' is both an aspiration and, increasingly, a recognition of reality. Global governance is incrementally being provided by international organizations and institutions.

Nisha Mukherjee and Jonathan Krieckhaus (2012, pp. 120–750) have examined the phenomenon of globalization including such diverse processes as the greater mobility of capital, goods, and services, as well as increasing diffusion of ideas, technology, and norms and the effect of economic, social, and political global integration on human well-being. They find that, on balance, all three forms of globalization positively affect well-being. Indeed, the post-Cold War world has seen a dramatic shift from focusing upon external threats to the state to focusing upon direct and indirect violence upon individuals within the state. Anticipated post-Cold War peace dividends and supposed universal economic benefits from globalization have not, however, materialized, with the number of the world's population exposed to extreme poverty persisting in spite of pockets of rapid economic development in East Asia.

Good governance means different things to different people depending on their disciplinary, cultural, and organizational background. Indeed, it is an essentially contested concept with no single and exhaustive definition, nor a delimitation of its scope, that commands universal acceptance. From an international institutional perspective on governance derived from major international donor frameworks, good governance refers to efficiency in the provision of services and economic competitiveness, comparing ineffective economies or political bodies with viable economies and political bodies (Agere, 2000, p. 1). For instance, historically, the International Monetary Fund's (IMF) main focus has been on encouraging countries 'to correct macroeconomic imbalances, reduce inflation, and undertake key trade, exchange, and other market reforms needed to improve efficiency and support sustained economic growth' (IMF, 1997). Likewise, the World Bank has emphasized that overall economic growth is crucial for generating opportunity, and that market reforms can be central in expanding opportunities for poor people. Although the institutions further notes that 'access to market opportunities and to public sector services is often strongly influenced by state and social institutions, which must be responsive and accountable to poor people' (World Bank, 2000, p. 7).

Contemporary discourse focuses increasingly on the latter part of this policy statement, and therefore as much on the political and administrative as the economic, looking at the degree of accountability of public institutions. The way in which instruments of public administration operate, provide or restrict information, deliver services in an equitable or discriminatory manner, and provide or prevent opportunities for peoples' voices in the policy-making debate has a direct impact on the way citizens perceive the degree of legitimacy of the system (UN Secretary-General, 2007, p. 8). The terms 'governance' and 'good governance' are also being used increasingly in development literature, with bad governance regarded as one of the root causes of all evil within our societies, and major donors and international financial institutions basing their aid and loans on the condition that reforms ensuring 'good governance' are undertaken (UNESCAP, 2012). Thus, for the United Nations Development Programme (UNDP), good governance is participatory, transparent and accountable as well as effective and equitable, while also promoting the rule of law (UNDP, 1997, Ch. 1).

There are, however, a number of problems even with this modified emphasis. All the above policy prescriptions are essentially top-down in nature. The international community (however it is defined or configured) prescribes concepts of good governance for national governments. In response, national governments implement pro-growth economic policies, and, if they wish to receive international support, open up their public administrative practices. The practical implications of such policies are (1) that the measurement of success is of a macro or aggregate nature – for example whether a particular policy promotes an increase in GDP per capita, and may therefore overlook the impact of policies on the extreme poor, or even increase path dependency; (2) that exogenous values and primarily Western standards are used in all evaluations, over-riding cultural relativity concerns; and (3) that political rights such as those associated with democracy and the rule of law are seen to trump other entitlement rights. All of these, however, are subject to challenges if we revert to basics and ask in whose interest should governance primarily function? This volume answers that 'good governance', as opposed to merely efficient governance, is that set of policy prescriptions and practices which prioritizes the interests of the most vulnerable sections of society; that the most foundational interests of these individuals can be found in entitlement rights covered by the newly emerging paradigms of human security and human development; and that particular attention must be paid to the confluence of these two sets of concerns in conflict affected and environmentally challenged states.

In many cases, East Asian countries have prioritized economic development over social or political development. While this econophoria, whereby the solution of all society's ills is sought through economic development has contributed to remarkable patterns of economic growth, it has also seen the rise in importance of challenges to human security in both absolute and relative terms (Buzan and Segal, 1998, p. 107). In 2008, controversies over national and international responses to May's devastating cyclone in Burma/Myanmar[1] and Chinese rule in Tibet (with violent demonstrations in Tibet itself, in the surrounding region and, as a result of the Olympic torch relay, across the globe), as well as severe civil unrest in Thailand, the

Philippines, and Malaysia, gave an immediacy and urgency to the debate on the clash between state prerogatives, human rights, and the duties of the international community in particular with reference to the East Asian region. The year 2009 saw an ongoing concern with transnational human security issues in the region, including criticism of Chinese repatriation of North Korean refugees and Thai repatriation of ethnic Hmong from Laos. Many victims of the cyclone in Myanmar and also the earthquake which devastated parts of China's Sichuan province in the same month still find themselves victimized a second time by the insufficient responses of regimes that seem unable or unwilling to provide for them (BBC, 2009).

The year 2010 saw a resurgent specter of famine in North Korea, and the spillover of human insecurity in that country into the international arena. In the same year, floods in Pakistan highlighted the interrelated nature of human security and development. The crisis revealed the potentially devastating impact of natural catastrophes upon states in the region that possess insufficient resources to prevent further suffering, to go to the aid of those affected, or to facilitate the distribution of international assistance. It also demonstrated how security considerations can undermine aid efforts as Taliban sources issue threats against international aid agency workers, and how hardship can undermine security with increasing discontent and criticism of domestic and international aid efforts among those worst hit by the catastrophe. Finally, it raised questions concerning the role of international state and non-state entities when crises occur in strategically important but politically sensitive vulnerable states. Meanwhile, members of the international community are increasingly asserting a right to intervene to protect the human security of individuals against the prerogatives of states.

This volume focuses on the duties owed by those who govern to provide freedom from fear and freedom from want for those who are governed. Freedom from fear focuses on concrete physical threats that are experienced at the level of an individual and do not necessarily implicate entire societies. Warfare is the paradigm case, and much debate correctly focuses here. Warfare does not, however, exhaust the list, but rather needs to be partnered by additional threats in the contemporary world. These include not only the residual threats to be found in post-conflict operating environments but also the possibility of contamination through exposure to health hazards ranging from traditional diseases such as tuberculosis and malaria, through more modern infections such as HIV/AIDS, to contemporary challenges such as nuclear waste or fallout. Others include natural or man-made environmental disasters and the threats of unjust coercion and involuntary displacement. If people are to be free from fear, they need protection from all of these potential threats. In terms of enhancing human security, the World Bank (2000, p. 7) has also spelled out the need to reduce vulnerability to economic shocks, natural disasters, ill health, disability, and personal violence as an intrinsic part of enhancing well-being, requiring effective national action and effective mechanisms to reduce the risks faced by poor people. This statement further highlights the linkages between freedom from fear and freedom from need.

Freedom from want points to the basic needs debate. Doyal and Gough (1991, pp. 3–4) contend that, 'individuals have a right to the optimal satisfaction of [such] needs' and that 'all human liberation should be measured by assessing the degree to which such satisfaction has occurred'. This is a cardinal point, as is the contention that human need is both objective and universal. Against radical democrats, critics of cultural imperialism and ideologues from the New Right and Marxist traditions who insist that human need is a subjective or culturally relative concept, they counter that because 'all humans have the same potential to be harmed or to flourish', they must all have BHNs (*ibid.*, p. 1). For Doyal and Gough, 11 main items can be broken up into two somewhat overlapping sets. The five elements that address basic needs for physical health are adequate nutritional food and clean water, adequate protective housing, a non-hazardous work environment, a non-hazardous physical environment, and appropriate healthcare. The six elements that address basic needs for mental health are security in childhood, significant primary relationships, physical security, economic security, appropriate education, and safe birth control and child-bearing. The next section explores the evolution of security concepts in international affairs from national security prioritization to one focusing increasingly on the most vulnerable individuals in international society regardless of their nationality.

From national security to human security

In contemporary discourse and increasingly in practice, security is also an essentially contested concept. Definitions range from the traditional state-centric, through the systemic, to the consideration of insecurity or vulnerabilities – both internal and external – that threaten or have the potential to bring down or weaken state structures. State-centric security implies a relative freedom from war, coupled with a relatively high expectation that defeat will not be a consequence of any war that should occur. Systemic security references both coercive means to check an aggressor and alternative means for reconciling conflicting interests. The contradiction between state and systemic security is exposed by the concept of relative certainty of victory if one goes to war in the former, and the collective security principle and rationale of relative certainty of defeat of an aggressor in the latter. Beyond these essentially contested rational imperatives, security is also contested in terms of referent object, the scope of issues covered (the degree of securitization), and indeed within specific issues.

New thinking on security has gradually come to the fore in the field, with input from academics and also from practitioners in international organizations and states. In the early 1980s, Japan adopted a 'comprehensive security' policy under the direction of Prime Minister Zenko Suzuki. Comprehensive security not only looked beyond the traditional security elements of individual self-defense by focusing on regional and global security arrangements but also stressed the need to take into account other aspects vital to national stability, such as food, energy, environment, communication, and social security, as well as emphasizing collective security institutions (Akaha, 1991; Radtke and Feddema, 2000). NTS agendas are now in vogue in other parts of the world and are often termed 'new security challenges'. The characteristics of such challenges include some or all of the following: a focus on non-military rather than military threats, transnational rather than national threats. and multilateral or collective rather than self-help security solutions (Waever, 1995; Acharya, 2002). Japan has also been instrumental in pushing forward the next step in the evolution of security conceptualization, providing many of the policy initiatives and much of the impetus for the development of the human security discourse, and acting as the largest contributor to the human security related practices and intuitions of the United Nations (UN).

Human security suggests that international security, traditionally defined with its territorial emphasis, does not necessarily correlate with the concept of security for the individuals who comprise the state, and that an over-emphasis upon state security can be to the detriment of human welfare needs. Indeed, traditional conceptions of state security may constitute a necessary but not sufficient condition of human welfare (Newman, 2010, p. 79). Human security is non-hegemonic in that the major impetus for the development of the paradigm has come from academics, from middle-ranked powers like Canada and Japan rather than the United States, and from international organizations and their spokespersons (Mushajori, 2012, p. 1). Nearly 20 years after the seminal report of UNDP, and a decade or more after initiatives from the chief national proponents, 'the concept of human security has made significant contribution, not only by broadening the scope of security horizontally to non-military activities but also by shifting the reference point of security vertically from state to individuals' (Takaso, 2012, p. 2).

Human security is an emerging multi-disciplinary paradigm for understanding global vulnerabilities at the level of individual human beings, incorporating methodologies and analysis from a number of research fields including strategic and security studies, development studies, human rights, international relations, and the study of international organizations. It exists at the point where these disciplines converge on the concept of protection. The complexity of threats in people's daily lives now involve transnational dimensions and have moved beyond national security, which focused solely on the threat of external military aggressions. Such threats range from poverty, unemployment, drugs, terrorism, environmental degradation and social disintegration (UNDP, 1994, p. 11). The international community has also begun to see security threats not only *between* but also *within* states and focus on people in addition to states (WHO, 2002, p. 218).

The concept in fact had a significant pre-history in the work of scholars and international commissions, including the Brandt, Palme and Brundtland Reports from the 1980s. From within the UN system, it was first given explicit acknowledgement by Secretary-General Boutros Boutros-Ghali in the 1992 Agenda for Peace, where it was cited in relation to preventative diplomacy, peacemaking, peacekeeping, and post-conflict recovery. For two decades since, one branch of security studies has confronted traditional debates about national or nuclear security, premised on state sovereignty and territorial integrity, with a human security agenda of individual sovereignty and well-being. Its freedom from fear strand, often held to comprise a set of first-generation human rights, draws largely on the international relations tradition. Its freedom from want strand, envisioned as a set of second-generation human rights, builds on the development studies tradition. Moreover, in pulling the two strands together to focus on the freedom of an individual to live in dignity, the human security literature can be said to have moved beyond mere fusion of two hitherto separate academic sub-disciplines.

The twin concepts of freedom from fear and freedom from want that remain central to human security discourse are, however, at the basis of a schism within the academic and practitioner community when it comes to analyzing threats to human security and policy prescription. Proponents of a 'narrow' concept, a freedom from fear emphasis which underpins both the UN's *Responsibility to Protect* approach and the Human Security Report Project's *Human Security Report*, focus on violent threats to individuals while recognizing that they are strongly associated with poverty, lack of state capacity and various forms of socioeconomic and political inequity. Proponents of a 'broad' concept, a freedom from want emphasis articulated in the UNDP's *Human Development Report 1994*, and the Commission on Human Security's (CHS) 2003 report, *Human Security Now*, argue that the threat agenda should be broadened to include hunger, disease, and natural disasters because these kill far more people than war, genocide, and terrorism combined. Nevertheless, all proponents of human security agree that its primary goal is the protection of individuals and that a clear distinction is to be made between human security and national security, although the two may be seen as complimentary rather than contradictory (Thomas and Tow, 2002, p. 178).

While national security focuses on defense of the state from external attack, human security is about protecting individuals and communities from any form of threat to their well-being or even their very existence. Although still relatively new, the term is now widely used to describe the complex of interrelated threats to individual human well-being associated with interstate war, civil war, genocide, ethnic cleansing, population displacement, natural disasters, and pandemics. Some of the broadest interpretations include aspects of security related to food, health, the environment, communities, politics, and human rights (UNDP, 1994). As such, the concept is quite protean, and one key task has been pinning it down through a clear definition and associated principles of measurement. In this regard, perhaps the most promising approach was made more than a decade ago by King and Murray (2001–02, p. 585), who proposed a 'simple, rigorous, and measurable definition' whereby human security is 'the number of years of future life spent outside a state of "generalized poverty"'. In turn, generalized poverty consists of 'an individual [falling] below the threshold of any key domain of human wellbeing'.

There is in fact an international security continuum wherein 'new' human-centered approaches are intimately related to 'old' state-centric considerations. While it may no longer solely be a question of focusing exclusively on threats *between* states, it remains a utopian dream to think that we can now focus exclusively on threats *within* states. Although distinct in terms of focus and (when looking at elements of human security) referent objects, there remains a close relationship between traditional and NTS approaches. On the one hand, national insecurity may lead to human insecurity along various paths. It can divert resources from human development. It can drain energy. It can create a permissive political circumstance where national security is privileged over human rights. Furthermore, it is likely to produce and perpetuate an operating environment within which the exceptional use of internal as well as external violence by the state becomes a permanent feature of the state. Fear on a national level percolates down to fear on an individual level.

On the other hand, human insecurity in turn can threaten national security in a number of ways. Fear on an individual level, for example caused by violence from other individuals or even the state, can lead a group of victims to take refuge in a neighboring country, impacting upon its human security condition. Worse, those refugees may regroup, recruit, and rejuvenate to strengthen their capacity to undermine the security of those who forced them to flee in the first place. Also, want on an individual level, such as lack of food or energy – especially if it is spread unevenly across the nation – can undermine national cohesion and weaken national strength, increasing national insecurity. Fear on an individual level percolates up to fear on a national level. Desperate conditions among the disaffected youth of refugee camps or inner cities have the potential to produce fertile breeding grounds for religious extremism or terrorism. Thus, human insecurity becomes a source of insecurity for states.

Mass cross-border migration patterns, whether in terms of refugees or economic migrants, and whether legal or illegal can contribute to an increase in interethnic tensions in the new host country, and also, potentially an increase in crime, whether petty or organized transnational. Security concerns related to Asian trans-border migration and refugee flows feature prominently on the traditional security radars of China (Vietnamese, North Koreans, and Burmese nationals), Thailand (Burmese and Lao nationals – particularly ethnic Hmong), Malaysia (Indonesians and Philippine nationals), and Australia (Chinese and Pacific Island nationals). In 2007, Australian Federal Police Commissioner Mick Keelty identified climate change and food insecurity in the Asia-Pacific region as the greatest security threats faced by Australia as they would force an exodus of refugees to seek illegal residence in Australia, further exacerbating social unrest (Lauder, 2007).

NTS issue therefore has the potential to become a traditional security threat, and issues of human security can morph into ones of pressing concern for the survival of states themselves or the peace and security of a region or even the globe. Thus, it is in the enlightened self-interest of states and statesmen as well as the international community, however broadly defined, to pay attention to non-traditional and human security concerns. This rings particularly true for the NTS security imperatives of Japan and South Korea outlined in Chapters 9 and 10 of this volume. Once the vicious cycle between national and human insecurity is recognized, therefore, it becomes at least plausible that one way to address human insecurity is to help the target state ameliorate its national security concerns, and vice versa, with the amelioration of human security concerns helping a target state feel less vulnerable. To seek freedom from fear is to provide for national security. Freedom from fear is integral to national security and vice versa, although one does not necessarily guarantee the other. Table 2.1 places the human security approaches in the wider theoretical and practical discourse on security studies.

All of these approaches are interrelated and non-exclusionary. Thus, for instance, as developed further in Chapter 4 of this volume, human security considerations in North Korea have the potential to spill over into national and international security challenges and vice versa. The major implications of the newly emerging human security paradigm for the concept of good governance are the need to protect individuals rather than states; to provide freedom from fear and freedom from want; that all human beings are 'entitled' to these rights; that the broadest interpretations include aspects of security related to food, health, the environment, communities, politics, and human rights; and that in providing safe havens we need to take into account the interrelated threats to individual human well-being associated with interstate war, civil war, genocide, ethnic cleansing, the displacement of populations, environmental degradation, natural disasters, and pandemics. Policies which fail to address these requirements of global governance not only do a disservice to the most vulnerable sections of international society but also can prove ineffective or even counter-productive when dealing with

Table 2.1 Approaches to international security

Type of security	Main actors	Threats from	Main targets	Issues
Traditional	States	States	States	Defense, deterrence, balance of power
Comprehensive security	International organizations, states	Non-state actors, environment	States and communities	Water, food, environment, energy, terrorism, international crime
Human security/narrow definition	International organizations, states, NGOs	States and non-state Actors	Individuals and communities	Genocide, humanitarian intervention, explosive remnants of war (ERW), peacekeeping, responsibility to protect
Human security/broad definition	International community	Environment, states and non-state actors	Individuals and communities	Shelter, food, water, stability, infant and maternal mortality, education, health, conflict transformation, responsibility to provide

some of the most pressing international security concerns. The next section addresses the complex relationship between human security and development under the rubric of governance.

Human security and human development

Human (in)security, development, and poverty are connected in a complex web of causality revolving around the twin concepts of reconciling conflicting interests and generating collective good first identified in this chapter as lying at the core of the governance. According to the UN Public Administration Programme, governance and violent conflict are intimately related with most occurrences of the latter being 'caused and sparked off' by failures in the former, while there is also a reverse causality with conflicts pulling down governance and public administration institutions and structures. The process of reconstruction is not only long and highly expensive but also it requires careful analysis of the causes of the conflict and the nature of the governance and public administration that should be put in place to avoid its recurrence (UN PAP, 2012). Likewise, bad governance can nullify the impact of pro-poor policies. In addition, conflict creates specific constraints for the formulation of a poverty reduction strategy and a good governance program. 'Conflict not only creates specific manifestations of poverty, but also affects wider structures and institutions' (Musoni, 2003, p. 3). A conflict-affected country is likely to experience low economic growth due to:

> low investment, disruptions to infrastructure and declining production, macro-economic instability (inflation, high expenditure pressures especially for defence resulting in low levels of poverty related spending), poor governance, low political legitimacy and corruption, a small donor presence which may focus mainly on humanitarian aid, limited civil society organisation and eroded community and national spirit. In addition to these general problems there will also be conflict related poverty, including factors such as: the emergence of specific vulnerable groups (e.g. child combatants, orphans, and war-wounded, children and female headed households, the aged whose social support networks have been eroded etc.), internally displaced populations and refugees, the problems of re-integration of demobilised combatants, psychological effects of war trauma, and communities fragmented by hostility. (ibid., p. 4)

The closest relationship between security and development in both theory and practice is that found between human security as the protection of persons and human development as the provision of BHN. Human security and human development are both people-centered. They challenge the orthodox approach to security and development – that is to say, state security and liberal economic growth respectively. Both emphasize people are to be seen as the ultimate ends but never as means, and treat humans as agents who should be empowered to participate in the process of their own need-satisfaction. Both perspectives are multidimensional, and address people's dignity as well as their material and physical concerns. Both impose duties on the wider global community.

Human security and development can be seen as mutually reinforcing. A peaceful environment frees individuals and governments to move from a focus on mere survival to a position where they can consider improvement of their situations. Likewise, as a society develops, it is able to afford more doctors, hospitals, welfare networks, internal security operations, schools, and de-mining operations. Conversely, as former UN Secretary-General Annan (2005) observed in his UN Report *In Larger Freedom*, 'we will not enjoy security without development, development without security, and we will not enjoy either without respect for human rights. Unless all these causes are advanced, none will succeed'. Conflict retards development, and underdevelopment can lead to conflict.

The UN Millennium Development Goals (UN MDGs) have highlighted the importance of security in the context of poverty reduction. In particular, *The Millennium Development Goals Report 2008* addresses the issue of 'conflict' as an important cause that has led to recent increases in poverty (UN, 2008). Along with causing rising food prices, conflict affects well-being through the displacement of people from their homes and livelihoods as refugees and into poverty. Indeed, '[m]ore than 42 million people are displaced by conflict and persecution, both within and outside the borders of their own countries' (*ibid.*, p. 7). Not only is there a direct causal relationship between insecurity and poverty but also the solution for poverty must encompass means to address security problems. In the past three decades, 21 of the 49 least developed countries (LDCs) have experienced grave episodes of violence and instability (Ghai, 2006, pp. 333–6). Indeed, the prevalence of warfare around the globe has resulted in post-conflict development 'becom[ing] the norm rather than the exception' (Junne and Verkoren, 2005, p. 318). The negative reinforcement of insecurity and underdevelopment can continue long after the official cessation of hostilities. Post-bellum threats to both life and well-being include the breakdown of law and order, the spread of disease as a result of refugee camp overcrowding, poor nutrition, infrastructure collapse, scarcity of medical supplies (although ironically often a proliferation of illicit drugs), and continued criminal attacks on civilian populations, unemployment, displacement, homelessness, disrupted economic activity, and stagflation. In addition to these complexities, in many post-conflict environments, the most immediate threat to both human security and human development is the legacy of ERW.

As developed extensively in Chapter 6, with its examination of the People's Democratic Republic of Laos, land mines, unexploded munitions (UXM), unexploded ordnances (UXO) such as bombs, shells, and grenades which have been employed but failed to detonate, and other ERW are widely encountered in the aftermath of international and internal conflicts, wreaking havoc for decades after hostilities have ceased (Watson, 2004, p. 4). They hinder the safe return of internally displaced persons (IDPs) and refugees to their communities, damage infrastructure essential for economic development, increase rebuilding costs, prevent the use of assets vital to sustainable livelihoods, such as water sources and irrigation channels, and are fatal impediments to land use. They prevent land use for agriculture, grazing, housing or resettlement, and commerce. In addition, they deter public and private investment and economic development through increased uncertainty, costs, and delays resulting from their suspected presence (GICHD, 2007). They harm otherwise productive members of society, and maim or kill children trying to salvage them for scrap metal (Rees,

2008). According to the UNDP (2009), as many as 78 nations are affected by landmines and about 85 by explosive remnants of war. Conflict can also have a disastrous impact on the environment. Likewise, irresponsible development practices can lead to pollution and climate change which impact on both human security and human development of the most vulnerable sections of global society. Finally, environmental challenges can lead to migration which can lead to insecurity. Table 2.2 reflects the relationship between security, poverty, and development under the rubric of governance.

This table demonstrates not only how the two central strands of governance can be reflected in policy prescription but also how they have gradually come together under the concept of a responsibility to provide, or at least to facilitate the production of conditions conducive to promoting these BHN. Indeed, the fundamental purpose of governance is to provide for the BHN of all, but particularly those whose needs are most endangered or threatened. Human security and development may be considered aspects of international entitlement rights –what states and the wider international community should provide for or guarantee the citizens of the world as each

Table 2.2 Theoretical and practical elements of global governance

Global governance				
Reconcile conflicting interests/protect interests against others			**Generate collective good/ facilitate cooperation**	
Traditional state-centric security	***Non-traditional security/new challenges***	***Human security***	***Human development***	***Traditional development/ governance***
Defense, deterrence, arms-racing, balance of power, security dilemma, conflict management	Natural disasters, disease, climate change, pollution, terrorism, transnational crime, resources, conflict resolution	R2P, freedom from fear genocide, humanitarian intervention, ERW, peacekeeping	Recipient focused, human-centric, participatory, new donors and actors, partnerships, non-hierarchical, NGOs, human development index (HDI), accountability	State-centric development, IGOs (UN, WTO, IMF, World Bank, etc.), foreign direct investment, free trade, traditional ODA, efficiency
		Responsibility to Provide/Facilitate Safe havens, shelter, food, water, meaningful occupation, stability, life expectancy, infant mortality, maternal mortality, education, health, conflict transformation, freedom from want		

individual has certain rights and entitlements by virtue of being a human being. The next section further explores entitlements under the human security paradigm and related perspectives.

Entitlement rights and obligations

Despite two decades of discourse and conceptual development, many analysts continue to argue that human security is by nature incoherent and useless. Paris (2001, p. 93), for instance, argues that, 'human security seems capable of supporting virtually any hypothesis – along with its opposite – depending on the prejudices and interests of the particular researcher'. He concludes that, 'if human security means almost anything, then it effectively means nothing'. Likewise, Buzan (2004, p. 369) insists that grouping various issues from traditional security to human development under the broad umbrella of 'human security' has no practical merit or use as an analytical tool. Moreover, he writes, human security 'drives towards a reductionist understanding of international security and reinforces a mistaken tendency to idealize security as the desired end goal'. Many argue for a confusion of categories, with Buzan, for instance, holding human security to be essentially the same as human rights. This volume however argues against such a conflation. Essentially, as represented in Figure 2.1,

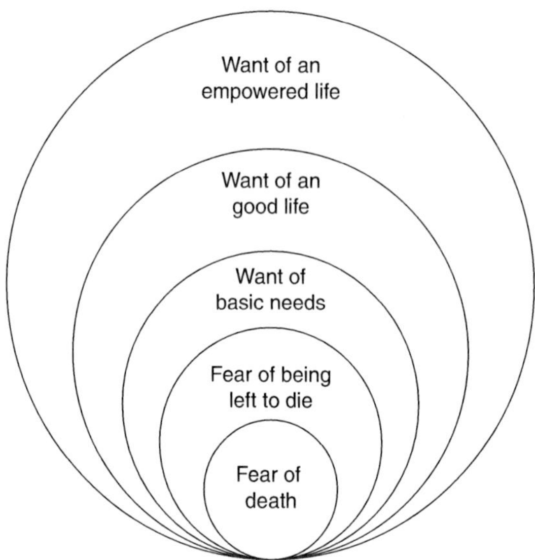

Figure 2.1 Spheres of entitlement to freedom from threat

the relationship between human security, human development, and human rights, can be viewed as concentric spheres of entitlement.

At the core, human beings are entitled to live their lives free from the fear of imminent and arbitrary death – a narrow definition best represented by Canadian approaches to Human Security. As a major contributor to UN Peacekeeping Operations in the former Yugoslavia, Rwanda, Somalia and other conflict areas, the Canadian government began to advocate the need to protect civilians in armed conflict situations within state borders and stressed the need to rethink the notion of humanitarian intervention (Axworthy, 1997). Therefore, the Canadian conceptualization of human security is closely associated with crisis prevention and conflict-management tools. The UNDP approach was rejected as an unwieldy policy instrument which emphasized the threats associated with underdevelopment while largely ignoring the continuing human insecurity resulting from violent conflict, and for Canada the concept of human security has increasingly centered on the human costs of violent conflict (DFAIT, 1999, Ch. 2).

This has led to Canada being closely associated with international initiatives which take a narrow focus on human security such as the Ottawa Convention to Ban Anti-Personal Landmines, the creation of the International Criminal Court (ICC), the International Commission on Intervention and State Sovereignty (ICISS) and its final report *The Responsibility to Protect* (2001). The implications of Canada's stance for human security in challenging case studies are further developed in Chapter 7 on Burma/Myanmar. This narrow interpretation of human security focusing on threats to individuals and the relationship between human security and national security is also championed in the *Human Security Report 2005: War and Peace in the 21st Century* for both pragmatic and methodological reasons.

Logically however, if individuals have an entitlement right not arbitrarily to be put to death, and those with the power to do so have an obligation to provide safe havens for them, free from the fear of being killed, this could also, conceivably be extended to freedom from the fear of being left to die. This resonates particularly strongly when one considers that death caused by bad governance, lack of capacity, neglect, and the (un)natural contributions of disasters, disease and famine, kill far more than those slain by the bomb or bullet. This, therefore, necessitates a second sphere under the freedom from fear concept whereby individuals have an entitlement right not to have their lives arbitrarily and dramatically ended as a result of the action or inaction of those in positions of authority and responsibility. This logical extension is introduced by the landmark *1994 Human Development Report: New Dimensions of Human Security* produced by the UNDP. Former UN Secretary-General Kofi Annan's address (2000a) at the 2000 Millennium Summit, stated that the concept of security should be human centered and placed the concept center stage for the global governance mission. In addition, at the workshop on human security during the Millennium Summit, he defined human security as much broader than 'the absence of violent conflict' (2000b). Yet the UN approach also crosses over the boundary into a third sphere of entitlement as it stresses the need for human security, broadly defining it as 'freedom from fear' *and* 'freedom from want'. Here, human security means 'safety from such chronic threats as hunger, disease, and repression', as well as 'protection from sudden and hurtful disruptions in the patterns of daily life – where in homes, in jobs or in communities' (UNDP, 1994, p. 23).

The third sphere brings us into the realm of human development or at the very least represents an overlapping between human security and human development. Here, the individual is entitled to provisions protecting against the arbitrary foreshortening of life. This is closely related to concepts of BHN – what an individual must have in order to have a reasonable chance of living a full life-span. These entitlements include but are not limited to, food, water, shelter, clean air and other environmental conditions, and basic medical supplies and services. According to the seminal 1994 report listed above, human security includes seven components, five of which (an assured basic income, basic food access, freedom from disease and infection, freedom from the dangers of environmental pollution, personal security/physical safety) are directly related to preserving life. Human security thus defined is also seen as preventive and is people-centered (*ibid.*, pp. 22–33). The CHS established under the chairmanship Sadako Ogata, former UN High Commissioner for Refugees, and Amartya Sen, Nobel Economics Prize Laureate, in its final report *Human Security Now,* defines human security as the protection of fundamental freedoms – freedoms that are the essence of life; protecting people from critical (severe) and pervasive (widespread) threats and situations; and creating political, social, environmental, economic, military, and cultural systems that together give people the building blocks of survival.

This is where Chapter 3 situates the UN and other international organizations, which have focused increasingly on the economic and development related elements of human security, at the broader end of the spectrum. As detailed in Chapter 9, Japan's approach to human security promotion closely correlates with (and to a considerable extent drives) that taken by the UN. The implications of the different approaches taken by Canada and Japan (narrow and broad) are further explored in Chapter 7, which looks at national and international governance challenges in Myanmar. King and Murray's number of years of future life spent outside a state of 'generalized poverty' then serves as a bridge between this sphere and the next, in that the number of years constituting a full life-span are often related to the provision of resources beyond those BHN essential for the survival of the individual.

The fourth sphere therefore encompasses the broader entitlement rights found in the human development paradigm and reflected in the Human Development Index (HDI) and the MDGs. The HDI was introduced by the UNDP as a new way of measuring development by combining indicators of life expectancy, educational attainment, and income into a single composite measurement of human-centered development. It refers to the process of widening the options of persons, giving them greater opportunities for education, health care, income, and employment. The MDGs were developed out of the eight chapters of the United Nations Millennium Declaration, signed in September 2000. The eight goals and 21 targets include: (1) eradication of extreme poverty and hunger, (2) universal primary education, (3) promotion of gender equality and empowerment of women, (4) reduction in child mortality, (5) improvement in maternal health, (6) combatting HIV/AIDS, malaria, and other diseases, (7) environmental sustainability, and (8) a global partnership for development. Thus, in this sphere, the focus is not only upon living a longer life but also upon living a better off, more equitable, stable, secure, and fulfilling life. International organizations increasingly address these issues, at times almost to the exclusion of freedom from fear considerations, so that the approach could almost be considered a second narrow definition of human security.

Finally, in the fifth sphere, we have the concept of human rights which springs most readily to mind when the topic is raised in connection with governance, whether national or global – political rights associated with liberal concepts of freedom, equality and justice. Human rights form backdrop of many contemporary political debates both within and between countries. The Cold War was, in many ways, fought on battleground of human rights. During this period of global hostility, the West promoted a purely political concept of human rights resulting on the 1966 International Covenant on Civil and Political Rights, whereas the East emphasized economic and social rights, culminating in the 1966 International Covenant on Economic, Social and Cultural Rights. Most countries are now signatories of both these covenants, and the growth of the international human rights regime can be seen as one of the prime examples of globalization. Rights have increasingly been enshrined in domestic constitutions and have gradually become embodied in international legislation. The tradition of the international human rights of the governed and obligations upon those who governs has evolved from League of Nations mandates, whereby states administrating territories granted to them in trust were answerable to the global body for the treatment of citizens therein, through UN Trusteeships, the UN Charter, and the Genocide Convention, to the ICC.

Contemporary thinking distinguishes between three generations of rights: first, broadly political; second, economic and social; third, the rights of peoples. The final two components of human security identified by the 1994 UNDP Report fit in here – (6) community security which ensures survival of traditional cultures and ethnic groups and (7) political security which means protection of BHN and freedoms (*ibid.*). Likewise, the CHS, in its ten starting points on human security goes beyond the protection of the individual and provision of basic living standards, health care, and education, to clarifying the need for a global human identity while respecting the freedom of individual to have diverse identities and affiliations (CHS, 2003, p. 133). As noted by the Office of High Commissioner for Human Rights, good governance and human rights can be mutually reinforcing: human rights principles provide a set of values to guide the work of governments and other actors, and a set of performance standards against which these actors can be held accountable, whereas without good governance, human rights cannot be respected and protected in a sustainable manner (OHCHR, 2007, p. 1). Shyama Kuruvilla *et al.* (2012, p. 141) stress that strategies that link the MDGs and human rights would facilitate more comprehensive, equitable, and sustainable progress in health and development.

Yet as mentioned above, there are a number of problems with expanding the human security paradigm to this fifth sphere. Controversies surround issues of selectivity (in terms of accusations of bad governance); the notion of human beings as rights bearers being European in origin; universalism versus cultural relativism; and the hierarchy of economic, social, and political rights. David Chandler (2008, p. 428) claims that in the post-Cold War world, 'human security approaches have been easily – and willingly – integrated into the mainstream because they have sought to (1) exaggerate new post-Cold War security threats, (2) locate these threats in the developing world, and (3) facilitate short-term policymaking in the absence of clear strategic foreign policy visions'. This is one of the numerous challenges raised in Chapter 8 with regard to state-building and nation-building in Timor-Leste. At the very least, many national governments are reluctant to implement measures which appear to reflect Western values or prioritization of individual political rights, or to support their promotion on the international stage, thereby hindering the protection of more fundamental entitlement rights.

While addressing each of these debates in both theoretical and practical policy terms, this volume restates the concept of human security by going back to basics. Whatever else is said, human security must be a subset of security, classically defined as freedom from danger, risk, care, anxiety, doubt, and so on. This focus not on factors that are present, but on ones that are absent, universal wrongs rather than rights, indicates that the inverse or negative manner in which the concept was expressed by UNDP in 1994 is essentially correct: 'freedom from' a specified list of challenges and threats. Then, human security has to mark out a sphere in which each and every human being attains that list of freedoms. This gives the concept an individualistic foundation. Human security is not an attribute of groups or classes but rather of discrete persons.

At the same time, the absence of threats dimension means that while human security has much in common with related concepts of human empowerment and flourishing, it is in fact quite different. Security is a limited and even cramped notion. The wider human rights discourse engages ideas of empowerment and participation which if denied certainly could lead to a less fulfilling and enriched life, but need not necessarily lead to a shorter or more arduous one. Divisions within the discourse and in policy communities over what constitutes a human right, which rights are important, and what can be done to protect and promote them make practical action in their name problematic and can lead to charges of or actual crusaderism.

The wider development discourse includes laying down conditions for communities to flourish and for their citizens to lead a 'better' or at least a better-off life. Yet not only is equating wealth with well-being contentious, but also once there is movement beyond a fairly basic level of material resources, further development may do little to protect individual human beings, and in fact may endanger them. Ideas of human empowerment and flourishing are much bigger and broader, pointing toward the good life. While taking human security as foundational, they move beyond it to construct much fuller conceptions of the human condition. Hence, in this volume a fairly restrictive notion of entitlement rights is used – essentially understood as the notions of safe havens, freedom from fear, and freedom from absolute or extreme want.

Even East Asian states known for their exceptionalism when it comes to global governance norms, and emphasis on relativism, have found themselves able to sign up to this sort of interpretation. Indeed, due to their epistemological backgrounds and historical experiences, such actors may in fact have unique contributions to make to the promotion and protection of human security in East Asia. This concept is explored in Chapter 10 (addressing the newest member of the OECD DAC, South Korea) and Chapter 11 (exploring new regional actors and initiatives in the field) of this volume. The key questions concern what duties are imposed on others when the leaders of a community fail in their R2P the human security of their citizens or fail to provide for their basic needs. The next section looks at how the obligations of good governance have gradually evolved into an internationally recognized R2P, and also how, logically, the same set of entitlement rights implies a responsibility to provide or at least facilitate the production of supportive conditions.

A responsibility to protect and to provide/facilitate

A reinterpretation of the concept of state rights as privileges granted to them in trust by their citizens has allowed the international community to consider violating the norm of non-intervention and the legal rights of states to political sovereignty and territorial integrity (Luban, 1985, p. 210). A R2P derives from the freedom from fear strand of human security. It focuses attention on what states and the wider international community should provide for the citizens of the world in terms of protecting the core right to life enjoyed by virtue of being a human being. This constitutes a different emphasis from a focus on the sort of political rights (freedom of speech, of assembly, to stand for office, and so on) that are often championed by external agencies attempting to provide impetus for reform in a fragile state. As such they may be considered less politically charged than a liberal 'crusade' to change the governance systems of target states. Nevertheless, questions arise concerning the duties imposed on the international community when the leaders of a community fail in their R2P the human security of their citizens.

During the Cold War, considerations of national interest dominated the decision-making of all the major powers. The end of the Cold War, combined with increased media penetration and dissemination capabilities, did much, however, to render amoral foreign policy untenable, at least in Western liberal democracies. Therefore, the governing dictates of that time may be seen as no longer suitable for the regulation of international politics, national interest as no longer a sufficient normative guide for action, and even the normative value long attached to the sovereign state open to question. Indeed, historically, a limit to state sovereignty was first established by the Nuremberg trials in 1945–46. States could no longer do as they wished with their citizens. The Convention on the Prevention and Punishment of the Crime of Genocide has now been ratified by 140 countries and, according to the International Court of Justice, holds to generally accepted values which oblige all states, even those with few links with the international community, to 'punish and prevent genocide'. Since the end of the Cold War, the process of normatively shifting from an emphasis on state rights and prerogatives to an emphasis on their duties to citizens and the rights of citizens against states has gathered speed.

Analyzing the post-Cold War period, Finnemore (2003) argues that two features stand out in the global pattern of military intervention: most of it is multilateral and typically the geostrategic or economic interests of the interveners are negligible. In particular, she notes the extraordinary costs of the missions to Cambodia and Somalia as mitigating against material interests of intervening states presenting the determining factor whether or not to intervene. National interest dominated when the international community decided not to intervene during the 1994 Rwandan genocide. The UN and member states were, however, ultimately compelled to take some form of action by pressure from international and domestic public opinion fuelled by information from NGOs and the media. In addition, what prevented other members of the Security Council from admitting that genocide was taking place was awareness that if such were proven, then international law would compel them to intervene, regardless of costs and the dictates of individual national interest.

Guilt at the failure to act over Rwanda subsequently increased international normative pressure for action in Kosovo, which was the first explicitly humanitarian intervention in the post-Cold War world. Indeed, when questioned, Madeleine Albright (2002), former US Ambassador to the UN and Secretary of State, confirmed that the previous cases where the United States and the international community had 'waited too long to go in' had 'played a huge role' in determining policy over Kosovo. The eagerness to get involved here contrasted most vividly with reluctance over Rwanda and Bosnia, as did the relative absence of considerations of material national interest compared with the Gulf. Not surprisingly, therefore, realists such as Henry Kissinger and Colin Gray repeatedly and convincingly argued from their theoretical standpoint against the intervention, holding that no vital US military or political interests were at stake.

Secretaries General of the UN have been to the fore in the promotion of the UN's global governance mission, and their words have stimulated governments and other organs to act. In the aftermath of the 1991 Gulf War, UN Secretary-General Boutros Boutros-Ghali (1992, p. 44) noted that '[t]he time of absolute and exclusive sovereignty ... has passed ... It is the task of leaders of States today to understand this and to find a balance between the needs of good internal governance and the requirements of an ever more interdependent world'. That is to say, as pointed out by Boutros-Ghali's successor, Kofi Annan (2005), no state is immune to the demands and rights of its internal and external constituencies, and the UN, as the embodiment of the international community will not tolerate the hindrance of its 'great objectives' of peace and security, justice and human rights, and 'social progress and better standards of life in larger freedom'. Similar sentiments can be found in Secretary-General Annan's Millennium report where he pointed out that states exist to protect citizens and not vice versa, and that they could no longer use sovereignty as a shield to hide behind. 'The charter is written in the name of "We the peoples". It's a document that is humane and centred on individuals ... The fact that we cannot protect everyone does not mean we cannot help where we can' (Annan, 2000a). This Report formed the basis of the Millennium Declaration adopted by Heads of State and Government at the September 2000 Millennium Summit, held at UN Headquarters.

In December 2001, ICISS (2001) released its final report entitled *The Responsibility to Protect*. This declaration included a specific endorsement of humanitarian intervention and the use of force by expressing willingness 'to take timely and decisive collective action for this purpose, through the Security Council, when peaceful means prove inadequate and national authorities are manifestly failing to do it'. Thus, the declaration of a R2P can be interpreted as a duty to use force to intervene humanitarianly. In the intervening years, this new paradigm has gained momentum and garnered international recognition.

In response to this international normative shift, at the High-Level Plenary Meeting for the 2005 World Summit (14–16 September), the world's leaders at the General Assembly agreed on a 'R2P' which included a 'clear and unambiguous acceptance by all governments of the collective international R2P populations from genocide, war crimes, ethnic cleansing and crimes against humanity'. Resolution 1674, adopted by the United Nations Security Council (UNSC) on 28 April 2006, 'Reaffirm[ed] the provisions of paragraphs 138 and 139 of the 2005 World Summit Outcome Document regarding the responsibility to protect populations from genocide, war crimes, ethnic cleansing and crimes against humanity', and commits the Security Council to action to protect civilians in armed conflict. This resolution was adopted unanimously. On 14 September 2009, in the course of the closing plenary of its 63rd session, the UN General Assembly adopted resolution A/63/L80 Rev.1 entitled 'The Responsibility to Protect' which had been co-sponsored by 67 member states from every region in the world. Only seven states sought to play down the importance of the document, stressing that in their opinion the resolution was strictly procedural, none of which was from the East Asian region (GCR2P, 2009).

Non-violent challenges and the related inactions or incompetence of states may, however, actually pose a greater threat to human security, especially in terms of a freedom from want, than that of violent actions in terms of freedom from fear. A responsibility to provide can thus be said to derive from the duty states owe to their citizens not only not to harm them but also to provide for or promote their basic needs. Once normative duties are placed upon states to generate freedom from fear and freedom from want for their citizens, and concurrent obligations are placed upon the international community to protect and to provide for the most vulnerable members of societies when their own governments are unwilling or unable to provide such safe havens, it is necessary to consider whether there are conditions under which a normative imperative operates for the international community to intervene even if there is opposition from the government of the target state.

As previously mentioned, in policy debates and the academic literature, freedom from want is becoming more important in both absolute and relative terms than freedom from fear. This is not only because non-conflict deaths are increasing while war-related deaths have been declining but also because the international community is both more likely to be informed of internal acts of aggression and more likely to act against them than in previous decades. It is for this reason that the most assertive champions of human security are beginning to provoke controversy by calling for 'aid invasions' when states contribute massively negative impacts to the human security of their citizens through deliberate action, incompetence, obstruction, or neglect (Evans, 2008).

There is no more dramatic manifestation of ethical dilemmas in international politics than humanitarian intervention, defined as 'the threat or use of force across state borders by a state (or group of states) aimed at preventing or ending widespread and grave violations of the fundamental human rights of individuals other than its own citizens, without the permission of the state within whose territory is applied' (Holzgrefe, 2003, p. 18). In contemporary western or universalist society, utilitarianism still operates as a tacit background against which all other theories have to assert and defend themselves. The morally right course of action is that which produces the greatest happiness (or least misery) for the greatest number of people. Utilitarianism can claim a degree of legitimacy based on a supposedly universal (value neutral) rational appeal rather than metaphysics. An action or policy is bad to the extent that someone suffers as a result. It is good to the extent that someone gets more happiness as a result. Therefore, the morality or 'fairness' of sets of rules, policies or actions becomes a simple question of mathematics. An intervention is justified if fewer people would suffer and more would be happy than if it were not to occur.

There are, however, a number of problems with taking a utilitarian approach to humanitarian intervention. It is impossible to know in advance the costs of intervention in terms of human suffering, or the costs associated with non-intervention. Furthermore, how do we measure utility in terms of human happiness or suffering, and worse, how do we aggregate it? How many rapes equal a death, for instance? If we only focus on body counts for our measurements of human suffering, we will get lost in the numbers game and miss a great deal of other human suffering that could, perhaps, be prevented with a minimum sacrifice of human life. In addition, if we wait until we know how many are likely to die in order to justify our intervention, we may be too late to save many individuals, and therefore would, ironically, lose our utilitarian justification. Finally, utilitarian calculations are always likely to sacrifice minorities to the interests of majorities, and any form of consequentialism contributes to the concept of 'anything goes' in global affairs, as long as the numbers work out right in the end.

In international relations and international law, state-centric traditions have tended to treat all states 'as if' they are legitimate representatives and guardians of the well-being of their citizens (Walzer, 1985, p. 51). Standing behind this practice is a fear of the breakdown of international order as states use humanitarian justifications for furthering their own agendas and interests. For communitarian commentators like Michael Walzer (1983, p. 5), there are human rights, but due to the problem of the particularism of history, culture, and membership, the political community to which individuals belong, rather than uninformed external interference, is the best agency for their defense. The political community (*qua* state) is the closest we can come to a world of common meanings as it is where language, history, and culture come most closely together to produce a collective consciousness (Walzer, 1985, p. 218). Walzer is unable to accept intervention for any reason other than to counter aggression. Individual members of each community are solely responsible for evaluating their own social rules and the behavior of their political leaders. Only members of the community are entitled to take action to make governance changes. Nobody has the right to 'force others to be free'. The most important normative considerations focus therefore on the sovereign rights of states, territorial integrity, and the principle of non-intervention. Aggression (or intervention) is the only crime in international affairs (everything else is a misdemeanor), and is the only justification for military action (Walzer, 1992, p. 51).

From a liberal viewpoint, however, the strict non-interventionist communitarian perspective is unacceptable. Human beings are viewed as individual bearers of inviolate human rights, as a result of which there is a limit to the degree to which they may be utilized for the collective good of society. Thus, morality replaces utility for considerations of the legitimacy of a certain action or rule, and intervention dilemmas become explicitly normative. Liberals are suspicious of state prerogatives, preferring a social contract concept of duties. Individuals cede powers to the state only if the state is committed to using them to protect citizens from the uncertainties and scarcities of social life. For David Luban (1985, p. 201), 'if the rights of states are derived from the rights of humans, and are thus in a sense one kind of human rights, it will be important to consider their possible conflict with other human rights'. He points out that an illegitimate and tyrannical state cannot derive sovereign rights against aggression from the rights of its own oppressed citizens, when it is itself denying them those same rights. In his opinion, the majority of states have forfeited their rights which in truth are only privileges granted them in trust. Thus, although not every infringement is a *casus belli*, he implies a duty to intervene. Unless morality is conditional upon the nationality of the aggressor, we have a duty to defend the victims of internal as well of external aggression.

Liberals therefore simultaneously and somewhat contradictorily support the concepts of individual human rights, global consensus, or shared norms, and a lingering respect for states as the legal persons of international society. What is needed is a way to reflect these competing demands upon our evaluation of justice. Perhaps Rawls comes closest to providing an answer. Starting with a value neutral liberal approach to the rights of individuals, he takes on board much of the criticism of relativists. He accepts that we are historically situated, but that we have become historically situated in liberal individualism (Rawls, 1987). Any state which conducts itself in a manner toward its own citizens that any rational being would find abhorrent is guilty according to the shared norms of international society, the works of eminent publicists, the practice of states, and the intents and purposes of the UN. That being the case, should the abuses be sufficient to outweigh the possible harm that would be done by external intervention, then the international community not only has the right but also the duty to intervene.

Yet even if we question the ontological underpinnings of communitarian commentary on humanitarian intervention, we may still side with non-intervention on more pragmatic grounds. Given that any weakening of the principle of non-intervention threatens international order, and could generate more warfare, and given the high human costs of modern warfare, we might side with the idea of treating states 'as if' they are legitimate on rule-utilitarian grounds. That is, the value of following the rule of non-intervention is greater, in normative terms, than the value of any good to be gained from a particular act of humanitarian intervention. On another pragmatic level, however, calls for humanitarian intervention from internal constituencies that have had pictures of bloated corpses beamed into their living rooms may prove too insistent for statesmen to resist, and on a normative level, in the most extreme examples, it is hard to make a case for them to do so. Even Walzer (1997, p. 21) concedes something along these lines, stating that, 'sovereignty also has its limits, which are fixed most clearly by the legal doctrine of humanitarian intervention. Acts or practices that "shock the conscience of humankind" are, in principle, not tolerated'.

Non-intervention is thus not tenable in the most extreme cases of human rights violation, and only a very few absolute pacifists or relativists would contend that there is no cause for which it is worth going to war. It is therefore possible to argue that imminent and gross endangerment of the human security of a significant portion of the population of a target state either by the government of the state or as a result of its incapacity or unwillingness to act constitutes such a cause. This is a narrower and more pragmatic position than perhaps would be the case under a liberal human rights regime. It would not support 'forcing people to be free' or the political objective of regime change, and it would only be permissive of an 'aid invasion' if conditions of human insecurity were sufficient to provoke global outrage. It may well be that no overarching normative or legal regulations for humanitarian intervention can be constructed, that every case necessitates debate about the morality of each side's position, and 'seat-of-the-pants practical judgment is a necessary supplement to one's principles in such matters' (Luban, 1985, p. 216). To be at a point, however, where such a decision needs to be made represents a failure on the part of both national and international policymakers to take sufficient account of humanitarian interests in their day-to-day endeavors. By committing firmly to a R2P, and paying greater attention to a responsibility to provide, or at least to ensure the promotion of conditions conducive to the production of havens free from fear and want, the international community can move to a situation in which fewer instances arise in which the responsibility to intervene needs to be debated.

Conclusion

This volume does not support the concept of aid invasions, acknowledging that in many cases it may be politically, militarily, or geographically impossible or undesirable in humanitarian terms to launch such an action. Nevertheless, it is beneficial to conceptualize human security as both a R2P and a responsibility to provide, as often fear and want, or insecurity and underdevelopment, are inextricably entwined. It also acknowledges the dangers of 'provision' in terms of Western neo-imperialism or 'benefitting' and dependent development, but highlights that global governance responsibilities extend beyond simply stopping the killing. A purely development-focused approach is unlikely to do much for the human security of vulnerable individuals. Similarly, focusing exclusively on protection of the population is unlikely to do much to fulfill their BHN. Narrow definitions of human security tend to focus on the physical threats to individuals, and prescribe a responsibility to protect individuals from the threats they face. Many examinations of development and ODA take a macro approach focusing on statistical data and measurements of aggregate well-being and improvement while missing the impact of underdevelopment and development on the most vulnerable sections of society.

From its first introduction in the academic literature, human security has been characterized by its emphasis on the individual as a referent of security. The approach sketched here seeks to embrace individuals faced with the contemporary world's most desperate security challenges and to indicate how their security needs can be encapsulated in a dual responsibility initially to protect and subsequently to provide or promote the conditions which facilitate the production of BHN. King and Murray's 'number of years of future life spent outside a state of "generalized poverty"' is an important formulation as it implicitly draws together the two strands of threat – years of future life implying a freedom from harm allowing the continuation of life, but the reference to outside a state of generalized poverty implying a freedom from want which must somehow be provided. The individual must not only be protected from acts and threats of violence in order to live in a state of freedom from fear but also BHN must be met in order to live a life free from want, and therefore truly secure.

If the objective of the paradigm is to minimize human suffering by maximizing the number of years of future life spent outside a state of generalized poverty, clearly the onus upon state and international actors in to protect and also to provide for, or provide needs-supportive conditions for, individual human beings by virtue of our shared humanity, irrespective of the artificial normative boundaries of states. The democratization of the media has made it harder for governments to perpetrate, cover up, or to turn a blind eye to inhumane practices or suffering within their jurisdictions or within those of their fellow states. In the contemporary international security environment, it is simply indefensible to fall back on the state-centric justification of national interest for actions or inaction.

At the same time, however, national sovereignty and international security concerns mean that it is necessary to set a reasonably high threshold for cross-border interventions of any kind. In principle, it is not difficult to work out where to put this, though in practice there may need to be extensive debate about specific cases, with voices from a truly global conversation given a chance to be heard. The bar proposed by Walzer when he pointed to 'acts that shock the conscience of humankind' is equally applicable to interventions falling under both protocols. That is, to trigger either R2P or responsibility to provide interventions, fear or want in the relevant society must attain the level of crisis generated by an immediate emergency situation. When this does happen, human security interventions are justifiable through a global responsibility to protect and to provide safe havens.

At the domestic level, good governance equates to those responsible for governing doing so in a way that not only helps resolve conflicts of interests and generates collective good, but is also equitable, accountable, and broadly in the interests of the most vulnerable sections of society. At the international level, when a national government fails in its duty to its citizens through either incompetence, incapacity, or malice, this responsibility to act in the interests of the most vulnerable transfers to those who possess the requisite competence and capacity. According to the R2P doctrine, when there are threats of violence of sufficient magnitude, the international community has a duty to intervene in their defense, even if this violates political sovereignty considerations. According the responsibility to provide/facilitate doctrine mooted in here, there is a similar duty to act (although not necessarily to intervene militarily) in cases where the fundamental well-being of the most vulnerable sections of society is being threatened. Indeed, global governance implies an awareness of the close relationship between the two responsibilities, and a desire to provide safe havens encompassing freedom from fear, and freedom from want.

Note

1. While the author is aware of the controversy surrounding the use of either Burma or Myanmar, hereinafter this volume will use Myanmar as it is the name officially recognized by the United Nations.

References

Acharya, A. (2002) 'Human Security: What Kind for the Asia Pacific?' in D. Dickens (ed.), *The Human Face of Security: Asia-Pacific Perspectives* (Canberra: Australian National University).

Agere, S. (2000) *Promoting Good Governance: Principles, Practices and Perspectives* (London: Commonwealth Secretariat).

Akaha, T. (1991) 'Japan's Comprehensive Security Policy: A New East Asian Environment', *Asian Survey,* 31(4), 324–40.

Albright, M. (2002) Interviewed by author in Seoul, South Korea, 12 November 2002.

Annan, K. A. (2000a) 'We the Peoples: The Role of the United Nations in the 21st Century', http://www.un.org/millennium/sg/report/.

Annan, K. A. (2000b) *Secretary-General, Addressing Closing Session of the Millennium Summit,* press release SG/SM/7540, 8 September 2000, http://www.un.org/News/Press/docs/2000/20000908.sgsm7540.doc.html.

Annan, K. A. (2005) *In Larger Freedom: Towards Development, Security and Human Rights,* http://www.un.org/largerfreedom/contents.htm.

Axworthy, L. (1997) 'Canada and Human Security: The Need for Leadership', *International Journal,* 52(2), 183–96.

BBC (2009) 'Burma Rejects EU, Asian pressure', *BBC,* 25 May 2009, http://news.bbc.co.uk/2/hi/asia-pacific/8066513.stm.

Boutros-Ghali, B. (1992) *An Agenda for Peace: Preventive Diplomacy, Peacemaking and Peace-keeping,* http://www.un.org/docs/SG/agpeace.html.

Buzan, B. and Segal, G. (1998) 'Rethinking East Asian Security' in M. T. Klare and Y. Chandrani (eds), *World Security: Challenges for a New Century* (New York: St. Martin's Press).

Buzan, B. (2004) 'A Reductionist, Idealistic Notion that Adds Little Analytical Value', *Security Dialogue,* 35, 369–70.

Chandler, D. (2008) 'Review Essay: Human Security: The Dog That Didn't Bark', *Security Dialogue,* 39(4), 427–38.

Commission on Global Governance (CGG) (1995) *Our Global Neighborhood* (Oxford: Oxford University Press).

Commission on Human Security (CHS) (2003) *Human Security Now: Final Report* (New York: CHS).

Department of Foreign Affairs and International Trade (DFAIT) (1999) *Human Security: Safety for People in a Changing World* (Ottawa: DFAIT).

Doyal, L. and Gough, I. (1991) *A Theory of Human Need* (Basingstoke: Palgrave Macmillan).

Evans, G. (2008) 'Time for an Aid Invasion?' *The Age,* 19 May 2008, http://www.theage.com.au/news/opinion/time-for-an-aid-invasion/2008/05/18/1211049061508.html.

Finnemore, M. (2003) *The Purpose of Intervention: Changing Beliefs about the Use of Force* (Ithaca: Cornell University Press).

Global Centre for the Responsibility to Protect (GCR2P) (2009) *GCR2P Summary on Statements on Adoption of Resolution RES A/63/L80 Rev.1,* http://globalr2p.org/media/pdf/GCR2P_Summary_of_Statements_on_Adoption_of_Resolution_on_R2P.pdf.

Ghai, D. (2006) 'Least Developed Countries' in D. Clark (ed.), *The Elgar companion to Development Studies* (Cheltenham: Edward Elgar Publishing).

Geneva International Centre for Humanitarian Demining (GICHD) (2007) *Lao PDR Risk Management and Mitigation Model* (Geneva: GICHD).

Holzgrefe, J. L. (2003) 'The Humanitarian Intervention Debate' in J. L. Holzgrefe and R. O. Keohane (eds), *Humanitarian Intervention: Ethical, Legal, and Political Dilemmas* (Cambridge: Cambridge University Press).

International Commission on Intervention and State Sovereignty (ICISS) (2001) *The Responsibility to Protect* (Ottawa: International Development Research Centre).
International Monetary Fund (IMF) (1997) *Good Governance: The IMF's Role* (Washington, DC: IMF).
Junne, G. and Verkoren, W. (2005) *Post Conflict Development: Meeting New Challenges* (Colorado: Lynne Rienner Publishers).
King, G. and Murray, C. (2001–02) 'Rethinking Human Security', *Political Science Quarterly*, 116, 585–610.
Mushajori, K. (2012) 'Three Reasons Why We Should Study Human Security', *Journal of Human Security Studies,* 1(Winter), 1.
Kuruvilla, S., Bustreo, F.*et al.* (2012) 'The Millennium Development Goals and Human Rights: Realizing Shared Commitments', *Human Rights Quarterly,* 34(1), 141–77.
Lauder, S. (2007) 'Climate Change a Huge Security Problem: Keelty', *ABC News*, 25 September 2007, http://www.abc.net.au/news/2007-09-25/climate-change-a-huge-security-problem-keelty/680208.
Luban, D. (1985) 'Just War and Human Rights' in C. R. Beitz and L. A. Alexande (eds), *International Ethics* (Princeton: Princeton University Press).
Mukherjee, N. and Krieckhaus, J. (2012) 'Globalization and Human Well-being', *International Political Science Review,* 33(2), 150–70.
Newman, E. (2010) 'Critical Human Security Studies', *Review of International Studies,* 36(1), 77–94.
Musoni, P. (2003) *Innovations in Governance and Public Administration for Poverty Reduction in Post-conflict Countries in a Globalised World,* http://unpan1.un.org/intradoc/groups/public/documents/un/unpan007601.pdf.
Office of the High Commissioner for Human Rights (OHCHR) (2007) *Good Governance Practices for the Protection of Human Rights* (New York and Geneva: UN Publications).
Paris, R. (2001) 'Human Security: Paradigm Shift or Hot Air?', *International Security,* 26, 87–102.
Radtke, K. W. and Feddema, R. (2000) *Comprehensive Security in Asia: Views from Asia and the West on a Changing Security Environment* (Boston: Brill).
Rawls, J. (1987) 'The Idea of an Overlapping Consensus', *Oxford Journal of Legal Studies,* 7, 1–27.
Rees, D. (2008) 'Clinton, Obama, and Cluster Bombs, *Huffington Post,* 4 February 2008, http://www.huffingtonpost.com/david-ress/clinton-obama-and-clust_b_84811.html.
Takaso, Y (2012) 'Mainstreaming Human Security in the Global Agenda', *Journal of Human Security Studies,* 1, 2–7.
Thomas, N. and Tow, W. T. (2002) 'The Utility of Human Security: Sovereignty and Humanitarian Intervention', *Security Dialogue,* 33, 177–92.
United Nations (UN) (2008) *The Millennium Development Goals Report* (New York: UN).
United Nations Development Programme (UNDP) (1994) *Human Development Report: New Dimensions of Human Security* (New York: Oxford University Press).
UNDP (1997) *Governance for Sustainable Human Developmen*t, http://mirror.undp.org/magnet/policy/.
UNDP (2009) *Mine Action,* http://www.undp.org/cpr/documents/mine_action/FastFacts/mine_action_fast_facts_march09.pdf.
United Nations Economic and Social Commission for Asia and the Pacific (UNESCAP) (2012) *What Is Good Governance?,* http://www.unescap.org/pdd/prs/ProjectActivities/Ongoing/gg/governance.asp.

UN General Assembly Resolution 55/2 (2000) *United Nations Millennium Declaration*, http://www.un.org/millennium/.

United Nations Public Administration Programme (UN PAP) (2012) *Governance and Public Administration*, http://www.unpan.org/DPADM/AboutUs/OurWorkAreas/GovernanceandPublicAdministration/tabid/538/Default.aspx.

UN Secretary-General (2007) *Guidance Note of the Secretary-General on Democracy*, http://www.un.org/democracyfund/Docs/UNSG Guidance Note on Democracy.pdf.

Waever, O. (1995) 'Securitization and Desecuritization' in R. D. Lipschutz (ed.), *On Security* (New York: Columbia University Press).

Walzer, M. (1983) *Spheres of Justice: A Defense of Pluralism and Equality* (New York: Basic Books).

Walzer, M. (1985) 'The Moral Standing of States: A Response to Four Critics' in C. R. Beitz, L. A. Alexander and L. Alexander (eds), *International Ethics* (Princeton: Princeton University Press).

Walzer, M. (1992) *Just and Unjust Wars: A Moral Argument with Historical Illustrations*, 2nd ed. (New York: Basic Books).

Walzer, M. (1997) *On Toleration* (New Haven: Yale University Press).

Watson, A. M. S. (2004) *An Introduction to International Political Economy* (London: Continuum).

World Health Organization (WHO) (2002) *World Report on Violence and Health* (Geneva: WHO).

World Bank (2000) *World Development Report of 2000/2001: Attacking Poverty* (New York: Oxford University Press).

3
East Asian Perspectives on Human Security and Governance

Introduction

The European governance experience can be seen as a benchmark for the protection and promotion of human security through legal and humanitarian mechanisms, through enhancing qualitative and quantitative democratic measurements, and, despite recent economic turmoil, through a generally positive development experience. In addition, the European Union (EU) has made tremendous strides in eradicating the scourge of war between its member countries, which, as outlined in other chapters in this volume, remains one of the major obstacles to providing freedom from fear and freedom from want.

Key to the European good governance experience at both the domestic and regional international levels are the three sides of the Kantian or liberal virtuous triangle – democratic peace, economic interdependence, and international organization. O'Neal and Russett (1999) and Russett and O'Neal (2001) have found the three sides of the Kantian triangle each to have an independent pacifying effect. Europe was also the testing ground for another new and important element of liberal governance and security strategy, with international norms established by the 35 states participating in the Conference on Security and Cooperation in Europe (CSCE) signing the Helsinki Final Act empowering civil society and contributing directly to the demise of communism in the former Eastern Bloc (Thomas, 2001, p. 3).

Thus, perhaps not surprisingly, the efficacy of the three sides of the liberal virtuous triangle, combined with the Helsinki process, in constructing a zone of perpetual peace, human security, and development in Europe, has also led many commentators and practitioners in East Asia in general, and in particular in Northeast Asia, to consider the viability of a similar liberal internationalist project in the region. All three sides of the liberal triangle are, however, at best limited in East Asia. There is little hope for a Helsinki process in the region, and it is still a decidedly state-centric environment in which governments jealously guard their monopolies of authority both in domestic contexts (reflected in a pre-occupation with non-interference) and in international relations (strong support for the principles of sovereignty and equality). The EU model of 'pooling sovereignty' therefore finds little support in East Asia. 'Sovereignty is jealously guarded by most states, some of which were still colonies only a generation ago' (Lawson, 2005, p. 112). This chapter therefore begins by examining the regional differences between Europe and East Asia, and how local particularities pose challenges for both the national and international liberal governance projects in the latter region.

Nevertheless, there is hope for the evolution of a regional operating environment more supportive of human security and development based on rational and socially constructed pragmatic instruments rather than those of the liberal paradigm. As a result of a regional overlapping consensus, proliferation of media outlets beyond national government controls, democratization of security norms, and increased assertiveness and independence of key actors in the region, East Asian governance holds promise as never before. The second part of this chapter addresses reasons for optimism regarding the evolution and growth of policy prioritization increasingly supportive of safe havens in East Asia. Overall, this chapter outlines the unique historical development and characteristics of East Asian governance, but also ways in which the region can develop operational characteristics similar to those possessed by Europe even if starting from a radically different base.

Challenges to liberal economic governance in East Asia

The side of the liberal virtuous triangle which seems to hold most promise for East Asia is that of economic interdependence. As mentioned in Chapter 2, the region has been described as suffused with a remarkable econophoria, where all governance problems, whether domestic or international, are seen as surmountable through development and growth – an outlook which has emerged alongside the dynamic economic success stories of most states in the region (Buzan and Segal, 1998, p. 107). Edward Morse (1970) contends that national policies have been transformed radically wherever high levels of modernization exist. And there is no doubt that high levels of modernization are being achieved throughout East Asia, with first Japan, then the Asian Tigers, (South Korea, Hong Kong, Taiwan, and Singapore), and finally China itself and the Asian Tiger Cubs (Thailand, Malaysia, Indonesia, and the Philippines) becoming increasingly developed and integrated into the international economy. Indeed, one of the underpinnings for South Korean President Kim Dae-jung's 'Sunshine Policy' and also the proposals for Northeast Asian energy cooperation was the anticipation that even North Korea could be encouraged to liberalize politically in the event of being helped to develop economically.

The great liberal hope for East Asia is that as a number of the countries in the region continue to experience phenomenal economic progress, a natural and inevitable by-product will be the emergence of numerically significant and politically influential middle classes who will stimulate civil society that in turn will press for political liberalization. China is of course the paradigmatic example of hope for this process, but it could be argued that South Korea, Taiwan, and Indonesia have already experienced something along these lines. Other potential transformation case studies in the region include Vietnam and Malaysia. With regard to China, Lowell Dittmer predicts 'under such circumstances, previous experience suggests that a full-blown civil society – albeit still with distinctive Chinese cultural characteristics – is apt to emerge as quickly as bamboo shoots after a spring rain', while Zbigniew Brezezinski agrees that it is 'impossible to envision a long-term process of increasing economic pluralism without the appearance of civil society in China that eventually begins to assert its political aspiration' (both quoted in Nau, 2002, p. 165).

Commerce is spreading in East Asia. Not just the major modern capitalist export-driven economies of the region (Japan, South Korea, Taiwan, Hong Kong, and Singapore) but also the countries formerly wedded to authoritarian models of governance such as Thailand, the Philippines, Malaysia, and Indonesia; the developing former socialist economies of Russia and Mongolia; and the still nominally socialist economies of China, Vietnam, Cambodia, the Lao PDR, and even North Korea, are driven to improve the lives of their citizens through selling what they can produce both globally and regionally. Special economic zones are flourishing and most of the economies in the region are pressing to join global and regional economic organizations. Russia and China have long given up on autarky, and the Juche philosophy of North Korea is failing so clearly that, as further developed in Chapter 4, even the 'Dear Leader' accepted reality and appeared a convert to international trade, showing enthusiasm for a Buick plant near Shanghai, and a consistent interest in establishing special economic zones (Gregg, 2003).

Thus, a 'liberal economic order divorces wealth and welfare from control over territory, and thereby removes one of the main reasons for the use of force' (Buzan and Segal, 1998). The impact of economic development on policies and practices of good governance is seen therefore to operate at both the micro level within states in the region and at the macro level between them. In both these arenas, however, there remain serious obstacles to the effective protection and promotion of human security regardless of, and in some cases perhaps even because of, economic development in East Asia.

In some ways, economic development is serving to restrict democratic pressures in China by strengthening the hand of the central government and channelling the enthusiasm of the most dynamic elements of society into getting rich rather than getting rights. In a similar way, as pointed out by Haggard and Noland (2008), in a country such as North Korea, even nominally private economic exchanges can be monopolized by the state and military sector and provide fungible resources that support the regime. At the very least, both countries have a long way to go before the beneficial effects of economic liberalism will be felt. North Korea remains an economic basket case, and one reason for the prolonged and much remarked double-digit growth of the Chinese economy is that it was starting from such a low base. In GNP per capita terms, China remains a low-income developing country, still ranked outside the top 100 in the world and has very limited resources (Wang, 2007) According to China's own strategic plans, it will take until the middle of the century before it can be called a 'modernized, medium-level developed country' and will face three big challenges before it gets there: a shortage of resources, environmental degradation, and a lack of coordination between economic and social development (Zheng, 2005). A market economy, by its nature, blossoms in commercial liberalism rather than the authoritarian pseudo-communist political system of China.

On a more general level, the consensual process of liberal transition is also under threat. The Western way of life, and associated governance models, only exert a positive attraction as long as they are perceived to be desirable and preferable to other alternatives. Should the capitalist democratic world system enter a pronounced downturn (as perhaps heralded by the ongoing global financial crisis which started in 2008), this may no longer be the case, particularly if increased interregional competition should lead to a new wave of protectionism and shrinking global trade. Furthermore, the promised benefits of liberal transition policies have been slower to materialize within transitional states than may have been hoped. An internal expectancy gap has developed within many transitional states, and in some cases, this could lead to a degree of discontent sufficient to undermine or even reverse the liberalization that has already taken place.

The processes of both economic and democratic transitions are themselves sources of considerable uncertainty and hardship. Some groups are bound to lose out, at least in the short term. Support for transition is only generated by the general optimism that ultimately all will benefit; the hope that even if this is not the case, then at least the majority will do so; and the common belief held by most, that they will form part of this majority. The longer that uncertainty regarding the distribution of democratic spoils persists, the greater the chance of an authoritarian relapse (Pridham, 1991).

More than any other form of government, democracy depends for its legitimacy upon the consent of a majority of those governed. In order to generate and maintain such consent, democracy must provide what the majority of people want. Political perceptions vary in accordance with economic circumstances, and the inevitable costs of transition include corruption, inflation, underemployment of capital and labour, allocative inefficiencies, and distributional effects (Maravall, 1997). No matter the universal aspirations, no reform makes all better off, and certainly some will always benefit more than others. Any group that perceives itself worse off in relative, let alone in absolute terms is therefore likely to resist the implementation of the reform. Rapid development has been matched by neither universal domestic good democratic governance nor the evolution in terms of international governance, of peace-inducing interdependence. The next section considers further the limits of political good governance in the East Asian region.

Challenges to liberal political governance in East Asia

Optimism about the inevitable universal triumph of liberal governance models is perhaps most famously summed up by Francis Fukuyama (1989) in his 'End of History' hypothesis, whereby the demonstrated superiority of liberalism in both the economic and political realms has led to a situation where there is no rational alternative. The notion of democratic contagion from the West provides further support for this hypothesis (although given the geopolitical progression it should perhaps be called contagion from the East). In a similar manner to that feared by Western Cold War strategists concerning the spread of communism, liberal economic and political transition has toppled one after another domino in the Communist Bloc (Whitehead, 1996).

Democratic values have spread from America through Japan to Korea and Mongolia, are increasingly felt in Southeast Asia, and have even impacted upon China. Post-totalitarian states, and the regimes representing them, have allowed considerable penetration of their societies by Western media, cultural, and economic organizations. Private organizations (from satellite television operators to car manufacturers), foreign state operations (from the BBC to overseas aid), and multi- and non-governmental organizations (NGOs) (from the World Bank to Save the Children) offer a constant diet of the advantages of belonging to the democratic club, and put pressure on transitional regimes to move in a direction acceptable to this club.

This phenomenon overlaps with another aspect of international pressure upon regime transition, that of consensual influence. Should the West rely upon forced democratization, there would be serious concerns regarding the legitimacy of such operations in forcing people to be free (Walzer, 1983, p. 5; 1997, p. 20) or the security achieved through the artificial transplantation of liberal methods of governance to societies unready to receive them (Carr, 1939; Kim, 1998). Yet many transitional countries are on the whole 'freely' choosing democracy because of the attraction of the West. Such 'democracy by convergence' relates 'how an almost universal wish to imitate a way of life associated with the liberal capitalist democracies of the core regions (the wish for modernity) may undermine the social and institutional foundations of any regime perceived as incompatible with these aspirations' (Regelsberger, 1997). Primarily the attraction is economic, but there is also a significant growth in support for the ideas of universal human rights and the rule of law both within and between states.

An overview of the body of research as a whole gives a strong statistical correlation between democratic dyads and peace (Ray, 1998, p. 27). Although there are doubts concerning the causal link between democratic dyads and peaceful interaction, as there may well be intervening variables that contribute to the causal effect, the best candidates for these intervening variables are the other sides of the liberal virtuous triangle, economic interdependence, and international organization. When all three variables are considered, there appears to be not only strong correlation but also causation. Henry Nau (2002, p. 153) claims that the United States and Japan form an incipient democratic security community in Asia, one which also includes the emerging democracies in South Korea, Taiwan, and Southeast Asia. He also asserts that peace between the strong democracies of America and Japan, expanding to include new democracies, is the key both to stabilizing the growth of Chinese power and to offering China a secure place in the peaceful and prosperous world community. With the United States, Japan, South Korea, and Taiwan, already consolidated democracies, a politically transformed China would not only lead to more democratic than conflictual dyads in Northeast Asia but would also defuse the potential flash point with democratic Taiwan, and reinforce the appeal of democracy in Southeast Asia with the Beijing consensus converging with that of Washington.

Were East Asia truly to develop into a zone of peace, the mutually reinforcing nature of the various sides of the liberal virtuous triangle would become apparent. Political transition would generate more trustworthy regimes, which in turn would be more ready to cooperate and come together in formal and informal political and legal institutions. New developments in the operating environment and new security agendas have not only reignited enthusiasm in the region for transnational governance but have also generated strategic imperatives for rational security cooperation. International organizations help set the international agenda, act as catalysts for coalition formation, and serve as arenas for political initiatives, leverage and linkage by medium and smaller powers (of crucial importance to intra-regional interaction and also to interaction with the United States). Liberal political principles of good governance at both the domestic and international level also, therefore, hold important implications for the promotion of peace, human security, and development in East Asia. Yet again, however, they come up short when the East Asian operating environment is examined in detail.

In China, the Tiananmen Square massacre has been but the most glaring symptom of stalled democratization. Tentative steps taken in Hong Kong under British rule were abruptly reversed when the territory returned to China's direct control. In 2002, the government launched an (on-going) attack on the Internet, attempting to restrict access and block sites. Crackdowns against the Falun Gong and other groups under Jiang Zemin's old guard continued under the leadership of Hu Jintao. Growth first, and building a domestic consensus among disparate power-brokers were the hallmarks of Hu's administration, and in these areas, he was remarkably successful (Brown, 2013). But in some ways, economic development has only strengthened authoritarian forces. President Xi Jinping is seen as an 'old school' member of the political elite and talks of the 'China Dream' – a Chinese renaissance so China can resume its rightful place in the world (Grammaticas, 2013). Such wording and strong support for the military has alarmed China's neighbors, and it is telling that the first overseas tour by the new president was to increasingly authoritarian Russia.

Despite the influence of the third wave of democratic transitions in the last quarter of the twentieth century, and the possible emergence of a fourth wave with the Arab Spring from December 2010, the region seems to support a number of consolidated authoritarian regimes. There seems little hope for democratic transition not just in the PRC but also in the DPRK, the one-party states of Cambodia and Laos, semi-democratic Malaysia and Singapore, or the monarchy of Brunei. Even those states in the region which are seen as democratic face challenges. Henry Nau notes that in general, 'Asia's emerging democracies suffer from deficiencies in peaceful rotation of opposing parties in power, divided and accountable institutions, and protection of civil liberties'. He finds bureaucratic politics in Asian democracies to be 'elitist, highly personalized, and often corrupt', with weak civil societies and institutions, subsidized and controlled media, corrupt judicial systems, brutal policing, and commonplace human rights violations (2002, pp. 163–4).

Both South Korea and Taiwan are plagued by disloyal oppositions, and in Japan, elites and a single political party exercise an inordinate amount of influence. In Southeast Asia, the supposed consolidated democracies of Thailand and the Philippines have experienced a military coup followed by a descent into ungovernability and into kleptocracy respectively. As discussed in detail in Chapter 8, Timor-Leste remains a fragile state beset with authoritarian temptations. Myanmar appears to be making progress in the right direction, but as reviewed in Chapter 7, reforms are both limited and tentative. Only Indonesia appears to be moving toward more solid democratic governance. Indeed, for Buzan and Segal (1998, p. 106), Asian politics leans toward authoritarianism and sudden changes of policy, with less transparent political and economic cultures making conflict and misunderstanding among the polities more likely.

European leaders are restrained by external constraints of international organizations and the external constituency of a regional normative community. By contrast, East Asia combines outstanding economic growth with minimal international organization. The needs of coexistence are provided by global organizations such as the UN or WTO or through bilateral agreements. Without regional organization, it is difficult for statesmen to foster a culture of common interests leading to cooperation rather than conflict. Part of the problem is historical, with the only prior experience of international organization, the Greater East Asia Co-Prosperity Sphere, established through Japanese conquest. Furthermore, because economic growth and development have been experienced in the context of a supportive transregional regime composed of the United States and global international organizations, there appears little need to change. Regional integration is therefore viewed as unfeasible, unnecessary, unlikely, and undesirable (Lee, 1996; Lim, 1996). This notion of East Asian 'difference' is broadly reflective of the Asian values debate detailed below.

The challenge of Asian values

Although few regions are as culturally and socioeconomically diverse, opposition to Western liberal or universal cosmopolitan values emanating from East Asia has tended to be identified collectively as the challenge of 'Asian values'. Asian societies are seen to operate within a value system of 'society over the self'. As pointed out by Acharya (2003, p. 12), what is important is, 'not the evidence that its proponents have been able to muster in support of this argument. Rather, the Asian values perspective has lent powerful ideological justification for enhancing state power at the expense of human security'. Furthermore, Henry Nau (2002, p. 163) notes that the lack of full protection for civil liberties in Asia 'reflects the significantly different traditions regarding the relationship of the individual to society. Nowhere in Asia is there a celebration of political individualism as we know it in the West, either in political thought or in historical events such as the Reformation or Enlightenment'. He claims that authority patterns 'infuse all social relationships – in the family (Confucianism), in religion (Buddhism and Islam), and in the state (Shintoism)' (ibid., p. 164).

The Asian challenge to solidarism can be seen in cultural, economic, and political terms. Culturally, it asserts that the Western liberal or universalist approach ignores the specific cultural traditions and historical circumstances of Asian societies, whose interpretations of human rights are different from those in the West. Economically, it maintains that the priority of developing Asian societies has to be the eradication of poverty. 'Asian values' have been invoked as a form of developmentalism, with the claim that until prosperity is achieved, democracy remains an unaffordable luxury (Thompson, 2004, p. 1085). Politically, it calls into question the motives of the West, accusing them of using human rights merely as an instrument for advancing Western economic or security interests – 'power politics in disguise' and a shallow pretense for the use of force against regimes which stand up to Western neo-imperialism.

Essentially, the Asian values debate poses a communitarian epistemological challenge to liberal individualism and solidarism. Communitarians address the necessity of attending to the demands of community alongside, or prior to, liberty and equality. In other words, we must not only pay attention to the shared practices and values within each society which constitute a distinct understanding of the common good, its generation, and its distribution, but also, society or community is itself a collective good which must at the very least be weighed against other rights. As mentioned in Chapter 2, for Michael Walzer (1985, p. 218), the political community (qua state) is the closest we can come to a world of common meanings as it is where language, history, and culture come most closely together to produce a collective consciousness.

A broad resistance to encroachment upon state prerogatives does seem to be reflected in the day-to-day diplomacy of the East Asian region. In December 1990, when the UN decided to convene a World Conference on Human Rights, several Asian states questioned the applicability of universal human rights in different cultural, economic, and social settings. The Asian regional preparatory meeting which took place in Bangkok between 29 March and 2 April 1993 provided an opportunity for Asian governments to put forward their definition of human rights on the global agenda. The Bangkok Declaration, signed by over 40 Asian governments, did not reject universal human rights, but the declaration suggested that universality should be considered 'in the context of a dynamic and evolving process of international norm-setting, bearing in mind the significance of national and regional particularities and various historical, cultural and religious backgrounds'. The Asian states also sought to link development issues with human rights questions and emphasize the importance of non-interference. Indeed for Kenneth Christie and Denny Roy (2001, p. 5), 'development has assumed cult-like status' in East Asia.

While the 'values' debate has toned down in recent years, it remains an important subtext 'especially in relation to issues that are now seen as part of the human security agenda' (Lawson, 2005, p. 110). Hence, East Asia remains a decidedly state-centric security operating environment, resistant to Western concepts of universalism, solidarism, and collective security, and 'is one of few areas in the world where most countries strongly defend traditional concepts of national sovereignty and firmly resist foreign intervention in the internal affairs of independent states' (Chu, 2001, p. 1). In part, as a result of experiences of colonialism, 'the collective autonomy and dignity of the state from foreign domination takes precedence over autonomy and dignity of the individual which lies at the core of human security' with Asian states remaining among the most ardent champions of Westphalian sovereignty (Acharya, 2003, p. 9).

Nevertheless, security norms in East Asia are evolving in such a way as not only to bring about a regional convergence, thereby stimulating and supporting collective security initiatives, but also to raise the possibility of a global synthesis of East and West on principles of human security and good governance. Much of the impetus for these developments comes from external pressure including the evolution of international law, the wider international community as represented by international organizations and regimes, and from Western liberal states and statespersons. The East Asian strong state security model is also, however, facing challenges from internal constituencies within regional polities. The final section therefore addresses reasons for optimism regarding good governance in East Asia.

Internal and external pressures for good Asian governance

With regard to international law, League of Nations mandates and UN Trusteeships established an international principle that states could be held accountable for the human rights of those governed. The Nuremberg trials further established a limit to state sovereignty – states could no longer do as they wished with their citizens, and the UN Charter Preamble reaffirmed faith in fundamental human rights without discrimination. This is also reflected in the wording of Articles 1(3), 55, and 56. The year 1948 saw the landmark Universal Declaration of Human Rights passed by the General Assembly, and this was followed in 1966 by the Covenants on Civil and Political Rights and Economic, Social and Cultural Rights. For Jack Donnelly, there is a 'remarkable international normative consensus on the list of rights' found in the Universal Declaration of Human Rights, and his claims are strengthened 'by the fact that in the daily round of diplomacy, state leaders justify their human rights policies in terms of these standards' (Dunne and Wheeler, 1999, p. 77).

The Nuremberg trials of Nazi war criminals, despite the dubious backdating of legal principles, helped undermine the principle of sovereignty with regard to a government's treatment of its own people, held individual officials accountable to a wider international court of public opinion, and reinforced the notion of an internationally accepted code of behavior. As put by US Supreme Court Justice Robert Jackson when trying to justify why the criminal statutes relating to wars of aggression and crimes against humanity that he proposed drafting would not be ex post facto laws: 'What we propose is to punish acts which have been regarded as criminal since the time of Cain and have been so written in every civilized code' (Linder, 2000). In 1946, East Asia also experienced a similar exercise in international 'justice' in the form of the International Military Tribunal for the Far East (IMTFE), otherwise known as the Tokyo War Crimes Tribunal. Given that the Tribunal was set up by order of General Douglas MacArthur, the supreme commander of Allied Forces in the South Pacific, this could still be viewed in the tradition of Western imperialism in Asia. Yet individuals representing numerous Asian countries (including China, India, and the Philippines) participated as judges and prosecutors. The defendants were accused of crimes against peace, crimes against humanity, and conventional war crimes (Tokyo). In addition, Asian countries (in particular China) held their own trials of Japanese war criminals, convicting and executing far more.

As briefly introduced in Chapter 2, the UN has been to the fore in championing the rights of peoples and the role to be played by the international community, even if these come at the expense of state prerogatives and sovereignty. Despite the misgiving listed above, East Asian states have been generally supportive of the normative endeavors, with their leaders voting in favor of the General Assembly and Security Council resolutions on the Responsibly to Protect. Other international actors have, however, also begun to pressure East Asian states to accept an ever broader international normative agenda and related governance obligations.

Myanmar has provided one of the focal points for Western criticism of Asian governance practices. In 2008, Madeleine Albright, the former US Secretary of State, called the response of the Burmese Government to Cyclone Nargis criminally neglectful and raised once again the complex question of when it is right to violate state sovereignty in the interest of the protection of the state's citizens. US Defense Secretary Robert Gates used very similar wording, and Gareth Evans (2008), president of the International Crisis Group (ICG) 2000–09 and a former foreign minister of Australia, reflected on whether it was 'time for an aid invasion'. Five of the world's leading international jurists commissioned a report from the International Human Rights Clinic at Harvard Law School, calling for the UN Security Council to act on more than 15 years of condemnation from other UN bodies on human rights abuses in Burma (IHRC, 2009). Finally, in response to what was seen as amounting to criminal incompetence by the authorities in response to the devastation of the cyclone, French Foreign Minister, Bernard Kouchner, proposed that the R2P be invoked to legitimize the forcible delivery of humanitarian assistance without the consent of the Government of Myanmar (Bellamy and Davies, 2009, p. 548).

The May 2009 Europe-ASEAN Meeting (ASEM) in Hanoi, Vietnam, was dominated by questions regarding an international response to the continued persecution of Burmese democracy leader, Aung San Suu Kyi, by the military junta. Interestingly, criticism of the regime came not only from the Western liberal individualistic states of Europe but also from Myanmar's fellow ASEAN members. In the week leading up to the meeting, ASEAN released a statement expressing 'grave concern' over her treatment, which attracted an old-school Asian values response from the military regime that Thailand (at that time holding the chair of ASEAN) was interfering in

Myanmar's internal affairs by releasing the organization's critical message (BBC, 2009). East Timor President Jose Ramos-Horta and the Burma Lawyers' Council announced that they were ready to go to the International Criminal Court (ICC) to charge Senior General Than Shwe with human rights abuses and violations of international law in Burma.

Meanwhile, European statesmen increased the pressure not only on the target state, Myanmar, but also on other Asian states and organizations to which the regime traditionally turns to support in their resistance against outside interference. The EU's External Relations Commissioner Benita Ferrero-Waldner called on Asian countries to 'commit themselves to engage with this government in such a way that there be changes' pointing out that China, India and ASEAN were 'the real neighbours here. They work with the country, and therefore they have the best influence' (BBC, 2009). ASEAN's on-going defense of Myanmar has proven a major obstacle to the establishment of a free trade agreement between the two regional blocs, and it may be that under the current economic conditions, member countries will see their interests to lie more closely with economic recovery through the reinvigoration of international trade than with the preservation of non-interference.

International pressures have also coalesced within the region. In July 1998, the then-Thai Foreign Minister Surin Pitsuwan proposed that ASEAN adopt a policy of flexible engagement, which involved discussions of fellow members' domestic policies. As noted by Pitsuwan (2008) himself, although flexible engagement was rejected to become enhanced interaction, ultimately the new ASEAN political and security community came to the fore, 'which is much more intrusive, much more aggressive, much more alien to the ASEAN mental perception than my initial idea in 1998 about flexible engagement'. On 6 May 2008, in a speech supportive of the concepts and critical of attachments to state sovereignty in the region by this time ASEAN Secretary-General Pitsuwan explicitly linked human security, the R2P and humanitarian intervention, emphasizing how the world has changed and that ASEAN and indeed the Asia-Pacific can do no less. In addition to Thailand's representatives, statesmen and spokespersons from Malaysia and even China have become critical of aspects of Myanmar's governance (The New York Times, 2007).

China is perhaps seen as the last champion of Asian values and bulwark against solidarist interventionary policies. Not only does China have its own human rights and governance issues, but alone among Asian states, it potentially has the resources to stand up to Western or universalist critique without the fear of intervention. Yet even the People's Republic is showing signs of normative shift. The opening and growth of China's economy has led to a greater enmeshing of the PRC in multilateral economic and political institutions with subsequent complex interdependence increasing the propensity of China to play the role of a responsible regional power.

Increasing confidence within China has led to a less defensive posture (Economy, 2008). China already contributes to regional conflict resolution and mediation initiatives through both formal and informal channels.

Although certainly not an ardent supporter of potential intervention, China is not the steadfast opponent of principles like the R2P that it is often portrayed. In fact, in its role as a permanent member of the UN Security Council, China has twice endorsed the principle specifically – at the 2005 World Summit and in the reaffirming Security Council Resolution 1674 (Bellamy and Davies, 2009, p. 556). Even with regard to Darfur, China supported the deployment of African Union peacekeepers, and its diplomacy was seen as key to getting Sudanese consent for their deployment. Likewise, with regard to Myanmar, it has provided diplomatic support for the use of the Secretary-General's good offices, securing a visa for the Special Representative, Ibrahim Gambari, and remains open to the idea of ASEAN playing a leading role in addressing Myanmar (ibid., p. 557). At the UNSC, China refrained from vetoing the 2011 R2P action against Libya and has supported international measures against the DPRK. Furthermore, even China is not immune to the penetration and diffusion of universal/solidarist interpretations of human rights among its own population.

It is interesting to note that most Asian states are in fact signatories to many of the humanitarian documents listed above. At the very least, as Dr Mahathir bin Mohamad discovered when questioning the applicability of the Universal Declaration of Human Rights to Malaysia, once a state has signed up to such a treaty, it is difficult later to repudiate its objectives and the implications of interpretation on the international stage. Furthermore, the existence of these documents, and the fact that many Asian states have signed up to them, may serve to stimulate the final challenge to authoritarian regimes in Asia and the principle of non-intervention: the internal constituencies of these very states; whether individuals, the media, human rights groups, religious groups, and/or NGOs. US Ambassador Leonard Garment noted with regard to the Helsinki Accords that, 'the existence of a formal, written document, to which the Eastern regimes gave their public consent and their formal stamp of legitimacy, has made a difference. The words matter and are beginning to move human minds' (Thomas, 2001, p. 257). In East Asia, there is no formal, written document to which target regimes may give public consent, but nevertheless, internal constituencies may be heartened by the normative turn international affairs that have taken in the post-Cold War operating environment.

China, for instance, already faces more than 90,000 protests annually as a result of poor governance involving endemic corruption and ongoing crises in public health and the environment (Economy, 2008). Political pressures for increased public services are in fact so strong and the current provision of education, health care, and pensions so inequitable and dysfunctional that the Chinese government will be compelled to continue to increase the share of output spent on these government services and transfers in the coming decades. China has to perform a delicate balancing act between expanding its economy to avoid domestic unrest and responding to calls, mainly from the West, for the country to act as a 'responsible stakeholder' (Gill *et al.* 2007). In recognition of the challenges of corruption and inequality which have soared along with growing wealth, President Xi Jinping has already visited two very poor areas in Hebei and Gansu where he was presented as a man of the people 'meeting peasants, tasting their food, chatting with them in their homes'. The party risks becoming viewed as the defender of privilege, so part of the new China Dream involves promises to tackle corruption, to spread China's wealth, and to create a fairer society (Grammaticas, 2013). These competing demands on their resources are one reason why the Chinese leadership may wish to pick its battles carefully rather than resist humanitarian intervention whenever and wherever it is mooted.

Authoritarian Asian states face a number of internal normative challenges when attempting to justify policies and actions that may negatively impact upon the human rights of their citizens. First, while it may be possible to talk of pluralistic principles of justice and distribution based on historically and culturally generated divergent understandings of social goods, these understandings of social goods may have been historically and culturally generated in the interests of only a small and distinct section of the community. Asian civil society groups are increasingly vociferous in condemning such unjust privilege and prioritization, whether with regard to caste (India and other South Asian societies), ethnicity (Malaysia), religion (the Philippines), age/generation (South Korea), or gender. As pointed out by Mely Caballero-Anthony (2004, p. 158), 'though found along the margins of subaltern security discourses, human security is the concept that embodies the security concerns of societies in the region and where the most vulnerable can find avenues to articulate their security in their own terms without being excluded and alienated', while civil-society organizations in the region have been playing a pivotal role through their transnational work in promoting human rights and human development.

Second, with democratization of the media, it has become harder for governments to perpetrate, cover up, or turn a blind eye to inhumane practices within their jurisdictions or within those of fellow Asian states. Reports and pictures of slavery, human trafficking, or bloated corpses beamed into living rooms may prove too insistent for statesmen rationally to resist, and in the most extreme examples, it is hard to make a case for them normatively to do so. In an overwhelmingly interconnected region, with heavy penetration of states by new media, and high levels of personal contact between the peoples of different states, ideas and norms are now able to diffuse much more rapidly, and state monopoly control of knowledge and opinion-forming is increasingly undermined.

Thus, David Shambaugh (2008, p. 3) has identified international relations in Asia as an increasingly two-level game, whereby societies of the region are interconnected to an unprecedented degree. What Nyan Chanda (2008, p. 307) refers to as the 'New Preachers' – NGOs and civil society community activists – have sprouted in many countries in the region to uphold humanitarian causes and issues and to pressure governments and corporations. These activists have also linked with international bodies and fellow activists in other countries for coordination and support. The authoritarian state's efforts to maintain its power are challenged by the mutually reinforcing trends of the constant diffusion of information and the rise of civil society activism (ibid., pp. 308–9). The region has experienced the growing influence of networks of NGOs and the growing activism of these networks. Civil society organizations have started to 'build constituencies for peace' wherein they seek to influence policies and programs that can engender 'people-centred security systems' instead of state-centric security systems deemed inadequate to address the growing threats to security of individuals and societies (Caballero-Anthony, 2004, pp. 166–7).

Here we must, however, introduce a caveat. Just because Asian states have signed up to international normative documentation, it does not mean that they understand such international principles to imply the same degree of obligation as might be understood among Western advocates. For instance, the Permanent Representative of South Korea to the UN, one of the most ardent supporters of the R2P among Asian states, stressed that 'the primary responsibility lies in the individual Government while the international community bears the secondary responsibility', that R2P is 'distinctly different from humanitarian intervention since it is based on collective actions, in accordance with UN Charter', and that 'not all humanitarian tragedies or human rights violations can or should activate R2P' (Park, 2009). Japan has been instrumental in pushing forward the next step in the evolution of security conceptualization, the human security discourse, and is the largest contributor to the human security related practices and intuitions of the UN. But in Japanese thinking, there is a significant difference between the two perspectives: 'while R2P recognizes the necessity for enforcement in certain circumstances, human security rules it out in every occasion;' therefore, the Japanese focus is one of preventions thereby reducing the need for intervention (Bellamy and Davies, 2009, p. 552).

Nevertheless, just because these states would prefer to avoid actual military intervention, this does not rule out a shift from a non-interventionary view of international relations. An increased willingness to resort to non-violent intervention, whether it be through aid (or its denial), criticism, or behind-the-scenes diplomacy, is nevertheless a significant departure from traditional views of Asian values in international relations. The evolution of the R2P doctrine itself is reflective of increased engagement between Asian states and the wider international community.

The initial ICISS report was very permissive of humanitarian intervention regardless of authorization by the UN Security Council. This report was drafted by an independent body of experts serving in an advisory capacity to the UN, and as such, their proposals are not legally binding. It might also be argued that East Asia was underrepresented on the panel given that the only member from the region was former President Fidel Ramos of the Philippines. The World Summit document, being a General Assembly resolution, was more binding than the ICISS report, in terms of both legality and, given the near universal representation at the General Assembly, in terms of legitimacy. It was, however, more restrictive in terms of the use of force. Security Council Resolution 1674 takes a similarly restrictive line. In doing so, it may be that the UN has managed to make the whole paradigm more palatable to Asian states. This might serve to explain Vietnam's dramatic shift 'from a position close to opposition to R2P in 2004–05 to one of relatively positive R2P engagement' at the World Summit and for Resolution 1674 (Ibid., p. 561).

In fact, the majority of states in East Asia have at least engaged with the idea of a responsibility to protect, having shifted from previously hard-line non-interventionary positions. In a recent study, Alex Bellamy and Sarah Davies examined the current degree of receptivity to the concept among regional states, identifying Australia, Japan, New Zealand, the Philippines (2004–05), and the Republic of Korea as advocates; Singapore, Indonesia, the Philippines (2006–08) China, and Vietnam (2008) as R2P-engaged; Vietnam (2005–07), Brunei, Cambodia, Laos, Malaysia, and Thailand as Fence Sitters; and only the DPRK and Myanmar as being opposed, with even these two countries not explicitly rejecting the idea that states have a responsibility to protect their own population (ibid., p. 551).

Conclusion

The idea of human security has been regarded as a Western legacy, stemming from liberalism (Rothschild, 1995, pp. 60–1) and is thereby challenged by claims of cultural specificity (Acharya, 2001a, p. 1). Despite the inherent claims of universality and solidarism within the Western liberal project, at both the domestic and international governance levels, distinct East Asian traditions and positions can be identified with regard to the rights and obligations of states and their citizens. Asian exceptionalism in the field of governance survives in the constitutive documents of regional international organizations and in many of the foreign policy priorities of Asian states. It is also found in the epistemological foundations of communitarian societies.

Asian perspectives do not, however, permit national governments to violate the entitlement rights of their citizens with impunity, or turn a blind eye to the violation of the safe havens of the most vulnerable sections of East Asian society by others. As pointed out by Acharya, 'human security protects the existence of entire social groups (including children, civilians in a war zone, ethnic minorities, and so on) from persecution and violence. This understanding of human security is eminently compatible with the alleged communitarian ethos of certain non-Western societies' (2001b, p. 449). Those authorities which hide behind claims of Asian Values to justify such abuses are facing an increasing challenge from internal and external communities and from the changing nature of international law and norms which may even lead to militarized humanitarian intervention.

There is, therefore, something like a global overlapping consensus emerging on governance regarding the need to simultaneously support the concepts of individual human rights, a universal R2P, and a lingering respect for state sovereignty and primacy. It may be possible to accept the claims of exceptionalists, communitarians, and relativists that we are historically and culturally situated, and that indeed in Asia these forces are particularly strong, yet nevertheless identify there being certain universal duties in terms of providing freedom from fear and freedom from want. As will be developed further in Part III of this volume, actors in East Asia are in fact becoming increasingly engaged in the practical provision of safe havens.

According to Paul Evans (2004, p. 264), after facing initial opposition, human security is now finding a place in regional discussion and some policy areas, and while individual states and regional institutions remain hesitant to embrace the terminology, the concept is affecting state practice and playing a catalytic role in changing the normative framework related to state obligations and the principles of sovereignty and non-interference. This does not mean that East Asian states have embraced human security in *preference* to state *security*. As Acharya (2001a, p. 15) cautions, the regional balance between national security and human security is not to be reversed in favor of the latter, but certain key, long-term developments have combined to create greater space for human security in the Asian security order.

East Asian perspectives on human security may still differ in terms of focus and intrusiveness from the Western liberal agenda in that prevention is emphasized over the use of force, development over security, a broad interpretation rather than a narrow interpretation with regard to human security, and a slow evolution and codification of international law. Nevertheless, East Asian states have demonstrated a capacity and willingness to change their positions on these issues. That being said, any attempt to rush this transformation, as for instance some of the more zealous advocates did with regard to the aftermath of Cyclone Nargis in Myanmar, are likely to backfire, strengthening conservative reaction and skepticism in the region of the principles being championed (Bellamy and Davies, 2009, p. 567).

Likewise in terms of human development, again, as will be developed further in Part III, East Asian actors are increasingly important in supplying development initiatives and assistance where it is most needed, but may have strategies and priorities which differ from traditional Western donors.

The strong tendency toward state-centricity and national interest in policy formation means that development assistance from East Asian actors will tend to involve more tied aid, securitization, and perhaps even confusion of motives. Yet this could also result in greater commitment to regional development from East Asian donors. Furthermore, the emphasis placed by regional leaders on social, cultural, and economic rights, often at the expense of civil and political rights – the 'bread before freedom' argument – could work in favor of economic engagement with challenging case studies (Lawson, 2005, p. 109).

East Asian case studies certainly generate divergent obstacles to those experienced in the Western development experience. While Europe dragged itself out of the ashes of two world wars, or was dragged out by American largesse depending on your perspective, most East Asian countries have suffered from colonial legacies and internal strife as well as those of international conflicts. The internal governance challenges are that much greater given, in many cases, not only the lower starting development threshold but also the much larger populations for whom safe havens must be provided. That East Asia is often viewed as a development success story speaks to the achievements of local and international governance actors. Nevertheless, as will be explored in the five challenging case studies, much is left to be done in the region in order to secure freedom from fear and freedom from want. The extent to which Asian solutions to Asian problems can be pursued with regard to human security may turn out to be of vital importance for peacebuilding and development in the region.

As outlined in Chapter 2, it is possible to identify universal entitlement rights common to and inherent in all forms of governance. This is not because we are all Western liberal individualists now. Rather it is because all normative traditions, including those in East Asia, accept that there are certain practices or operational circumstances which 'shock the conscience of humankind' and should be stopped, and that there exists a concurrent obligation on those in positions of authority (those with legitimized power) to protect and provide for those for whom they are responsible. Global governance norms and regional foreign policies/diplomacy in East Asia can be seen as following a mutually constitutive process. Rising Asia does not imply the beginning of the end of international normative consensus, but rather a stronger paradigm of overlapping consensus built on foundations in both the East and the West.

References

Acharya, A. (2001a) 'Human Security: East versus West', Institute of Defence and Strategic Studies (IDSS) Working Paper Series, 17, 1–20.

Acharya, A. (2001b) 'Human Security: East versus West', *International Journal,* 56(3), 442–60.

Acharya, A. (2003) 'Guns and Butter: Why do Human Security and Traditional Security Co-exist in Asia?', *Global Economic Review: Perspectives on East Asian Economies and Industries*, 32(3), 1–21.

Albright, M. (2008) 'The End of Intervention', The New York Times, 11 June 2008, http://www.nytimes.com/2008/06/11/opinion/11albright.html.

BBC (2009) 'Burma Rejects EU, Asian Pressure', BBC, 25 May 2008, http://news.bbc.co.uk/2/hi/asia-pacific/8066513.stm.

Bellamy, A. J. and Davies, S. E. (2009) 'The Responsibility to Protect in the Asia-Pacific Region', *Security Dialogue*, 40(6), 547–74.

Brown, K. (2013) 'What did Hu Jintao and Wen Jiabao do for China?', BBC, 14 March 2013, http://www.bbc.co.uk/news/world-asia-china-21669780.

Buzan, B. and Segal, G. (1998) 'Rethinking East Asian Security', in M. T. Klare and Y. Chandrani (eds), *World Security: Challenges for a New Century* (New York: St Martin's Press).

Caballero-Anthony, M. (2004) 'Revisioning Human Security in Southeast Asia', *Asian Perspective*, 28(3), 155–89.

Carr, E. H. (1939) *The Twenty Years' Crisis, 1919–1939: An Introduction to the Study of International Relations* (London: Macmillan).

Chanda, N. (2008) 'Globalization and International Politics in Asia', in D. Shambaugh and M. Yahuda (eds), *International Relations of Asia* (Plymouth: Rowman & Littlefield).

Christie, K. and Roy, D. (2001) *The Politics of Human Rights in East Asia* (London: Pluto Press).

Chu, S. (2001) 'China, Asia and Issues of Sovereignty and Intervention', Pugwash Occasional Papers, 2(1), http://www.pugwash.org/reports/rc/como_china.htm.

Dunne, T. and Wheeler, N. (1999) *Human Rights in Global Politics* (Cambridge: Cambridge University Press).

Economy, E. (2008) 'Leadership Gap in China', Washington Post, 1 December 2008, http://www.washingtonpost.com/wp-dyn/content/article/2008/11/30/AR2008113001690.html.

Evans, G. (2008) 'Time for an Aid Invasion?', The Age, 19 May 2008, http://www.theage.com.au/news/opinion/time-for-an-aid-invasion/2008/05/18/1211049061508.html.

Evans, P. M. (2004) 'Human Security and East Asia: In the Beginning', *Journal of East Asian Studies*, 4, 263–84.

Fukuyama, F. (1989) 'The End of History?', *The National Interest*, 16, 3–18.

Gill, B., Blumenthal, D., Swaine, M.D., and Mathews, J.T. (2007) *China as a Responsible Stakeholder* (Washington, DC: Carnegie Endowment for International Peace), http://carnegieendowment.org/2007/06/11/china-as-responsible-stakeholder/wmb

Grammaticas, D. (2013) 'China's New President Xi Jinping: A Man with a Dream', BBC, 14 March 2013, http://www.bbc.co.uk/news/world-asia-china-21790384.

Gregg, D. (2003) 'My Turn: Kim Jong Il – The Truth Behind the Caricature', Newsweek, 3 February 2003, http://stacks.msnbc.com/news/863858.asp.

Haggard, S. and Noland, M. (2008) 'North Korea's Foreign Economic Relations', *International Relations of the Asia-Pacific*, 8(2), 219–46.

International Human Rights Clinic (IHRC) (2009) 'Crimes in Burma', Harvard Law School, http://www.law.harvard.edu/programs/hrp/documents/Crimes-in-Burma.pdf.

Kim, Y. (1998) 'Patterns of Military Rule and Prospects for Democracy in South Korea', in R. May and V. Selochan (eds), *The Military and Democracy in Asia and the Pacific* (Canberra: ANU Press).

Lawson, S. (2005) 'Regional Integration, Development and Social Change in the Asia–Pacific: Implications for Human Security and State Responsibility', *Global Change, Peace & Security*, 17(2), 107–22.

Lee, CJ. (1996) 'Promoting Northeast Asian Economic Cooperation: Korea's Role', in R.G. Rich Jr (ed.), *Joint U.S.-Korea Academic Studies Volume 6: Economic and Regional Cooperation in Northeast Asia* (Washington, DC: Korean Economic Institute).

Lim, L. Y. C. (1996) 'Whither Northeast Asian Regional & Economic Cooperation', in R. G. Rich Jr (ed.), *Joint U.S.-Korea Academic Studies Volume 6: Economic and Regional Cooperation in Northeast Asia* (Washington, DC: Korean Economic Institute).

Linder, D. (2000) 'The Nuremberg Trials', http://www.law.umkc.edu/faculty/projects/ftrials/nuremberg/nurembergACCOUNT.html.

Maravall, J. (1997) *Regimes, Politics, and Markets: Democratization and Economic Change in Southern Europe and Eastern Europe* (New York: Oxford University Press).

Morse, E. (1970) 'The Transformations of Foreign Policies: Modernization, Interdependence and Externalization', *World Politics*, 22(3), 371–92.

Nau, H. (2002) *At Home Abroad: Identity and Power in American Foreign Policy* (Ithaca: Cornell University Press).

O'Neal, J. R. and Russett, B. M. (1999) 'The Kantian Peace: The Pacific Benefits of Democracy, Interdependence, and International Organizations, 1885–1992', World Politics, 52(1), 1–37.

Park, I. K. (2009) 'Permanent Representative of the Republic of Korea to the United Nations', Plenary Meeting of the General Assembly on Responsibility to Protect, New York, United States, 23 July 2009, http://www.responsibilitytoprotect.org/Korea_ENG.pdf.

Pitsuwan, S. (2008) Transcript of ASEAN Secretary-General Keynote Address, RSIS Centre for Non-Traditional Security (NTS) Studies Launch, Traders Hotel, Singapore, 6 May 2008, http://www.rsis.edu.sg/NTS/Events/Launch/keynote_address_by_Surin_Pitsuwan_-transcript.pdf.

Pridham, G. (1991) *Encouraging Democracy: The International Context of Regime Transition in Southern Europe* (New York: St. Martin's Press).

Ray, J. L. (1998) 'Does Democracy Cause Peace?', *Annual Review of Political Science*, 1, 27–46.

Regelsberger, E. (1997) *Foreign Policy of the European Union: From EPC to CFSP and Beyond* (London: Lynne Rienner).

Rothschild, E. (1995) 'What is Security?', *Journal of the American Academy of Arts and Sciences*, 124(3), 53–98.

Russett, B. M. and O'Neal, J. R. (2001) *Triangulating Peace: Democracy, Interdependence, and International Organizations* (New York: Norton).

Shambaugh, D. (2008) 'International Relations in Asia: The Two-Level Game', in D. Shambaugh and M. Yahuda (eds), *International Relations of Asia* (Plymouth: Rowman & Littlefield).

The New York Times (2007) 'Chinese Diplomats Criticize Myanmar's New Capital', The New York Times, 23 May 2007, http://www.nytimes.com/2007/05/23/world/asia/23iht-myanmar.1.5837710.html.

Thomas, D. (2001) *The Helsinki Effect* (Princeton: Princeton University Press).

Thompson, M. R. (2004) 'Pacific Asia after "Asian Values": Authoritarianism, Democracy, and "Good Governance"', *Third World Quarterly*, 25(6), 1079–95.

Walzer, M. (1983) *Spheres of Justice: A Defense of Pluralism and Equality* (New York: Basic Books).

Walzer, M. (1985) 'The Moral Standing of States: A Response to Four Critics', in C. R. Beitz, L. A. Alexander, and L. Alexander (eds), *International Ethics* (Princeton: Princeton University Press).

Walzer, M. (1997) *On Toleration* (New Haven: Yale University Press).

Wang, Y. (2007) 'China's Rise: An Unlikely Pillar of US Hegemony', *The Harvard International Review*, 29(1), 56–60.

Whitehead, L. (1996) 'Three International Dimensions of Democratization', in L. Whitehead (ed.), *The International Dimensions of Democratization: Europe and the Americas* (New York: Oxford University Press).

Zheng, B. (2005) 'China's "Peaceful Rise" to Great Power Status', *Foreign Affairs*, 84(5), 18–24.

Part II

East Asian Challenging Case Studies

4
Human Security and National Insecurity in North Korea

Introduction

As addressed in Chapter 2, there is an international security continuum wherein 'new' human-centered approaches are intimately related to 'old' state-centric considerations, NTS issues have the potential to become traditional security threats, and issues of human security can morph into ones of pressing concern for the survival of states themselves or the peace and security of a region or even the globe. Perhaps the best example of this relationship is to be found in the DPRK, and the failure of national and international policymakers to address adequately the complexities of the situation. This chapter examines the causes and consequences of the failure of policies of the national government, aid agencies, donor states, and the international community (strategic partners and competitors), in addressing the insecurity of the citizens of North Korea, and suggests possible policy prescriptions.

With regard to security on the Korean Peninsula, this chapter challenges the traditional belief that diplomats should ignore the internal affairs of states in order to preserve international stability. Regarding states as unitary rational actors misses alternative explanations for the behavior of statesmen, leads to the adoption of self-fulfilling worst-case-scenario planning, is inherently confrontational, and contributes to the likelihood of the emergence of a traditional security dilemma whereby an increase in one state's capabilities is considered a threat to the security of its neighbors. Indeed, this chapter posits that it is North Korean weakness rather than strength that most threatens international peace and security in the region. It is important therefore to take a critical stance toward the exclusive use of traditional security analysis in terms of conceptual area, rational implications,

---

This chapter draws on work previously published with Kahul Kim (2011) as 'North Korea: Policy Failures, Human Insecurity, Consequences, and Prescriptions' *Korea Observer*, 42(2), 281–310.

and referent object. Although all conclusions must be tentative due to lack of hard data from North Korea, traditional security analysis clearly has shortcomings when addressing this case study in particular, and alternative rational models can be constructed on the basis of the information available.

While hostility is understandable among neighbors previously victimized by North Korean aggression or forced to address aggressive statements and actions emanating from Pyongyang, taking a hard line in response may contribute toward a vicious cycle whereby the DPRK either perceives a dangerous external security environment necessitating further internal sacrifices and military prioritization or uses the environment as justification for such measures. These measures are likely to hasten regime collapse in the DPRK and thereby increase further the NTS threats posed by North Korea to surrounding countries, and/or the traditional security threats in terms of diversionary acts of aggression to divert internal constituencies from the problems generated at home by Pyongyang's policies. Thus, state-centric security considerations can filter down to the level of human security, and in turn further destabilize a fragile regime. Unpalatable as it may seem, some process of engagement with North Korea might mitigate Pyongyang's security concerns and also help the internal situation remove both justifications and motivations for dangerous policy prioritization in the DPRK.

North Korea certainly poses a traditional security threat to its neighbors. There has been considerable exaggeration, however, of the degree of traditional threat posed by Pyongyang's military prioritization, weapons systems, and aggression. At the same time, North Korean insecurity poses perhaps a greater threat – one which has often been underestimated or left underexplored. Although some commentators have referred to this phenomenon, generally the emphasis has been on the weakness of the North Korean state rather than the internal dynamics of sub-state structures and threats at the level of individual well-being percolating up to pressure the leadership. This chapter thus emphasizes the interconnectedness of human security and national/international security on the Korean Peninsula.

This in turn demonstrates the need, in this case, for a broadening of both referent objects and policy arena with regard to security. Hence, the logic of a critical approach to North Korean security concerns forces us along a 'securitization' pathway, whereby an issue is first politicized (requiring state action *within* the standard framework of the political system), and then securitized (requiring emergency action *outside* the boundaries of the established norms), which in turn frames the issue as one of an existential threat to a referent object (Emmers, 2007, pp. 110–3). It could be argued that securitization is a self-fulfilling prophecy in that an issue labeled and framed as a security problem becomes such, warranting critical action as recognized by both the actor (typically the state) and the audience (public, collective groups, and so on) (Buzan and Wæver, 2004, p. 71), but this chapter posits that such a process has already occurred in practical terms; thus, in order to grasp the unique complexities of the North Korean security situation, we must likewise broaden the scope of our analysis.

Although North Korea has pursued a political and economic strategy that is enormously destructive for human security internally, in part this has been exacerbated by actions, policies, and at times inactions or sanctions from actors in the international community. Thus, if those who engage strategically with the DPRK truly wish to reduce the threat posed by the rogue regime, it is essential that all aspects of the security spectrum be considered: traditional and non-traditional, state-centric and human security, internal constituencies, and external operating environments. This chapter provides an overview of the relationships between traditional, non-traditional/new, comprehensive, and human security studies, and policy implications for external actors of different security foci with regard to North Korea.

Traditional and non-traditional security in North Korea

The inter-relatedness of state and sub-state security issues is being increasingly recognized in policy-related and academic fields. In 1945, the US Secretary of State, Edward Stettinius Jr, reported to his government the conclusions reached at the San Francisco meeting that led to the establishment of the United Nations:

> The battle of peace has to be fought on two fronts. The first is the security front where victory spells freedom from fear. The second is the economic and social front where victory means freedom from want. Only victory on both fronts can assure the world of an enduring peace ... No provisions that can be written into the Charter will enable the Security Council to make the world secure from war if men and women have no security in their homes and their jobs. (UNDP, 1994, p. 4)

This fundamental recognition of the interconnectedness of diverse threats has continued with the development of the NTS discourse in general, and, more particularly, with the development of the human security paradigm. Furthermore, the human security paradigm has been broadened by its inclusion of 'freedom from want' alongside 'freedom from fear'. Given the horrific impact of shortages in North Korea, human security therefore constitutes an eminently suitable paradigmatic lens through which to view the security challenges in, and policy failures of, the DPRK. Once the vicious cycle between national and human insecurity in North Korea is recognized, it becomes at least plausible that one way to address human insecurity is to help the target state ameliorate its national security concerns, and vice versa, with the amelioration of human security concerns helping a target state feel less vulnerable.

To seek freedom from fear is to provide for national security. Freedom from fear is integral to national security and vice versa, although one does not necessarily guarantee the other. All security approaches are inter-related and non-exclusionary. Thus, human security considerations in North Korea have the potential to spill over into national and international security challenges and vice versa. Again as pointed out in Chapter 2, there is a close relationship between human security envisioned as the protection of persons, and human development as the provision of BHN. Poor governance combined with a number of exogenous forces and events have undermined the human security and development of North Korea, but internal insecurity and underdevelopment have contributed to regional international instability.

North Korea has a long history of brinksmanship. Actions such as restarting its nuclear program, testing nuclear devices and missiles, and in 2010, sinking the South Korean naval corvette *Cheonan*, and shelling the South Korean island *Yeonpyeong* near the Northern Limit Line (NLL) have heightened the trepidation of near neighbors and the wider international community. In traditional security and strategic analysis, a security dilemma exists when the military capabilities of one state, even if they are perceived by that state as being for defensive purposes to deter others from aggression, are viewed by other states as a potential threat. Thus, North Korean acquisition of enhanced military capabilities, particularly those with long-range force projection (such as missiles) or mass destruction potential (such as nuclear weapons), is seen as posing a threat to the security of other parties. It is not necessarily the increasing strength of North Korea that threatens, however, but rather Pyongyang's increasing weakness – an 'insecurity dilemma' rather than a security dilemma, where in addition to posing a threat to its own people, the insecure state's vulnerability is projected outward as a diversionary and unifying tactic causing international uncertainty and instability and security threats to neighboring states.

One explanation for the attack on the *Cheonan* is that it was an attempt by the leadership to show solidarity with the armed forces and improve their morale through gaining revenge for the earlier 2009 naval clash and humiliating defeat (Song, 2010). O Kuk-ryol, a North Korean hardliner and Kim Jong-il loyalist, was not only implicated in the *Cheonan* incident, but was also deeply enmeshed in the succession politics, supporting the controversial candidature of Kim Jong-un, the young third son of the former leader (Kim, 2010). Likewise, the shelling of a South Korean island near the NLL could have been the product of internal insecurity – on the one hand in the face of South Korean live fire operations and joint exercises with the United States, and on the other with regard to the succession crisis as the candidature of Kim Jong-un was promoted within and through the military. Thus, the roots of these military operations with far-reaching international security ramifications can be seen in domestic mass and elite politics.

In other words, the overly-aggressive nature of Pyongyang's actions and statements could be a product not of strength based on new capabilities, but rather of weakness generated by internal crisis. The decline of North Korean capabilities rather than their augmentation is what truly threatens. Civil war or implosion could lead to an even greater exodus of refugees over the border into China than has currently been caused by famine and political oppression in North Korea (30,000–50,000 according to the US State Department, up to ten times this number according to some NGOs), and this time, any criminals or desperados in their midst could be armed (CRS, 2007, p. 1). Most worryingly, both military technology and weapons of mass destruction could diffuse to other undesirable state and non-state actors (Chestnut, 2007).

Shortages in skilled personnel as a result of the isolation of the hermit kingdom and shortfalls in its own training and education programs led to the criminal abduction of citizens of neighboring states, estimated at a total exceeding 180,000. Although this process started during the Korean War when almost 83,000 South Koreans were abducted, it has continued ever since with thousands more South Koreans abducted, around 93,000 ethnic Koreans lured from Japan and then denied the right to leave, and several hundred Japanese and Chinese citizens (the latter mostly ethnic Koreans) taken to North Korea against their will (Yamamoto, 2011, p. 11).

In its desperation for hard currency, Pyongyang has been involved in the production and trafficking of illicit drugs, counterfeit currency, cigarettes, and pharmaceuticals. North Korea is also a source of insurance fraud, human trafficking, and wildlife trafficking. The illicit activities garner about US$500 million in profits per year, or about one-third of DPRK's annual exports (CRS, 2008, p. 1). Thus, economic vulnerability within North Korea may have led to a proliferation of activities that impact negatively on the security of other states. There is also a concern that the profits from these activities are in part funneled to weapons programs that further threaten regional security. Although some of the CRS figures are open to question, regardless of the actual physical impact of increased North Korean criminal activity, regional and global perceptions of the issue and its securitization could further contribute to the international security dilemma.

China's security is particularly threatened by North Korean insecurity. According to Melinda Liu (2003), hunger and oppression inside North Korea have spawned an epidemic of crime over the border in neighboring Chinese provinces. Perhaps most worrying, some of these crimes have been attributed to instruments of DPRK national security, specifically, border guards and other impoverished North Korean soldiers who have apparently gone on a violent crime spree along the 870-mile border (Bennett, 2003). Meanwhile, a recent *Newsweek* report noted how an underground economy, border transients, poverty, and desperation are fuelling a drug scourge in the Chinese hinterlands (Fish, 2011).

If North Korea collapses, the resulting power vacuum could lead to conflict among neighboring states, which would rush to fill the void. As pointed out by Kei Koga (2009, p. 30), 'without any coordination on contingency among them, it is highly likely that the other five states will face grave security risks, including flows of refugees and the proliferation of nuclear weapons and cruise missiles to such non-state actors'. Not surprisingly then, Russia has already increased security on the short border it shares with the DPRK (Blomfield, 2009), and China is reinforcing fences and has stepped up patrols along its much longer border as fears mount of another catastrophic famine in the North (Foster, 2011). Thus, North Korea potentially poses a greater threat because of its inherent internal instability and deliberate generation of external instability in order to distract from the internal fault lines, than because of greater military capability or intent to use such capability against its enemies.

While Pyongyang's aggression could conceivably be ideologically based, along with many of the internal policies such as *juche* (self-reliance) and *songun* (military-first), the acknowledged failure of these ideological foundations to produce what they promised for the citizens of North Korea itself could contribute to internal paranoia and insecurity as well as making North Korea a greater threat to its neighbors. Even should Kim Jong-il's successors harbor lingering dreams of Korean unification through conquest, they cannot fail but to recognize the impracticality of this option, and in January 2010, Kim Jong-il himself had already accepted the shortcomings of internal policies. Indeed, according to Brian Reynolds Myers (2010), while North Korea's outward projection is 'like a fascist's guess of what communist propaganda should look like', the inward self-perception is that 'virtue has rendered them as vulnerable as children to an evil world'. If ideology drives North Korea's aggressive foreign policy, it is an ideology that reflects vulnerability, either at source, as a result of its own shortcomings, or as a result of the failure of regimes with similar ideologies.

Although largely the architect of its own internal insecurity dilemma, North Korea has also been disadvantaged by developments in its international operating environment, which have fostered a belief in the need for, or justification of, policies that further undermined internal development and human security. Previously reliant on the former Soviet Union and China to supply critically needed resources, with uncertainty surrounding continued largesse from its allies, Pyongyang has highlighted energy sovereignty by privileging domestic sources and minimizing its reliance on trade. The sense of insecurity at the national level has, in other words, led Pyongyang to adopt energy policies that contribute ultimately to the underproduction and inefficient use of energy. North Korea has also emphasized sovereignty in its food policies, again with disastrous results. In the 1980s, the growth rate of rice production began to slow, and when North Korea was hit in the 1990s by the combination of natural disasters and the collapse of the Soviet bloc, which cut off petroleum and other inputs essential for agricultural production, the limitations of the food sovereignty policy became undeniable as what had been widespread hunger exploded into massive starvation and famine (Haggard and Noland, 2005, p. 14). The next section examines the extent of distress in the DPRK.

Human security and domestic governance failure in North Korea

Human security is most noticeable when it is absent, as in the case of North Korea. The country lags behind in terms of human development and fares particularly poorly when it comes to respect for basic human rights and civil liberties. Misguided in its pursuit of the warped dual policies of *juche* and *songun*, the government itself is a major source of threat to its own people. Already one of the worst violators of the human rights of its citizens, the DPRK has recently been reported as expanding its notorious prison camps. Amnesty International has published satellite imagery and new testimony that shed light on the horrific conditions in the camps, which hold an estimated 200,000 people, and a comparison of the latest images with satellite imagery from 2001 indicates a significant increase in the scale of the camps (Amnesty International, 2011). Economic mismanagement, governance failure, negligence and oppressive behavior by the state has had grave consequences for ordinary citizens, and the country remains deep in distress despite recent, flawed attempts at reform and the inflow of international aid.

At the end of World War II, Korea was placed under temporary UN protection after being released from 30 years of colonial rule by imperial Japan. Divided by ideologies and mindful of the growing Cold War spheres of influence, the UN Security Council was unable to come to an agreement over the path toward an independent and united Korean nation; therefore, the peninsula was divided along the 38th Parallel. In 1948, the Soviets administering the northern part of the country established a communist-type regime headed by Kim Il-sung, while, in the southern part, an anti-communist administration under President Rhee Syng-man came to power with the support of the United States. Hopes of unification were put on indefinite hold when a civil war broke out in 1950, which ended with an armistice – a cease fire that fell short of permanently resolving the conflict.

As a newly established country, North Korea was arguably in better shape than was its southern counterpart. Historically, the mountainous northern part of the country was more industrially developed and endowed with more natural resources such as coal. Unlike the capitalists in the South, who pursued export-driven growth, the North Korean government sought economic prosperity based on the socialist mode of production and distribution, refraining from participating in the global market and pursuing *juche*.

Nevertheless, North Korea continued to receive heavy economic assistance from the Soviet Union and later from China, after the demise of the former country. Aided by its ideological allies and initial industrial advantage, North Korea was able to achieve a high growth rate of over 20 per cent during the post-war period that lasted from the mid-1950s through the 1960s, finally leveling off at approximately 5 per cent in the 1970s and 1980s. The country also maintained a well-budgeted, strong military force.[1] Yet the chimeral nature of apparent DPRK success was brutally exposed with the ending of North Korea's privileged position due to the collapse of the Soviet bloc, combined with drought and crop failure.

The DPRK does continue to score surprisingly well when it comes to certain categories used to measure human security and development. It is estimated that 100 per cent of the urban and rural population currently uses improved drinking-water sources and that 58 percent of the urban and 60 per cent of the rural population has access to improved sanitation facilities (WHO, 2010a; 2010b, p. 102). With the aid of international medical assistance, the percentage of the population receiving vaccination is believed to be almost 90 per cent (KDI, 2010, p. 104). Virtually, all the population is literate, and 11 years of free formal education (one year of pre-school, four years of elementary and six years of middle school) is mandatory for all citizens (Kwak and Lee, 2006; KINU, 2009). Although job security in a socialist country like North Korea has a different significance than it does for outsiders, and will be discussed subsequently in greater detail, most people in North Korea have some form of employment.

The state of North Korean human development, however, when gauged in terms of many of the other indexes used to measure conformity to the MDGs, is disturbing. Life expectancy at birth for North Koreans is around 67 years – significantly lower than that for South Koreans, which is around 79 years (WHO, 2010b, p. 48). These gap indicators are even more pronounced for particularly vulnerable groups such as women and children. The infant mortality rate, under-five mortality rate, and maternal mortality rate in North Korea are estimated to be around 42, 55, and 77 per cent, respectively, for every 1,000 live births, while it is 5, 5, and 18 per cent, respectively, for the same categories in South Korea (*ibid.*, pp. 48–53). Approximately, 33 per cent of the population is undernourished and the percentage of children under five who suffer from moderate to severe growth stunting is around 45 per cent (WFP, 2010), a statistic that indicates an effect that is likely to endure into the next generation.

A chronic shortage of food is by far the most pressing problem faced by the majority of vulnerable North Koreans. Although the actual extent of the record-setting famine in the 1990s is still under debate, a minimum of 580,000 and possibly as many as 1.12 million people are believed to have died from hunger and other famine-related causes from 1994 to 2000 (KINU, 2009, p. 294). People continue to die of starvation at a steady rate, even though North Korean police and village offices do not report malnutrition to be the cause of these deaths (North Korea Today, 2010a). Indeed, according to a joint FAO/WFP Crop and Food Supply Assessment Mission (CFSAM) conducted in late 2008, there has been only marginal improvement in household food security in recent years (WFP, 2010). As many as 300,000 people are estimated to have violated the state ban on travel and fled to China in order to escape hunger, where they live in constant fear of being caught and forcibly repatriated (Freedom House, 2011).

Being cut off from the agrarian South, which had traditionally been the breadbasket of the peninsula, posed a serious challenge to food security in the DPRK, particularly after agricultural reform in the 1970s and 1980s failed to increase farmland (Kwon, 2004). Only approximately 22.4 per cent of all land is arable in North Korea (CIA, 2010), and deforestation resulting from poorly planned land conversion policies led to topsoil erosion and river silting. This proved disastrous in a country where seasonal flooding is a fixture, and floods repeatedly destroyed crops and damaged farmlands, thereby further reducing yield. To make matters worse, agricultural policy failed to ensure adequate crop rotation and soil depletion intensified as farming became heavily dependent on chemical fertilizers, which then had to be imported in order to meet the high domestic demand for food output (DLA Piper *et al.*, 2008, pp. 3–6). Unable to attain self-sufficiency in domestic cereal production, commercial import of food and external aid became unavoidable and the government began to cut back on rations.

Growing hunger in North Korea was anticipated by external observers when the government reduced daily food rations following the end of Soviet support in the late 1980s; it became increasingly likely with the implementation of the 'let's eat two meals a day' policy in 1991. Pyongyang, however, made no overt appeal for international assistance until a series of natural disasters in 1995 made it politically viable to do so without losing face (Haggard and Noland, 2005, pp. 11–9). While bad weather may have exacerbated the situation, the North Korean leadership is guilty of mismanagement and negligence before and during the crisis, and Pyongyang's policies constituted the real source of food insecurity for ordinary people in North Korea. Once international assistance began to arrive, Pyongyang redirected aid and reserved rations for priority groups, such as government officials and the military, further undermining the human security of the most vulnerable sectors of society. Perhaps the most draconian policy implemented was the cutting-off and abandonment of people in the extreme northerly provinces, where the food shortage was believed to be the most acute, in order to prevent news of starvation and famine-related deaths from reaching the remainder of the population (Amnesty International, 2004, pp. 9–13).

The gravity and impact of policy failure in such a highly controlled and centrally planned country cannot fully be grasped without discussing the social security structure and restrictions on individual coping strategies. The

North Korean rationing system, known as the Public Distribution System (PDS), was initially designed as a multi-purpose mechanism that was meant not only to distribute scarce resources but also to form one pillar of a wider social security scheme and population control mechanism (KINU, 2009, pp. 305–33; Kim, 2010). Along with State Social Insurance, which included the Industrial Accident Compensation System as a secondary social safety net, the PDS distributed food, clothing, and shelter through both cash and in kind payments as a type of social welfare system (KINU, 2009, pp. 305–33). The pinnacle of this centrally planned welfare arrangement was the 'free medical treatment' system touted as superior to health care policies of any other nation. Under this system, the government was to provide doctors and hospitals with 'medical payment' in the form of medical supplies (Lee, 2003; KINU, 2009, pp. 305–33).

Unfortunately, these instruments required tremendous commitments that could not be fulfilled because Pyongyang lacked both the resources and necessary capacity (Lee, 2003; Kim, 2010). By 1990, the North Korean economy was recording a negative growth rate of –4.3 per cent and, as the country experienced increasing economic difficulties, adjustments were made to downsize the PDS along with large portions of the social security system, which would eventually be abolished in July 2002 (Kim, 2003; KINU, 2009). For example, the 'free medical treatment' system has become completely inoperative and patients are now required to purchase their own medicines and meals (KINU, 2009, p. 15).

In addition to the breakdown of state-guaranteed social security and extreme food insecurity, the human security of North Koreans is uniquely handicapped by prohibitions that severely limit the coping strategies of its people. The overhaul of management systems in 2002 decreased government assurance of welfare and increased the responsibility of individuals to provide for themselves; however, the ban on free movement and limitation on market participation remained intact. In North Korea, traveling from one town to another as well as buying and selling goods in markets require the permission of authority figures, which, in turn, usually requires bribery. Unable to relocate to regions where the PDS is still functioning, many people are trapped in rural and mountainous regions where rations have been discontinued. There is also a legal ban on small-plot farming and trade without authorization, which means that even growing and selling one's own foodstuff is restricted (North Korea Today, 2010b).

Even in Pyongyang, where the situation is comparatively less grim, economic hardship has made it difficult for many people to live on their normal income alone. For example, an increasing number of '8.3 workers' bribe their supervisors so that they can be absent without leave to engage in supplementary activities that are more profitable. The term itself originates from Kim Il-sung's announcement on 3 August 1984, in which people were encouraged to 'produce consumer goods using by-products and wastes from factories in self-reliant way' (Kim, 2010). In North Korea, everyone must join and report to some form of organization; thus, the right to labor and duty to work is essentially one and the same. Rather than choosing an occupation based on individual preference and aptitude, all citizens are assigned a workplace according to the personnel supply-demand plans of the Party (Kim, 2003; KINU, 2009, p. 16; Lee, 2010, p. 119). As in the case of rations, preferential treatment, such as better-paying jobs, is given on the basis of the 'degree of loyalty' to the Party. Violating the prohibition on alternative means of survival that require venturing outside the system, whether by seeking another job or traveling to escape hunger, can result in being sent to North Korea's infamous gulags or labor camps for punishment and intensive 'rehabilitation' during which offenders are made to overwork and deprive of adequate rest, food, and shelter.

In essence, the government has failed to provide for its people while also restricting individuals from seeking the means to cope with economic hardship, thereby leaving ordinary citizens trapped between accepting starvation and breaking the rules at the risk of severe punishment. Rising rates of violent crimes, such as homicides, and non-violent ones, such as raids on food storage facilities, among an increasingly desperate population contribute to a concurrent rise in fear (North Korea Today, 2010c). Community security is also being threatened and the effect this has on the North Korean society and families is alarming (Yi, 2009). Children who have been orphaned due to parents' deaths or abandoned by parents who can no longer care for them are banding together in city slums and generating a phenomenon called *kkotjebi* (literally 'flower swallows', which means child vagrants). The breakdown of family continues to intensify and, as traditional sources of community and family protection wither, personal security is exposed to the threats of increasing crime and poverty (KINU, 2009, pp. 363–5; Lee, 2010, pp. 120–1).

In particular, increasing violence against women and under-aged girls has become a major concern. During the food crisis, many North Korean women started vending, peddling, and trading to support their families. They conducted these activities under the constant threat and fear of theft, robbery, human trafficking, and sexual assault (KINU, 2009, p. 354). Incidents in which officials demand sex from women who have committed minor offenses in markets or on trains are believed to have increased, although exact figures are unavailable as such events are under-reported. In addition, the human trafficking of women and girls who are forcibly abducted, enticed with false promises, or volunteer in order to support their families has come to the fore as a serious cross-border problem (KINU, 2009, pp. 416–26; Liebelson, 2010; Lee, 2010). In 1999, the ratio of men and women who crossed the China-Korea border was roughly equal; however, by 2006, women outnumbered men in a ratio of three to one (ICG, 2006, p. 5). Furthermore, sexual violence against North Korean women who are forcibly repatriated to North Korea from China is particularly heinous; in addition to rape and torture, those women who return pregnant by Chinese men are beaten until the fetus is aborted in order to prevent the mixing of races (KINU, 2009, p. 354).

Sexual violence is not the only threat to women's health in North Korea. The mortality rate of women and girls who die from pregnancy-related complications is estimated to be 370 per 1,000 live births, which is by far the highest rate in Northeast Asia (KDI, 2010, p. 103; WHO, 2010b, p. 62). The same indicator for Mongolia stands at 46, China at 45, South Korea at 14, and Japan at 6. Resorting to commercial and survival-motivated prostitution exposes women to further risks since contraceptives are difficult to obtain in North Korea. In addition to being exposed to sexually transmitted diseases, pre-marital and extra-marital sex is illegal according to state law, and many women perform dangerous, self-administered abortions in order to avoid punishment (KINU, 2009, p. 354). The health risks associated with starvation, malnutrition, pregnancies, childbirth, child rearing, and abortion, seen against the background of the added physical stress and psychological burden of supporting a family, are believed to account for the significant increase in the number of North Korean women who suffer from various illnesses, such as cancer and diabetes (*ibid.*).

Thus, North Koreans are neither 'free from fear' nor 'free from want', and threats to their security come from diverse economic, social, and political sources. It is debatable whether the North Korean state, with its over-sized military and nuclear leverage, is strong or weak; however, it is certainly an insecure state in that it endangers its own people. Even recent government measures, such as the currency reform aimed at restructuring the economy, have caused more harm than good for ordinary citizens. Since the famine of the 1990s and the collapse of the PDS, vulnerable people have adopted coping strategies, such as stashing cash and buying food from small- and large-scale entrepreneurs who have left the state sector and become food suppliers (ICG, 2010, pp. 8–9). The latest currency reform that took place on 30 November 2009 – in which a new currency was issued with the conversion rate of the old won to new won set at 100:1 – had the effect of confiscating excess savings, further lowering the purchasing power of ordinary people and wiping out the assets of small-scale traders who had not managed to convert to foreign currency as had large-scale operators (ICG, 2010, pp. 8–9; North Korea Today, 2010a).

Although the government of North Korea has faced many obstacles beyond its control that have contributed to these human security challenges, such as limited natural resources, multiple natural disasters, and a changing geopolitical operating environment, Pyongyang's policies have served to exacerbate or even be the cause of some of the worst manifestations of human insecurity to date. Economic mismanagement, governance failure, negligence, and oppressive behavior by the state have had grave consequences for ordinary citizens, and the country remains deep in distress despite recent, flawed attempts at reform and the inflow of international aid.

With regard to North Korean brinksmanship, the generation of an external threat has traditionally been used as a tool for uniting a divided country in time of crisis through rallying round the flag, the party, or perhaps, in this instance, the army. In the case of North Korea, the 'hostile' international environment is used to justify domestic policy. Furthermore, if other states become sufficiently concerned by the deterioration of the systemic security of Northeast Asia, they may ultimately be willing to grant the comprehensive peace treaty for which North Korea has been pushing (Walker, 2010). As a result, 'the "military first policy" becomes a useful tool both domestically and internationally' (Koga, 2009, p. 29).

Nevertheless, the governance and human security challenges in North Korea may now be greater than can be managed by the domestic administration alone, even if Pyongyang was willing to reform. Kim Kwan-jin (2011), an economist and banker from North Korea who defected in 2003, recently noted that essentially, the DPRK has already collapsed, and that just the skeleton of the regime is left, with a shrinking economy, the execution or defection of scapegoats, and a loss of public trust. The international community has a moral obligation to aid the most vulnerable in North Korea not only because of the latter's entitlement rights due to a shared humanity but also because of the negative impact of some of the policies which have been adopted toward the DPRK by actors on the international stage. Furthermore, international actors may also have a rational obligation to help, as a North Korean collapse serves nobody's interests. Thus, the next section evaluates the efficacy of international efforts to alleviate the dire human security situation in the DPRK.

International policy failures

From a traditional security perspective, the way to deal with a rogue state is through coercion – increase the costs of them pursuing a course of action that adversely affects the security interests of the enforcing state(s). The coercive measures and policies that have been considered for engagement with North Korea span a broad range, from political pressures, through economic sanctions, to potential military intervention. Some of these measures, however, have proven counterproductive, while others are not practical to implement. It has proven impossible fully to isolate Pyongyang and drive a wedge between North Korea's leadership and their tacit backers. As long as North Korean officials remain welcome in Beijing, and to a lesser extent in Moscow, political sanctions will have little effect other than to increase Pyongyang's paranoia.

The United States and other countries have imposed a number of economic sanctions on North Korea. According to a CRS Report for Congress, US economic sanctions are imposed against North Korea on four primary grounds: (1) North Korea is seen as posing a threat to US national security, (2)North Korea is designated by the Secretary of State as a state sponsor or supporter of international terrorism, (3) North Korea is a Marxist-Leninist state, with a Communist government, and (4) North Korea has been found by the State Department to have engaged in proliferation of weapons of mass destruction. In accordance with US law, the United States limits some trade, denies trade in dual-use goods and services, limits foreign aid, and opposes entry into or support from international financial institutions (Rennack, 2003). The international community through the UN Security Council imposed further sanctions on North Korea in response to Pyongyang's nuclear tests in 2006 and 2009.

Given that the United States has virtually no economic relationship with North Korea, however, the imposition of direct US sanctions against Pyongyang has no real impact on policy elites, especially given Beijing's willingness to continue to trade with the DPRK and to supply most commodities that the leadership in the North might require (Foster, 2011). The freezing of DPRK funds as a result of the Banco Delta Asia scandal has denied the North Korean elite a vital source of patronage relied upon in order to secure the support of the Korean Workers Party rank and file, but this may merely contribute to the insecurity dilemma detailed above, forcing ever more ambitious provocations of foreign policy crises to shore up support and distract from internal problems. Contrary to US claims, the sanction regime does have a serious negative impact on the human security and development of the most vulnerable sections of North Korean society. Constraints on foreign capital and financial transactions severely limit infrastructure and development projects. They also discourage foreign direct and private investment. Thus, even if the North were to implement sound economic policies, Pyongyang is being denied the resources to develop the country out of internal insecurity.

Of more direct concern from a non-traditional and human security perspective are accusations of denial of humanitarian assistance to the North. After a three-day private visit to Pyongyang, former US President Jimmy Carter accused the United States and South Korea of human rights violations against North Koreans by withholding food aid (BBC, 2011a). Charities and the UN have reported that after a disastrously harsh winter, North Korea was in imminent danger of repeating the experience of famine that proved so costly in terms of human suffering in the 1990s. Even if something of an exaggeration, this potentially represents a grave escalation of NTS challenges to governance in North Korea, and again as detailed above could spill over into regional traditional security threats. US officials have denied the accusations, noting that Pyongyang was primarily responsible for the plight of the North Korean people given that US food aid was suspended in 2009 after the North said it was not wanted (BBC, 2011b). Yet, this is precisely because Pyongyang fears a loss of sovereignty and national security if aid is accepted, especially if it comes with strings attached.

Unfortunately, unconditional aid, such as espoused by the Sunshine Policy and pursued for ten years by successive liberal administrations in Seoul, has also appeared to have little or no impact on international, national, or human security considerations on the Korean Peninsula. At the international level, it was unable significantly to contribute to solving the nuclear issue as it concentrated solely on improving inter-Korean relations through constructive engagement and unilateral benevolence regardless of reciprocity (Chun, 2009, p. 2). It turned out to be a 'wrong policy based on wrong assumptions' (Park, 2010, p. 7). To date, other international aid efforts have also failed to alleviate human security challenges in the DPRK and their consequent spillover into traditional security considerations in Northeast Asia.

Distrust on both sides (DPRK government and the international community) hampers the effectiveness of aid and contributes to donor fatigue. In the first ten years of the Consolidated Appeals Process by various international organizations and NGOs, total humanitarian assistance to North Korea amounted to about US$2.5 billion not including bilateral and multilateral commitments made by the United States, China, Japan, and South Korea (Haggard and Noland, 2005, Appendix 2.1). Donations had, however, started to dwindle by 2005, and yet another series of floods devastated the nation in 2006. The World Food Programme (WFP), which feeds nearly one-third of the population, spoke out in 2008 about the increasing difficulty of getting donations, and a senior UN official warned that the Pyongyang office risked closure (Oliver, 2010). Currently, the WFP is assisting 65 districts in seven provinces in North Korea, including parts of the northeast, although access to the population is still severely hampered and it struggles to operate while adhering to its 'no access, no food' principle (WFP, 2010). Unlike food aid distributed to selected target groups, such as flood victims and pregnant or nursing women, aid that passes through local PDS warehouses before being distributed via schools, orphanages, and hospitals is subject to diversion, which exasperates donors (Haggard and Noland, 2005, p. 24).

At the same time, Pyongyang is suspicious of outside interference that it perceives as intruding on its sovereignty, and the DPRK is not a member of any organizations that can provide comprehensive technical assistance in a relatively depoliticized manner, such as the World Bank, the IMF, or the ADB (Haggard and Noland, 2007, p. 231). Although the country accepts help from international aid organizations and NGOs, the government distrusts them, restricts their operation by demanding long notice periods before visiting rural areas and banning the use of independent translators, and has on occasion asked some of them to leave altogether.

Indeed, the giving of any assistance to North Korea is controversial. On the one hand, international aid can be seen as keeping the existing regime in Pyongyang afloat indirectly by ameliorating the suffering of the masses to a manageable level, thereby removing the motivation for a revolution from below. On the other hand, critics of aid point to the direct succor provided to Pyongyang when resources intended for those in need are diverted to those less deserving, such as government officials and the military. Yet while these are arguments worth rehearsing and addressing in terms of policy prescription, it is morally untenable to prescribe a solution that involves standing by and doing nothing in the face of suffering of such magnitude in the hope that things will deteriorate to the critical point needed for a desirable future political outcome. Even if there is a sure guarantee that regime collapse or fundamental reform will occur relatively swiftly, there still remains the question of collateral damage and whether any political triumph would ever justify the humanitarian sacrifice entailed.

Furthermore, the right of North Korean refugees, or 'economic migrants', in China to receive international assistance has also proven to be a thorny topic. Only a portion of those who make it out of North Korea eventually find safe passage to new host countries, mostly to South Korea; however, after resettlement, they continue to face discrimination and legal complications due to their refugee status. Indirect violation of international human rights norms, repatriation of North Koreans who are caught is conducted in accordance with state-level agreements such as the defector deportation agreement between North Korea and China (Kim, 2006, pp. 71–5). For international agencies and NGOs involved in rescue work, this poses an operational challenge that precedes the policy quandary outlined above, and many have chosen the apolitical path of remaining silent. Others have aligned themselves in support of one policy over the other and thus further politicized the international network of aid agencies that is already divided along lines of religious mandates, ideological agendas, and operational philosophies. Efforts to deal with basic human security concerns related to freedom from fear and want have been complicated and undermined by a focus on human rights and other political issues.

In fact, thus far, neither the hardline approach adopted by the United States and the South Korean administration of Lee Myung-bak nor the constructive engagement policies of the EU and previous liberal South Korean administrations have yielded much in terms of results (Kim, 2006, pp. 79–84; Lee, 2009). The final section of this chapter addresses policy prescriptions aimed at overcoming the distrust that acts as an obstacle to securing freedom from fear and want in North Korea. It must be noted that these prescriptions are merely attempts to think beyond the constraints of the conventional approach that has failed thus far. They may not all be feasible, and, undoubtedly, to a certain extent they are contradictory; however, they require serious consideration by the international community not only because of the dire conditions facing ordinary citizens of the DPRK but also because of the implications that such a great level of human insecurity has for traditional security considerations in the region.

Potential policy prescriptions

Engaging North Korea in human security dialogue, let alone policy implementation, is challenging in many ways. Perhaps key to the conundrum is finding a way to make the receipt of aid acceptable to North Korea in order to alleviate internal human security challenges, thereby also reducing the impetus for destabilizing national policies. If the provision of aid is to succeed as a policy for improving the food security of North Koreans, there must be a more constructive relationship between the recalcitrant North Korean government and the donor community. Currently, distrust on both sides hampers the effectiveness of aid and causes donor fatigue. Unlike the food-related aid that the WFP distributes to selected target groups, such as flood victims and pregnant or nursing women, the aid that passes through local PDS warehouses before being distributed among schools, orphanages, and hospitals is subject to diversion, a complication that often exasperates donors (Haggard and Noland, 2005, p. 24). At the same time, the North Korean government distrusts aid agencies and restricts their operation by demanding lengthy advance notice periods before allowing such agencies to visit rural areas and banning the use of translators that are not provided by the government.

One possible solution involves both parties giving up ground. In other words, if the donors accept that a certain level of diversion will occur and that the central North Korean government will demand a degree of oversight, while the latter accepts the internationally recognized obligation of aid recipients to facilitate the operation of aid agencies, this will ease the distribution of aid and ensure that the WFP obtains both the funding from donors and access to the population that it requires. For this to occur, a consensus among donor countries is needed to empower the existing aid framework comprised of the WFP and other international organizations and NGOs who operate under the same norm. Agreeing to support the existing aid framework implies that bilateral donors must also attach the condition of 'no access, no food' to any arrangements made with North Korea. A coordinated policy that enables the continued delivery of food aid, while simultaneously treating North Korea in a manner consistent with internationally recognized norms, constitutes a responsible policy choice that is likely to build trust.

Haggard and Noland (2007), whose ideas represent a second potential approach to changing aid policies, have caused controversy by arguing that China and South Korea must channel a greater portion of their concessional food assistance through the WFP. They asserted that the two countries' shared policy of bypassing WFP and providing concessional sales or grants of food with little or no conditions or monitoring attached undermines the efforts of the broader aid community. Moreover, 'if China and South Korea remain suppliers of last resort, the North Korean government gains the opportunity to weaken the multilateral regime that is in place and to challenge the WFP's most basic mandate; in mid-2005, that is exactly what Pyongyang did by asking the WFP to leave' (*ibid.*, p. 232).

The provision of only conditional aid, however, is a long-standing point of controversy within the aid community, both in theory and practice. Deals between the vested state actors in the region have complications on a higher political level that are separate from the fundamental goal of food aid, which is to free people from the want of food and fear of starvation; thus, tying aid agencies to bilateral aid restrictions may not always be possible or desirable. Furthermore, the carrot that aid represents is transformed into a stick by such processes and can consequently be used to beat an opponent, which makes it unlikely that such efforts will result in constructive dialogue. Hence, the North Korean Human Rights Act promulgated by the United States not only failed to bring about significant improvement in either the human rights or the human security of ordinary North Koreans but it also alienated important actors on both sides of the demilitarized zone (DMZ) (Howe, 2006).

Thus, a third alternative process could be used; instead of insisting that aid be tied to Pyongyang behaving in ways acceptable to the international community, international actors that Pyongyang already deems acceptable can be identified and aid can be funneled through them. North Korea's only remaining ally of note, the PRC, could serve this purpose. China has demonstrated itself to be an increasingly responsible actor in international affairs. Zheng Bijian (2005, p. 19) claims that this is part of China's advocacy of 'a new international political and economic order, one that can be achieved through incremental reforms and the democratization of international relations'. This assertion is fundamental to China's 'peaceful rise' paradigm. The paradigm was first introduced at the 2003 annual session of the Boao Forum for Asia (an Asian economic forum similar to the Davos World Economic Forum) (Da, 2005). The policy asserts that China can thrive economically in a peaceful environment and serve as a catalyst for global peace – a kind of virtuous cycle intended to maximize China's economic benefit. Hence, in 2004, Premier Wen Jiabao declared China's rise 'will not come at the cost of any other country, will not stand in the way of any other country, nor pose a threat to any other country' (Pan, 2006). Chinese leaders and academics have repeatedly iterated this claim. China itself, however, remains wary of even the term 'human security', as it is considered too close to the sensitive topic of human rights; thus, more effort needs to be made for separating the issues.

As noted above, China is perhaps most at risk from the consequences of a failing DPRK. The PRC should therefore recognize both its traditional and human security interests in supporting such initiatives. Likewise, opponents of Pyongyang are coming around to the idea of working through Beijing. Admiral Mike Mullen, Chairman of the US Joint Chiefs of Staff, recently called on China to use its close relationship with Pyongyang to build regional security, and noted that the United States 'wants a positive, cooperative and comprehensive relationship with China – one that comes to be defined by our common challenges and our shared interests in Asia and globally. Global cooperation advances China's interests, and it advances US interests' (News Corp, 2011).

South Korea's interests also lie in the reform and development of the North in a sustainable fashion. While the majority fleeing a collapsing DPRK would most likely head to China due to the difficulties of penetrating the fortified border between the two Koreas, some would still brave the seas, becoming Korean 'boat people', or would find their way in sufficient numbers via third countries to have a major impact on the support services and resources of South Korea. Furthermore, even absent a dramatic collapse, a gradual move toward Korean unification also requires that the North be developed significantly. Numerous reports in recent years have estimated the cost of Korean unification, from the Rand Corporation's US$50 billion for doubling Northern income so that it reaches nearly 10 per cent of Southern income to the Credit Suisse's US$5 trillion for raising Northern income so that it reaches nearly 60 per cent of Southern income. Even this level might not be enough to persuade North Koreans to remain in the shell of their failed state. Thus, as Peter Beck (2010) points out, 'building a modern economy in North Korea would be a wise investment in peace and prosperity in North Asia'.

Although emergency aid and economic assistance funneled through a Chinese version of the Sunshine Policy are unlikely to prove a panacea for the DPRK's internal problems or for the regional security spillover generated by them, they are at least likely to buy some time for both the most vulnerable sections of North Korea's society and the international community. Through a process of functional incrementalism, it will be a step in the right direction and will be conducive to the production of an operating environment in which distrust is lessened and at least the possibility of cooperation realized. According to David Mitrany (1933, p. 101), collective governance and 'material interdependence' develop their own internal dynamic as states integrate in limited functional, technical, and/or economic areas. This promotes a peaceful outlook among actors because of increased prosperity, for economic interdependence increases the cost of war and the benefits of peace, and because of 'spill-over' into the high political sphere of security through the establishment of a culture of cooperation rather than conflict.

A fourth potential policy prescription would be for the international community to lower the world grain price (or at least the quote for the portion used in exchanges with North Korea) artificially and temporarily, thereby allowing Pyongyang to 'purchase' what the people of North Korea require. According to the FAO, North Korea needed to import 1.10 million tons of cereal for the 2009/10 (November/October) marketing year in order to meet the needs of approximately 24 million people (GIEWS, 2010). At the same time, the country was again experiencing severe financial problems due to the fact that it has no foreign exchange reserves upon which to draw; moreover, the earnings from arms exports and illicit activities are not enough to offset a trade deficit of approximately US$1 billion per year (ICG, 2010).

If even a token amount of what is needed can be paid for by the North Korean government, in contrast to its past practice of using international aid to substitute for commercial imports rather than supplement local production (Haggard and Noland, 2005, p. 16), this would still provide something for the country to build on. The policy would encourage the North Korean government to fulfill its responsibility of protecting its own people – a practice that does not wholly dismiss the potential for diplomatic talks – without provoking paranoia about losing its sovereignty and still allowing a degree of face-saving among key stakeholders and gate-keepers in Pyongyang.

A fifth prescription involves a shift in focus from traditional state-centric and monolithic engagement to one where non-threatening international non-governmental actors approach key stakeholders in Pyongyang and the North Korean provinces over specific NTS issues such as the disabled, education, and the environment. Substantial progress has already been made in these areas through unheralded and unreported 'back door' and 'side door' negotiations from both North Korea and the international community.[2] Yet such are the political sensitivities of such interactions for both sides that at least for the foreseeable future, they may have to remain not only non-traditional but also unacknowledged.

Finally, as mentioned in earlier sections, some causes of human insecurity in North Korea, such as the policies of *juche* and *songun*, are actually consequences of the insecurity felt by the regime in Pyongyang. Pyongyang has few friends and many powerful enemies and has been the target of three hostile policy initiatives from Washington in recent years (it was labeled part of the Axis of Evil, named one of the Outposts of Tyranny, and targeted by the North Korean Human Rights Act). Brutalized by Japanese occupation, North Koreans, similar to South Koreans, are likely to view Japanese moves to 'normalize' their foreign and security policy with trepidation; Tokyo has recently issued a number of anti-Pyongyang statements that support this fear (Kirk, 2010). Seoul has turned away from the constructive engagement of the 'Sunshine Policy', adopting a more hardline approach linking aid to progress on human rights and security and prompting Pyongyang to respond that 'the group of traitors has already reduced all the agreements reached between the North and the South in the past to dead documents'

(The Guardian, 2009). Alleviating North Korea's traditional security concerns may be a pre-requisite to addressing the human security concerns of its people.

Pyongyang has long craved a comprehensive peace treaty and, given the impracticalities of actually intervening in the DPRK to put an end to both traditional and non-traditional threats, it may be time to consider granting it (Hoo, 2003). To a certain extent, the international community is responsible for dragging its heels on this issue and is thereby indirectly responsible for the human security consequences. Section 3 of the 1994 Agreed Framework between the United States and DPRK pledges both sides to work together for peace, security, and a nuclear-free Korean Peninsula. Although Pyongyang clearly violated the second-half of this clause, it could be argued that more could have been done by Washington with regard to the first part. Section 2 discussed that the two sides will move toward full normalization of political and economic relations, yet little progress has been made in this direction and the United States refuses to even recognize the North Korean state and continues to impose economic sanctions (KEDO, 1994).

Conclusion

The changing nature of the international normative environment may well have imposed upon us an obligation to protect the lives of North Koreans, and even a duty to provide for their BHN or at the least support conditions in which their BHN can be realized. This chapter, however, has also demonstrated how it is in the narrow self-interest of the key actors in international affairs to address the insecurity dilemma facing the Pyongyang regime, lest it contribute to an international security dilemma. Human insecurity in North Korea has multiple dimensions. The developmental challenges of poverty and starvation exist side-by-side with social vulnerabilities such as the breakup of traditional family structure and rise in crime. The government of North Korea is hazardous to its own people in that it is unable to provide competent governance, unwilling to cooperate with external agents, and is restrictive of individual coping strategies. The cross-border movement of people that has ensued adds an international dimension to this human security crisis. When combined with the complex dynamics of the relationship between internal insecurities and the formation of North Korean national security, it is evident that the human security of the citizens of North Korea is of crucial importance to neighboring states and the wider international community.

Unfortunately, these concerns are more than just academic. North Korean refugees interviewed by Stephen Haggard and Marcus Noland (2011) showed absolutely no support for a transformed DPRK, instead favoring absorption by the South. Yet currently, the provisions in place for dealing with such an eventuality are woefully inadequate and amount to establishing 'aid magnets' in the heart of North Korea to which hopefully potential refugees will gravitate rather than looking to cross borders in the search for greater human security (Security Consultant, 2010). At the same time, the environment of mutual distrust among state actors has been hindering the delivery of aid to people in need. Thus, examined through the lens of human security, the situation in North Korea demonstrates that fear and want on the individual human level, generated by an insecure state, can form a vicious cycle.

The policies of the DPRK and those of external actors have failed to address the issue of human security of the North Korean people adequately. Domestic reform attempts, such as agricultural policy aimed at increasing food production, currency reform, and the downsizing of the government, have not increased the availability of food for ordinary citizens and have, instead, further undermined their chances of survival. The existing international aid framework operates with much difficulty due to donor fatigue, lack of a coordinated approach by bilateral donors, and inherent distrust and suspicion, thereby undermining efforts to procure the necessary level of compliance from Pyongyang. The carrot and stick approach to aid and sanctions has had mixed results in terms of facilitating desirable political change and has impeded the continued delivery of aid. Currently, Pyongyang is unable (or unwilling) to ensure either freedom from want or freedom from fear for its citizens; thus, the international community has a responsibility to both protect and provide such freedoms.

In order for the international aid community to enable North Korea to help itself in a manner consistent with international norms, this chapter proposes several alternative policy options. The first is strengthening the existing multilateral aid framework of the WFP and associated aid organizations by persuading bilateral donors to adopt the 'no access, no food' policy. The second attaches conditionality to aid provision in terms of 'good behavior' by the recipient regime toward its own people. Alternatively, aid could be funneled through a donor country that is already acceptable to North Korea, such as China. The fourth option is to assist North Korea to at least appear to be providing for the human security of its own citizens by allowing them to purchase grain at discounted prices, while a fifth shifts the focus from rational actor model-based donor and recipient relationships to sub-state activities. Finally, de-escalating the traditional security threat perception in Pyongyang may facilitate the development of policies that aid rather than undermine human security.

As previously mentioned, not all of these prescriptions may be feasible, and some of them are contradictory, but clearly something needs to change as not only are North Koreans continuing to suffer as a result of bad governance but also international security is threatened by the consequences of internal human insecurity in the DPRK.

Notes

1. It must be noted that statistics on the North Korean economy, from annual growth rates to military expenditures as a percentage of the total national budget released by different sources, are contentious because sources vary in their method of calculation and degree of reliance on official declarations by North Korea, which are controversial as well. This chapter has made generalizations based on the most frequently cited sources, such as the South Korean government (Korea Institute for National Unification before 1990, the Bank of Korea from 1990 onward, the Ministry of Defense, and the Korea Development Institute), US Arms Control and Disarmament Agency's (ACDA) World Military Expenditure and Arms Transfers, UK-based International Institute for Strategic Studies' (IISS) Military Balance, Stockholm International Peace Research Institute's SIPRI Yearbook, and UN statistics.
2. Substance of conversations held at workshop *Toward a Human Security Framework for North Korea: Promoting Human Rights through Pragmatic Approaches*, Chatham House, London, UK, 2–3 December 2010. The 'Chatham House Rule' allows no direct attribution to sources.

References

Amnesty International (2004) 'Starved of Rights: Human Rights and the Food Crisis in the Democratic People's Republic of Korea (North Korea)', http://www.amnesty.org/en/library/asset/ASA24/003/2004/en/f5daaf5b-d645-11dd-ab95-a13b602c0642/asa240032004en.pdf.

Amnesty International (2011) 'North Korea: Images Reveal Scale of North Korean Political Prison Camps', 4 May 2011, http://www.amnestyusa.org/news/press-releases/north-korea-images-reveal-scale-of-political-prison-camps.

BBC (2011a) 'Ex-President Jimmy Carter Calls for North Korea Aid', *BBC*, 28 April 2010, http://www.bbc.co.uk/news/world-asia-pacific-13221867.

BBC (2011b) 'US "not Withholding Food Aid from North Korea"', *BBC*, 30 April 2010, http://www.bbc.co.uk/news/world-asia-pacific-13247723.

Beck, P. M. (2010) 'The Cost of Korean Reunification', *The Wall Street Journal*, 4 January 2010, http://online.wsj.com/article/SB10001424052748704340304574635180086832934.html.

Bennett, C. (2003) 'China Moves to Curb Crime by North Koreans/Impoverished Soldiers Blamed for Rash of Killings, Robberies', *Chronicle Foreign Service*, 19 September 2003, http://www.sfgate.com/news/article/China-moves-to-curb-crime-by-North-Koreans-2587655.php.

Blomfield, A. (2009) 'North Korea: Russia Takes Extra Security Measures in Case of Nuclear Conflict', *The Telegraph*, 27 May 2009, http://www.telegraph.co.uk/news/worldnews/asia/northkorea/5394262/North-Korea-Russia-takes-extra-security-measures-in-case-of-nuclear-conflict.html.

Buzan, B. and Wæver, O. (2004) *Regions and Powers: The Structure of International Security* (Cambridge: Cambridge University Press).

Chatham House (2010) *Towards a Human Security Framework for North Korea: Promoting Human Rights through Pragmatic Approaches*, Personal communication, 2–3 December 2010.

Chestnut, S. (2007) 'Illicit Activity and Proliferation: North Korean Smuggling Networks', *International Security*, 32(1), 80–111.

Chun, C. S. (2009) 'ROK-US Alliance and Northeast Asian Security: A South Korean Perspective', *An ROK-U.S. Alliance for the 21st Century,* Seoul, Republic of Korea, 3 November 2009, East Asia Institute.

Central Intelligence Agency (CIA) (2010) *World Fact Book,* https://www.cia.gov/library/publications/the-world-factbook/geos/kn.html.

Congressional Research Service (CRS) (2007) *Report for Congress: North Korean Refugees in China and Human Rights Issues* (Washington, DC: CRS).

CRS (2008) *Report for Congress: North Korean Crime-for-Profit Activities* (Washington, DC: CRS).

Da, S. (2005) 'Peaceful Rise of China a Hot Topic', *China.org.cn,* 22 April 2005, http://www.china.org.cn/english/2005/Apr/126696.htm.

DLA Piper, the Committee for Human Rights in North Korea, and the Oslo Center for Peace and Human Rights (2008) *Failure to Protect: The Ongoing Challenges of North Korea,* http://www.dlapiper.com/files/upload/NK_Report_F2P_North%20Korea_Sep19_08.pdf.

Emmers, R. (2007) 'Securitization' in A. Collins (ed.), *Contemporary Security Studies* (Oxford: Oxford University Press).

Fish, I. S. (2011) 'North Korea's Meth Export', *Newsweek,* 19 June 2011, http://www.thedailybeast.com/newsweek/2011/06/19/north-korea-s-meth-export.html.

Foster, P. (2011) 'China Builds Higher Fences over Fears of Instability in North Korea', *The Telegraph,* 30 March 2011, http://www.telegraph.co.uk/news/worldnews/asia/northkorea/8415490/China-builds-higher-fences-over-fears-of-instability-in-North-Korea.html.

Freedom House (2011) *Freedom in the World 2011: North Korea,* http://www.freedomhouse.org/report/freedom-world/2011/north-korea.

Global Information and Early Warning System (GIEWS) (2010) *GIEWS Country Briefs: Democratic People's Republic of Korea,* http://www.fao.org/giews/countrybrief/country.jsp?code=PRK&lang=en.

Haggard, S. and Noland, M. (2005) *Hunger and Human Rights: The Politics of Famine in North Korea* (Washington, DC: US Committee for Human Rights in North Korea).

Haggard, S. and Noland, M. (2007) *Famine in North Korea: Markets, Aid, and Reform* (New York: Columbia University Press).

Haggard, S. and Noland, M. (2011) *Witness to Transformation: Refugee Insights into North Korea* (Washington, DC: Peterson Institute for International Economics).

Hoo, S. (2003) 'North Korea Demands Nonaggression Treaty with United States, Rejects International Setting', *Associated Press,* 31 January 2003, http://www.highbeam.com/doc/1P1-71430755.html.

Howe, B. (2006) 'Strategic Implications of the 2004 U.S. North Korean Human Rights Act', *Asian Perspective,* 30(1), 191–219.

International Crisis Group (ICG) (2006)'Perilous Journeys: The Plight of North Koreans in China and Beyond', *Asia Report No 122,* http://www.nautilus.org/publications/essays/napsnet/reports/0694IGC.pdf.

ICG (2010) *North Korea under Tightening Sanctions,* 15 March 2010, http://www.crisisgroup.org/en/publication-type/media-releases/2010/asia/north-korea-under-tightening-sanctions.aspx.

Korea Development Institute (KDI) (2010) *KDI BukhanKyungje Review* [KDI Review of North Korean Economy], May, http://www.kdi.re.kr/report/report_class_e4.jsp?pub_no=11467.

The Korean Peninsula Energy Development Organization (KEDO) (1994) *Agreed Framework between The United States of America and the Democratic People's Republic of Korea Geneva,* http://www.armscontrol.org/documents/af.

Kim, H. R. (2006) 'Transnational Network Dynamics of NGOs for North Korean Refugees and Human Rights', *Korea Observer,* 37(1), 57–92.

Kim, K. J. (2011) *Voices from the North: Personal Stories from North Korean Defectors,* Yongsan Army Garrison, Seoul, 20 June 2011.

Kim, S. H. (2010) 'What are Motives Behind the Cheonan Attack?', *The Korea Herald,* 26 May 2010, http://www.koreaherald.com/national/Detail.jsp?newsMLId=20100526000776.

Kim, Y. B. (2003) 'National Economic Management System' in Choong Yong Ahn (ed.), *North Korea Development Report 2002/03* (Seoul: Korean Institute for International Economic Policy).

Korea Institute for National Unification (KINU) (2009) *White Paper on Human Rights in North Korea 2009,* http://www.kinu.or.kr/eng/pub/pub_04_01.jsp?page=1&num=28&mode=view&field=&text=&order=&dir=&bid=DATA04&ses=&category=2672.

Kirk, D. (2010) 'North Korea Plays on Tokyo's Mind', *Asia Times,* 6 March 2010, http://www.atimes.com/atimes/Korea/LC06Dg01.html.

Koga, K. (2009) 'The Anatomy of North Korea's Foreign Policy Formulation', *North Korean Review,* 5(2), 21–33.

Kwak, N. U. and Lee, Y. J. (2006) *Bukhan Uimugyoyukjedowa Boyukjedo* [Obligatory Education System and Childcare System of North Korea] (Seoul: Korean Society for Early Childhood Education).

Kwon, T. J. *et al.* (2004) *Bukhaneui Nongeopbumun Gaehyeok Gaebang Jeongchaekkwa Nambukhyeomnyeok Bangan* [Strategies for Agricultural Reform in North Korea and Inter-Korean Cooperation] (Seoul: Korea Rural Economic Institute).

Lee, A. R. (2010) 'Wae Bukhaneui Yeoseong Talbukjaga Maneunga?', [Why are There So Many North Korean Women Refugees?], *Monthly Korea Forum,* 249, 118–23.

Lee, S. P. (2009) 'Europe Yeonhapeui Daebukhan Jeongchaekeseo Inkwon Jeong-chaekeui Euimiwa Yeokhal', [The Role of the EU's Human Rights Policy toward North Korea], *GukjejiyeokYoengu,* 13(2), 261–82.

Lee, S. S. (2003) 'Social Security System and Social Services', in Choong Yong Ahn (ed.), *North Korea Development Report 2002/03* (Seoul: Korea Institute for International Economic Policy).

Liebelson, D. (2010) 'Nine out of Ten Women Escaping North Korea are Trafficked', *Change.org,* 29 October 2010, http://news.change.org/stories/nine-out-of-ten-women-escaping-north-korea-are-trafficked.

Liu, M. (2003) 'Nukes and Crime: China's Borderline Troubles', *Newsweek,* 31 August 2003, http://www.thedailybeast.com/newsweek/2003/08/31/nukes-and-crime-china-s-borderline-troubles.html.

Mitrany, D. (1933) *The Progress of International Government* (New Haven: Yale University Press).

Myers, B. R. (2010) 'North Korea's Race Problem: What I Learned in Eight Years Reading Propaganda from Inside the Hermit Kingdom', *Foreign Policy,* http://www.foreignpolicy.com/articles/2010/02/22/north_koreas_race_problem?page=full.

News Corp (2011) 'Adm. Mullen Seeks China's Help on North Korea', *My Fox Boston,* 10 July, http://www.myfoxboston.com/story/17759081/adm-mullen-seeks-chinas-help-on-north-korea.

North Korea Today (2010a) 'North Korea Today No. 339', *Good Friends*, April, http://goodfriendsusa.blogspot.com/2010/04/north-korea-today-no-339-april-2010.html.

North Korea Today (2010b) 'North Korea Today No. 337', *Good Friends*, March, http://goodfriendsusa.blogspot.com/2010/04/north-korea-today-no-337-march-2010.html.

North Korea Today (2010c) 'North Korea Today No. 367', *Good Friends*, September, http://goodfriendsusa.blogspot.com/2010/10/north-korea-today-no-367-september-2010.html.

Oliver, C. (2010) 'Donor Fatigue Threatens Aid for North Korea', *Financial Times*, 3 May 2010, http://www.ft.com/cms/s/0/4008f910-26e2-11df-8c08-00144feabdc0.html#axzz1mqZbdoyX.

Pan, E. (2006) 'The Promise and Pitfalls of China's "Peaceful Rise"', *Council on Foreign Relations*, 14 April 2006, http://www.cfr.org/publication/10446.

Park, H. R. (2010) 'The Right Approach to Change North Korea: Consistent Pressure as Learned from Chicken Game Theory', *Korean Journal of Security Affairs*, 15(1), 5–30.

Rennack, D. E. (2003) 'North Korea: Economic Sanctions', *Report for Congress*, 24 January 2003, http://www.au.af.mil/au/awc/awcgate/crs/rl31696.pdf.

Security Consultant (responsible for briefing US Forces Korea commanders) (2010) Interviewed Confidentially by author in Seoul, South Korea, 12 November 2010.

Song, S. H. (2010) 'Spy Report after Cheonan Sinking Cited NK Attack', *The Korea Herald*, 23 April 2010, http://www.koreaherald.com/national/Detail.jsp?newsMLId=20100422000616.

The Guardian (2009) 'North Korea Says Military and Political Agreements with Seoul are "Dead"', *The Guardian*, 30 June 2009, http://www.guardian.co.uk/world/2009/jan/30/north-korea-south-korea.

United Nations Development Programme (UNDP) (1994) *Human Development Report* (New York: Oxford University Press).

Walker, P. (2010) 'North Korea Calls for Peace Treaty with US', *The Guardian*, 11 January 2010, http://www.guardian.co.uk/world/2010/jan/11/north-korea-peace-treaty-us-nuclear-talks.

World Food Programme (WFP) (2010) *Korea, Democratic People's Republic (DPRK)*, http://www.wfp.org/countries/korea-democratic-peoples-republic-dprk.

World Health Organization (WHO) (2010a) *Democratic People's Republic of Korea: Health Profile*, http://www.who.int/gho/countries/prk.pdf.

WHO (2010b) *World Health Statistics 2010*, http://www.who.int/whosis/whostat/EN_WHS10_Full.pdf, date accessed 14 March 2013.

Yamamoto, Y. (2011) *Taken! North Korea's Criminal Abduction of Citizens of Other Countries* (Washington, DC: The Committee for Human Rights in North Korea).

Yi, S. W. (2009) 'Bukhaneui Inkwonhyeonhwangkwa Hangukeui Inkwon Oegyo-jeongchaek', [South Korean Human Rights Diplomacy towards Current North Korean Human Rights Violations], *Jeju Peace Institute Policy Forum*, 2009–7, 1–15.

Zheng, B. (2005) 'China's "Peaceful Rise" to Great Power Status', *Foreign Affairs*, 84(5), 18–24.

5
Conflict Drivers in Muslim Mindanao

Introduction

This chapter continues the evaluation of spillover between the realms of traditional and non-traditional security analyses and practice begun in the previous chapter's consideration of the North Korean challenging case. This chapter, however, further deconstructs the negative and counter-productive impact of state-centric security and development foci while also broadening the analysis of human security contributions to include conflict drivers from the arena of human development. In other words, analysis of the spillover between traditional and non-traditional security perspectives is expanded along both the vertical and horizontal axes. The challenging case study considered in this chapter, the conflict between the Government of the Republic of the Philippines (GRP) and various armed groups claiming to represent the Muslim population of the southern island grouping of Mindanao, is, by some estimates, the second oldest on earth (after the conflict between North and South Sudan), and certainly the oldest and apparently one of the most intractable conflicts in East Asia (Judd, 2005, p. 1).

The conflict dates back to pre-independence days, but escalated in the late 1960s. From that time, growing numbers of Christians have settled in Mindanao, fostered by deliberate policy of the central government, ultimately leading to the island having a Christian majority overall, with Muslim-majority areas concentrated in the central and southwestern regions. Although the impact of some aspects of the conflict (kidnappings, terrorist events, smuggling, and other trans-regional and even trans-national crime) have been felt at the wider national, and on occasion, international level, it has primarily been concentrated in the Muslim-majority areas of the 17 regions of the Philippines: Region IX – Western Mindanao; Region

---

Research for this chapter was supported by the Yuchengco Center and International Studies Department of De La Salle University, Manila

XII – Central Mindanao and the Autonomous Region in Muslim Mindanao (ARMM); and four provinces in Region XI – Southern Mindanao (Davao del Sur, Sarangani, South Cotabato, and Sultan Kudarat) (*ibid.*).

Also for this reason (the concentration of human security to national security spill-over in Muslim-majority areas), despite there being a third party, potentially even more disadvantaged and vulnerable than the Moro communities, the non-Muslim and non-Christian tribal or cultural communities known as the Lumad, this chapter will concentrate on the human security-related drivers for the conflict in Muslim Mindanao. Rudy B. Rodil's (2010) concern that a true, just, and lasting peace in Mindanao can only be achieved through what he terms a tri-people approach is well taken, and it is substantially in line with the arguments presented here for a focus on conflict transformation rather than management or resolution. Unfortunately, the brevity of the challenging case studies in this volume only allow for consideration of the most pressing elements of conflict and crisis.

A focus on zero-sum games and positional negotiations, combined with a top-down aggregate approach toward what are seen as unitary rational entities, rather than concentrating on BHN, providing safe havens, and improving the lot of the most vulnerable, are substantially to blame for the failure to transform conflictual relationships on the island and between the Muslim population (historically and self-identified as Moros) and the GRP. By focusing on such indivisible or zero-sum concepts as identity and/or land, the available options for resolution of the conflict are inevitably limited. Furthermore, the roles played by human insecurity and underdevelopment as well as the mutually reinforcing nature of the two have been poorly understood and insufficiently addressed by successive administrations. It is important to ask why it matters that different communities share the same land, and why they cannot share the same political processes. The answer lies in the fact that one group perceives itself, not without cause, as structurally disadvantaged by the operation of the current sociopolitical and economic relationships in Mindanao and in the country as a whole (Abinales, 2010, p. x).

Muslims rally to secessionist banners because they feel that they are treated worse than Christian communities: that not only are they relatively disadvantaged but also that the Christian-dominated government in Manila has done little to ease well-being discrepancies, and, historically, has done much to worsen them, and that promises to them have been repeatedly broken. Thus, 'Amidst the manifold problems that dog the peace process – from primordial claims of ethno-religious difference, to suppressed Moro identity and sovereignty, and continual wrangling over the Memorandum of Agreement on Ancestral Domain (MoA) – one potent mixer, a recognized catalyst of conflict, is relatively sidelined: chronic poverty' (Dearn, 2009). This is not to suggest that economic considerations in Mindanao have been completely ignored by successive administrations in Manila, but rather that such considerations have not been prioritized in the hope of transforming the conflict, and the national government has tended to assign top-down funds to local leaders rather than focusing on alleviating the suffering of the least well-off.

Policy initiatives to end the conflict, or at least militate against its worst effects have focused on conflict management or conflict resolution. Conflict management refers to the long-term management of intractable conflicts – an ongoing process that may never have a resolution but focuses on relationships, or in Winston Churchill's famous words, 'jaw jaw rather than war war'. The term conveys the idea that even if resolution is impossible, conflicts and disputes can be managed constructively and the worst manifestations avoided. Conflict resolution on the other hand looks to bring about an agreed and formally recognized end to a conflict, usually through some process of dispute resolution, sometimes involving external actors and third parties, culminating in a public declaration, accord, or peace treaty. A managed conflict, however, always has an ever present liability to break down in the future, and even one apparently 'ended' by a formal agreement of some sort, is still liable to recur in the future when one or more parties to the accord finds themselves dissatisfied with the outcome. Hence, numerous processes of mediation and arbitration, as well as other alternative dispute resolution mechanisms have been put in place, peace treaties have been signed, but the conflict in Muslim Mindanao persists.

A true solution to the conflict can only lie in removing the underlying causes of desires to secede – conflict transformation (and transformation of the nature of the relationships between protagonists) rather than attempted management or resolution. As recognized by Mao Tse-Tung, 'the guerrilla must move amongst the people as a fish swims in the sea'. Denying them the cover, the sustenance, and the oxygen provided by this environment is far more effective than trying to use brute force, or imposing solutions from above, which are both only likely to spread discontent and increase support for insurgents and expand their freedom of operation.

In Mindanao, interaction at the level of negotiations between protagonists has also been carried out through positional bargaining rather than identification of interests, whether conflicting or mutual. It is important to realize that an individual's interests are not necessarily the same as the positions they take (Fisher *et al.*, 1991, pp. 40–55). Positions are an individual's demands or list of wants. Underlying these positions are the reasons parties demand something: their needs, concerns, desires, hopes, and fears. A negotiated agreement that satisfies the fundamental interests of all parties has a good chance of lasting success, and is also achievable, even when parties take apparently irreconcilable positions. A resolution of conflict that only addresses positions will either merely reflect power differentials or will result in an arbitrary meeting in the middle, leaving neither side satisfied and also leaving many potential collective gains on the table. Unearthing the fundamental interests of other parties and considering ways in which they may best be satisfied rather than attempting to coerce opponents into positions more satisfactory to one's own is the only way to secure a true end to a conflict and a transformation of the relationship between protagonists. The next section outlines how the frustration of fundamental development and security-related interests in Muslim Mindanao has generated an intensely conflictual relationship.

Genesis of a conflict: human insecurity and underdevelopment

The origins of the conflict can be traced back as far as the forcible and illegal annexation of Moroland to the Philippines under the Treaty of Paris in 1898 which ceded the Philippines to the United States for the sum of US$20 million (Hurights, 2008). Although there had been conflict between the Spanish and the Muslim entities, it was only once the United States took over in Manila that a program of conquest and military pacification ensued. The 2005 Philippine Human Development Report lists other major milestones along the path to full-scale conflict as including the imposition of confiscatory land laws; the 'Indionization' (or Filipinization) of public administration in Moroland and the destruction of traditional political institutions; government financed or induced land settlement and migration to Moroland; formal and informal seizure of Muslim lands; cultural inroads against the Moros; the Jabidah Massacre in 1968 (killing of Muslim army recruits by their superiors); Ilaga (the Rats – Christian vigilante groups) and military atrocities in 1970–72; and government neglect and inaction on Moro protests and grievances; with the declaration of martial law on 21 September 1972 by the then President Ferdinand E. Marcos serving as the triggering event of the contemporary Moro armed struggle (HDN, 2005, p. 66).

Reasons given for the enduring intractability of the conflict usually revolve around its perceived zero-sum nature, whereby any gain for one party comes at the expense of their opponent, and/or the issues at state are seen to be indivisible. Either mutually exclusive polities and identities, or territorial considerations are often seen to be at the root of the conflict in Mindanao. For Peter Gowing and Robert McAmis, 'the conflict might be viewed as a clash between two imagined nations or nationalisms, Filipino and Moro, each with their own narratives of the conflict ... This has made the conflict a veritable case of "irresistible forces, immovable objects"' (Santos, 2005). For Samuel Tan (2000), the government has ignored and belittled certain fundamental realities and facts that have remained active in Muslim consciousness: namely that independence was still the underlying essence of autonomy for all Muslim social movements (Moro National Liberation Front (MNLF), Moro Islamic Liberation Front (MILF), and so on) regardless of differences. For Jacques Bertrand (2000, p. 43), the Moros, 'were never given sufficient representation in the central government to advance their interests and more importantly, they lost control of their territory and of their system of governance'. For Thayil Jacob Sony George (1980, p. 8), 'the most persistent interpretation was that religion was the main issue in Mindanao. A variation on that theme was that a minority was challenging an oppressive majority'. The works of Nathan Gilbert Quimpo and Thomas M. McKenna consistently identify these zero-sum problems as the cornerstones of the conflict.

Some commentators emphasize that, 'the current armed-conflict in Mindanao reflects the recurring call for the fulfillment of the right to self-determination of the Muslim population in the Philippines in order to obtain sustainable peace' (Hurights, 2008). Abinales (2010, pp. 120–1) notes that this view has become orthodoxy among the Philippine and international left and has gained support not only among the Organization of the Islamic Conference (OIC) but also among 'unlikely' associations such as the BBC and the United States Institute for Peace. Self-determination can never, however, be a satisfactory outcome for either side. If left to an open vote for the whole of the region, the newly settled Christian majority will of course thwart any secessionist Muslim aspirations, thereby failing to address the apparent underlying causes of the conflict. If self-determination is afforded to each province, the region will fracture, and there would still remain the problem of Christians marooned in a newly independent Muslim state and Muslims left behind in the rump Christian-dominated entity. Furthermore, as can be seen by the ultimately successful campaign against the expansion of the ARMM waged by Christian settlers and other entities, secession would not necessarily end resistance to the peace process, and in fact could merely reverse the positions of dominant political group and insurgent minority. Quimpo (2001, p. 273) looks for solutions in secession, regional autonomy, or a federal system, and asks whether to resolve the problem, 'is a negotiated political settlement feasible or is war the only viable recourse left?'.

Certainly some of the roots of the conflict can be traced to competing identity and resource demands. At the beginning of the twentieth century, Muslims made up about three-quarters of the population of Mindanao, but by the late 1960s, as a result of immigration from the more densely populated Christian islands, they accounted for only one-quarter of the population. Therefore, any attempt at a democratic solution could only be perceived as the tyranny of the majority over those who now form a minority in their own ancestral lands. The Muslims further resented the physical loss of their lands through appropriations, including those idle but which formed part of their traditional community, and this resentment grew as Muslims witnessed the usurpation by Christian settlers of vast tract of prime lands. Indeed, the, 'question on land ownership and land disputes between Muslims and Christians was crucial during the post-war period' (Hurights, 2008). Different identities founded on culture and religion increased resentment of the alien other and doomed attempts to 'assimilate' the Moros into the wider Philippine body politic. Furthermore, 'interested ring-leaders deftly used religious prejudices to spread a sense of terror and gain their ends' (George, 1980, p. 2). Thus, for Marco Garrido (2003), 'it would seem that while Muslim insurgency may be a way of expressing grievance, it is also a means of capitalizing on and creating opportunities ... Muslim insurgency can be seen as an innovative way of continuing patrimonial politics on a local level'.

None of these explanations, however, sufficiently address the causal link between the frustration of entitlement rights and the generation of violent resistance to governance from Manila. Asymmetric conflicts are likely to be at their most intractable when communities from whence insurgents are drawn feel they have little left to lose in terms of human security envisioned as the protection of persons, and human development as the provision of BHN. As pointed out by Abinales (2010, p. 119), the various Moro campaigns of the contemporary period are better understood as 'modern mobilizations against the intrusive reach of the nation-state than as the latest edition of an epic Moro struggle against various colonialisms'. The next section, addresses the desperate economic state of affairs in Muslim Mindanao, and how this has particularly impacted on the most vulnerable section of society, the Moro population. The section, 'Insecurity in Muslim Mindanao', shows how a combination of this economic underdevelopment, national government policies, and the ongoing conflict has generated human insecurity in the regions considered, creating conditions for security spill-over into the national security realm.

Underdevelopment in Muslim Mindanao

The beginning of Muslim Mindanao resentment and resistance to perceived oppressive rule from Manila, and the relative impoverishment of the region, lies in the colonial era policies of land registration and confiscation of land from the ill-served Muslim then majority, combined with large-scale resettlement of Christians, and the allocation of land for rubber, bananas, pineapples, and logging to serve the demands of transnational corporations. As most of the Muslim population made a living from agriculture, loss of land meant a major loss of income to the extent that when combined with increased fishing competition and the limitation of Sulu's barter trade with North Borneo (redefined as smuggling), the 1948 census reported that 80 per cent of Muslims in the Philippines had no definite source of income and no property. Upon achievement of national independence, 'economic conditions in Mindanao were spectacularly backward, even by Philippine standards', and no matter intent, 'successive administrations carried out policies that left Muslims and the areas they inhabited lagging dramatically' (George, 1980, p. 6, 220).

According to Tan (2000), 'the socio-economic conditions certainly continue to worsen as population increase naturally exerts more pressures on the capacity of traditional sources of revenues and livelihood such as the land, rivers, lakes, and seas within reach of the inadequate local technologies and crafts'. This is supported by Mary Judd (2005, p. 6) of the World Bank who finds increased incidence of poverty – already the highest in the country – from 56 per cent in 1991 to 62.5 per cent in 1997 and 71.3 per cent in 2000. Indeed, more recent statistics continue to tell a very 'disheartening story of want in a place of wealth. Of poverty in a land of plenty' (ICCO and AFRIM, 2008, p. 11). Mindanao consistently ranks as the poorest of the Philippines' three major island groups, with almost 50 per cent below the poverty line (twice the national average), all five regions in the ten poorest in the country as a whole, and with 14 of the 20 poorest provinces. Areas where Muslims are in the majority do particularly badly within this island group, and in the ARMM, the poorest of the poor are to be found (NSCB, 2005). The Philippine Development Forum describes the rise in poverty in the ARMM between 1988 and 2006 as, 'alarming' (Dearn, 2009). Per capita GDP for ARMM in 1995 (PhP 3866) was a third of the national average of PhP 11,417. By 2009, the ratio had worsened to a fifth (ARMM PhP 3572; national PhP 15,528) (NSCB, 2010, pp. 3–48).

There have been some improvements in some measurements of development in recent years within the region, and other parts of the Philippines are equally poor. Under-five mortality has gone down considerably in ARMM from 98 (for every 1,000 live births) in 1998 to six (for every 1,000 live births) in 2006. Maternal mortality due to pregnancy-related causes has also gone down from 102 (for every 100,000 births) to 77 in 2006 (*ibid.*, pp. 9–17). Malnutrition among children aged 0–5, however, remains higher than the national average for ARMM (28.8 underweight; 34.7 underheight) (*ibid.*, pp. 9–36). Cohort survival rate in elementary and high school education from 2008 to 2009 in ARMM was also the lowest for the entire country (at 40 and 70, respectively). Mindanao as a whole, and the ARMM in particular, amount to a unique geopolynomic concentration of poverty, geographic proximity, and discontent. Fermin Adriano identifies four causes of this dire economic situation in Mindanao:

> First, before the 1990s, it had been assigned the traditional role of food-and-raw-materials supplier for the markets of Metro Manila and Cebu. Consequently, the fate of Mindanao's economy became highly dependent on the fortunes of those two markets. Second, partly because of its role as food-and-raw-materials supplier, the growth of its predominantly agricultural economy proceeded along a colonial mode of development ... Third, as a result of the above development paradigm, intra- and inter-regional trade within the island hardly occurred as the regions were not physically connected to each other [lack of infrastructure].

> Finally, the sociopolitical conflict generated by the massive influx of Christian settlers from the north led to the increasing marginalization of indigenous and Muslim groups in Mindanao. This resulted in an unstable peace and order situation and created an environment of political instability. This, in turn, discouraged investors from establishing business ventures in the island. (2007, p. 110)

The first two of these refer to the concept that as the breadbasket of the nation, as well as an increasingly important supplier of raw materials, Mindanao's economic fate was determined by fluctuating commodities prices, futures, and needs in the metropolis. Thus, conditions in Mindanao formed, essentially, a microeconomic version of world systems theory's vision of economic cores and dependent peripheries. As with the global macroeconomic model, declining terms of trade and structural dependency ensure that the commodity producing periphery is kept underdeveloped and underfinanced. The neocolonial positioning and exploitation through plantations, national, and multinational corporations (MNCs), means that little of the wealth extracted from the fertile land of Mindanao actually stays with, or finds its way back to the most vulnerable inhabitants. Thus Tan (2000) has noted how, 'the power elite, and the multinational and national entities have remarkably developed the mining and agro-industrial potentials of the region through the years and yet, have reserved to themselves the greater part of the resources and benefits of development leaving a very small portion to the indigenous people (IP) to divide among themselves'.

With regards to the second of the two factors, infrastructure construction is concentrated on fulfilling the needs of those entities involved in extracting this wealth rather than the development needs of the local communities themselves. In pre-independence times, US Army officers had called for the massive building of roads to connect towns, and engage and develop the Muslims and 'wild tribes' (Abinales, 2010, p. 156). But such plans had come to naught. For almost a decade, the current national government has generated programs focused on developing Mindanao's basic infrastructure such as roads, irrigation, ports and airports, energy, and telecommunications. Yet even now, numerous roads in main ARMM cities remain unpaved, communications infrastructure weak, the quality and quantity of water are still decreasing, and conflict-affected areas remain without electricity (USAID, 2009).

Hence Mindanao has the lowest percentage of paved national and local roads and the lowest percentage of irrigated areas, which when combined with the inadequacy of government services has been detrimental to its economy as it, 'increases business costs relative to the other island regions, thus eroding the competitiveness of existing enterprises and discouraging investment'. Likewise the ARMM has both the lowest national road-density ratio and proportion of paved roads in Mindanao and the lowest proportion nationally of irrigation development in potentially irrigable land (Concepciòn *et al.*, 2003, pp. 19–21). This even seems to have been confirmed in September 2009 by Defense Secretary Gilbert 'Gibo' Teodoro who noted in a discussion with Ateneo university students that 'infrastructure, major infrastructure has not been brought to several areas, making development suffer', and that it is a truism that when you build a road to an area, a security problem is reduced' (2009). Thus, the third factor in turn is related to the final, and perhaps most important element, that insecurity itself is leading to underdevelopment in Mindanao.

IRIN Asia, a project of UN Office for the Coordination of Humanitarian Affairs, has found perhaps not surprisingly that, 'almost four decades of armed conflict in Mindanao between government troops and the MILF fighting for autonomy have stunted growth in the mineral-rich province' (2010). Direct financial costs of the conflict have actually been relatively low, but have borne most heavily upon the poor Muslim areas. Indirect economic costs have been much more severe. The most important of these, as mentioned above, is investment deflection. Paul Collier (2007) notes that capital flight is a main result of civil conflict, with capital repatriation following a settlement of the conflict. In the case of Mindanao, however, such capital flight (limited by the low level of the initial capital) has been compounded by a failure to attract the equity investment that could be expected based on the area's location and factor endowments–investment which was deflected to other areas in the Philippines and East and Southeast Asia (Judd, 2005, p. 6). Hence, Sylvia Concepciòn *et al.* (2003, p. 19) note that foreign investors prefer to invest in Luzon rather than in Mindanao or Visayas, and that Mindanao's share of the country's total government services was only around 16 per cent in 2000, with approximately 84 per cent going to Luzon and Visayas. Other indirect costs of the conflict include plummeting returns on investments, rising unemployment, crops abandoned, seeds not sown, animals and implements lost, and limited household budgets redirected to finance the purchase of weapons for self-protection from bandits and other criminal elements which flourish under conflictual conditions.

Furthermore, Muslim areas in Mindanao have been neglected by the national government relative to other provinces in terms of budgetary allocation and have posted lower than national average economic growth. Of the 65.8 billion Philippine Pesos spent in 1995, 993 million (1 per cent) was spent for ARMM and 9.2 billion (14 per cent) for all of Mindanao provinces combined (NSCB, 2010, pp. 3–62). By 2009, the pattern had changed little. The national government spent 2 per cent of its budget to ARMM and 17 per cent to Mindanao provinces combined. These figures are paltry compared to how much the national government spends for the National Capital Region (50 per cent in 1995 and 41.5 per cent in 2009). Indeed, 'Muslim Mindanao continues to be excluded from the fruits of national growth, and the minimal growth in the region itself is unsustainable, and mainly dependent on election and reconstruction-related consumption spending' (Lara Jr and Champain, 2009, p. 4).

Three decades of conflict have further exacerbated this condition. Delivery of basic services has been undermined. Internal displacement has disrupted livelihoods and schooling for children. Private investments have turned away as security risks heightened. The conflict not only provides a convenient justification for government failure to establish health, education, and other services, but it does also present a real impediment to making services accessible to the population at large. In addition to the destruction of facilities, the insecurity prevailing in rural areas encourages government employees to stick to the safety of urban centers and discourages projects in the poor and dangerous rural areas. The impact of conflict on development in Mindanao is such that even if you control for geographic variables (climate, topography, and so on) and access and infrastructure variables (road density, presence of port, and so on) on average, in Muslim Mindanao poverty incidence is 32 per cent points higher and per capita income PhP 11,000 lower (2000 value) (Ducanes, 2005, p. 2). As noted by Amina Rasul (2003), however, 'poverty can just as likely cause conflict as result from it, particularly when it reinforces 'social inequities', and this certainly seems to be the case in Mindanao. Indeed the two form a mutually reinforcing vicious cycle in the Muslim regions of Mindanao. The next section turns to consider human insecurity in Muslim Mindanao.

Insecurity in Muslim Mindanao

Abinales (2010, p. 154) highlights the impact of the conception of Mindanao as a frontier, 'an area at the farthest end of the national geobody but also adjoining similar frontiers of neighboring nation-states, the state is always nervous about what is happening there'. It is densely endowed with natural resources, but (relatively) sparsely populated. Thus, there is considerable attraction in terms of both security and development, for the metropolis to implement settlement programs to relieve congested and politically unstable areas in the country by transferring the poor and subversive there, while at the same time filling up the frontier with loyal citizens – even if they are undesirable back home (*ibid.*). Yet such policies have undermined the human security of the indigenous populations, including the Moro, and led in turn by way of feedback and spill-over, to threats to Philippine national security.

As a frontier, further security challenges present as violence between groups in a relatively lawless environment, as well as between these groups and the national government. Lara Jr and Champain (2009, p. 4) thus point out that, 'rebellion-related violence relating to the vertical armed challenges against the infrastructure of the state combines with inter- or intra-clan and group violence relating to horizontal armed challenges between and among families, clans, and tribes'. Thus, governance failures relate not only to the failure of the national government to provide safe havens free from freedom of fear and want for the most vulnerable sections of society but also to similar failure by regional and local foci of authority.

The Transparency Accountability Governance (TAG) Project finds corruption and governance failures (such as human rights violations) to be deeply imbedded in the Philippines' traditional system of governance (TAG, 2012). The impact of these governance failures upon the most vulnerable sections of Philippine society has stimulated support for armed revolutionary groups. In an interview with the foreign press in 1999, the founder and chief ideologue of the MILF, Ustaz (teacher) Hashim Salamat (2002, pp. 130–1), claimed that the corrupt system of governance in the Philippines is the reason why MILF territories are predominantly underdeveloped. He added that the only way to break free from the corrupt system is to fight for a fully independent state. The MILF also views the repeated violent human rights abuses in Muslim Mindanao as a form of a 'genocidal war' against Muslims (Tuazon, 2008, p. 244).

Although data availability is very limited for the early years of the conflict, from the escalation in the early 1970s up to the early years of this century, it costs an estimated 120,000 lives, with uncounted numbers of wounded and disabled, and the displacement of more than two million people (Judd, 2005, p. 5). More than 1,000,000 have been rendered homeless, and over 200,000 Muslim refugees have fled to Sabah (Quimpo, 2001, p. 278). In August 2008, renewed hostilities broke out as a result of the controversial split decision by the Supreme Court to reject as unconstitutional the planned expansion of the ARMM to include lands claimed to be ancestral domain. Nearly 400 people were killed and 700,000 people displaced (IRIN Asia, 2010). Although over time some of the displaced do return home, there is ongoing concern regarding the levels of human security and services available to them when they do so, and large numbers choose instead to stay with friends and relatives in 'safer' areas, in turn overburdening the social and economic resources of these communities and creating Muslim ghettos.

As mentioned above, human security is not only undermined by direct threats to life and limb coming from open conflict but is also endangered by other elements which shorten lives or reduction in 'livability'. Mindanao in general, and the conflict affected Muslim areas in particular, rank poorly in all measurements of human security. Partly this is a result of the side effects of conflict, partly as a result of economic deprivation, and in part as a result of inadequate government provision of services to overcome these challenges. 'In 1970, the country as a whole had one doctor for every 2,800 people; Mindanao had one doctor to 3,954 people; "Muslim Mindanao" had one doctor to 6,959 people' (Concepciòn *et al.*, 2003, p. 7). This, along with poverty, contributed to infant mortality of over 150 per 1,000 live births in parts of Muslim Mindanao compared with around 90 per 1,000 nationally.

Meanwhile ARMM life expectancy in 1995 was 56.1 years; 15 less than in central Luzon, and 12 less than the national average (ibid., p. 139). In fact, the five provinces of the ARMM are consistently to be found at the bottom of the list for longevity (HDN, 2005, p. 98).

Educational provision is similarly inadequate. In 1959–60, only 17.75 per cent of children of school age (7 to 13 years) were in state schools in Lanao, 63 per cent in Cotabato, and 66.37 per cent in Sulu (the national average was 78.6 per cent), while on average, roughly one-fifth of secondary students in ARMM leave school before finishing the level, double the national average and five times higher than the average rate in the National Capital Region (NCR). Thus, not surprisingly, in 1994, simple literacy in the ARMM was 73.82 per cent, and functional literacy 61.12 per cent (compared with national averages 93.9 per cent and 83.79 per cent) (Concepciòn *et al.*, 2003, pp. 140–1). Again, if we look at a province by province breakdown, at the bottom for school enrolment are six provinces of Mindanao: Bukidnon, Basilan, Sulu, Sarangani, Maguindanao, and Lanao del Sur – which have consistently featured in the bottom ten since 1998, and all six appear in the bottom ten for at least one of the education indicators (HDN, 2005, pp. 100–1). IDP communities are particularly vulnerable to having their schooling disrupted.

The breakdown of law and order in the conflict-affected areas has led to an increase in criminal activities, many of which further endanger local people. These include rampant incidences of kidnapping for ransom, smuggling, bank robberies, arms dealing, illegal logging (leading to soil erosion, floods, loss of watersheds), and increased human trafficking of women and children (internally to urban areas and internationally). Only three out of ten families in the ARMM have access to potable drinking water, and only one out of four to sanitary toilet facilities (Rasul, 2003, p. 139). Obviously, a key contributor to some of these threats is underdevelopment. In terms of standard of living, three Mindanao provinces (Maguindanao, Zamboangadel Norte, and Sarangani) along with Guimaras are new additions to the bottom ten, replacing Western and Eastern Samar, Sorsogon. ARMM provinces figure prominently in the bottom four provinces. The corresponding HDI figures reveal seven out of the bottom ten belonging to Mindanao, of which five are from the ARMM. Sulu continues to record the lowest HDI (0.301), followed by Maguindanao, Tawi-Tawi, and Basilan, while the fifth ARMM province, Lanaodel Sur, is tenth from the bottom. Sarangani and Zamboanga are new additions to the bottom ten list, replacing Romblon and Agusan del Sur which rose in the ranks to 67th and 61st, respectively (HDN, 2005, pp. 102–3).

HDIs reflect both absolute and relative (to the rest of the country) shortfalls. During the benchmark year of 1994, the HDI scores for ARMM provinces were lower than the national average of 0.627, with Sulu and Tawi-tawi having the lowest HDI for the entire Philippines (0.357 and 0.387 respectively). Marginal improvements in the HDI scores of ARMM provinces were noted in 2000, but still well under the national average and among the lowest in the entire country. Sulu and Tawi-Tawi remained at the bottom of the pile (NSCB, 2010, pp. 1–46). Two regions in Mindanao (ARMM and Caraga) likewise posted below-national average and lowest incomes in 1997 (PhP 74,885 and PhP 71,726, respectively). In 2006, average income for ARMM was the lowest for the entire country and almost half of the national average (*ibid.*, pp. 2–13). With the exception of Basilan, all ARMM provinces also have the highest severity of poverty, with Lanao del Sur, Tawi-Tawi, and Maguindanao posting almost twice or three times the national average of 3.1 (*ibid.*, pp. 2–25). More than half (55.3 per cent) of families in ARMM were poor, with Tawi-Tawi and Maguindanao again posting the highest number (78.9 per cent and 62 per cent respectively).

Unsurprisingly under such conditions, underdevelopment combined with other grievances and a perceived lack of consideration of their plight by the national government has fueled the flames of rebellion in Muslim Mindanao. The Philippine Development Forum describes the rise in poverty in the ARMM between 1988 and 2006 as 'alarming', noting that, 'while income poverty alone does not automatically result in social unrest, international experiences have shown that an explosive political situation is created when poverty is combined with deprivation and injustice' (Dearn, 2009). Alistair MacDonald, visiting head of the Delegation of the European Commission to the Philippines noted that poverty, above religion and secessionism, is the root of the conflict and that the Philippines should be ashamed to have such low levels of basic social indicators as those found in Mindanao (*ibid.*). Concepciòn *et al.* (2003, p. 26) have identified a strong correlation between armed conflict and poverty in Mindanao: 'The poorest regions, ARMM, Western and Central Mindanao have been at the centre of armed conflict'.

Even when there is some progress in the region, this can often be deceptive as the starting base is so low that development figures appear artificially inflated. Significant development needs to occur for a prolonged period of time before the gap with other parts of the Philippines can be closed. Moreover, the anticipation of development (often as a result of grandiose government proclamations) can raise expectancy above a level than can reasonably be hoped achievable. Disappointment will naturally ensue (the expectancy gap), leading once again to the vicious cycle of resentment, rebellion and underdevelopment. 'Poverty fuels conflict – by magnifying the sense of marginalization and exclusion. Conflict, in turn, aggravates poverty – through its effects on people, institutions and the economy. Thus they create the very conditions for their continuation'. (Rasul, 2003, p. 145) Vellema *et al.* (2011) argue, therefore, that the conflict is 'symptomatic of social justice issues not addressed by a succession of the Philippine governments, the Mindanao elite and the mainstream Moro revolutionary organizations'.

Previous administrations in Manila have not put in sufficient effort, resources, or commitment to break this cycle. The clearest gap between predominantly Muslim areas and the rest of the country lies in the lack of government services and resources, and, 'even more than income disparity, awareness of this gap serves as a symbol of government discrimination and neglect, one of the key grievances in the conflict' (Concepciòn *et al.*, 2003, p. 27). Again, even Defense Secretary Teodoro (2009) acknowledged that the government had committed insufficient resources to ensuring peace and order compared not only to other countries in the region and the rest of the world but even with regard to smaller countries with fewer problems. The next section considers the shortcomings of the Philippine government policies and initiatives in more detail.

Policy failures related to Muslim Mindanao

Generations of strategic analysts and policy advisers have relied on the concept of protagonists as single unitary rational actors (the rational actor model or RAM) when drawing up scenarios through which the decision-making environment of the target can be altered in favor of producing outcomes preferred by the agent. From a power-political perspective, the costs of unfavorable decision-making outcomes can be increased either at the implementation means stage (defense) or at the post-action ends stage (deterrence). From liberal perspectives, rational states (or statesmen) can best be influenced through use of carrots rather than sticks, by divorcing wealth and welfare from territory, and transforming a zero-sum game into one of win-win economic cooperation. In this way, conflict can be resolved. Strategic actions and policies associated with these traditional approaches to international security have, however, been found to come up short when dealing with the demands of an asymmetric war-fighting operating environment. In particular, the top-down policy approach common to strategic actions and the RAM model of decision-making, while suitable perhaps for conflict management, does little to address the BHN of the most vulnerable, who form the well-spring of support for insurgency.

This problem is not unique to Philippine national policymaking toward Muslim Mindanao, but this does seem to form a paradigmatic example. While national capitals may grant local governments some powers or relax control over them, in certain strategic areas, they always seem to prefer the top-down arrangement, and while southeastern Mindanao may have received its share of official pronouncements favoring more autonomy or greater decentralization, Manila retains tight control over the security concerns (Abinales, 2010, p. 201). Despite the 1988 Act Providing for the ARMM promising to truly reflect the ideals and aspirations of the Moro people, the right to determine fiscal and monetary policies, the power to tax incomes and determine how much the ARMM will receive from the national government, and of course policing prerogatives, all remained with Manila. Indeed for Lara Jr and Champain (2009, p. 4) the 'core of the problem is the exclusionary political economy that is developed and sustained through a complex system of contest and violence'.

The previous sections have identified how in many cases the GRP either failed to act to address Muslim grievances or were perceived to have done so. Even when decision-makers in Manila did conceive of a course of action, it was often inappropriate, ineffective, or even counter-productive. The first cause of failure was precisely that policies were initiated in Manila and then imposed on the ground in Mindanao, thereby offending both Muslims and non-Muslims in the region over perceived lack of consultation and transparency. In general, policy failures in Mindanao can be placed in two broad categories: too great a focus on aggregate, macro or top-down unitary rational actor approaches, or attempts to deal with the problems of under-development and insecurity in isolation one from the other or prioritizing one over the other.

Examples of the first of these categories include the 1976 Tripoli Agreement, which provided for the creation of an autonomous region in Mindanao and Palawan (covering 13 provinces), and the establishment of an autonomous government, judicial system (for Sharia law), and special security forces; the 1987 Philippine Constitution which brought in a new legal basis for an ARMM; the actual creation in 1990 of the ARMM; the 1996 Final Peace Agreement (FPA) to complete the implementation of the 1976 Tripoli Agreement between the GRP and the MNLF; the establishment of a 'Special Zone of Peace and Development' (SZOPAD); and the policy output of the National Commission on Indigenous Peoples (NCIP). None of these were able to bring about peace and development in the region because of the top-down nature of implementation, and failure to address the needs and interests of the most vulnerable and therefore most discontented sections of society in Mindanao.

Despite its 'autonomous' nature, the ARMM receives approximately 98 per cent of its operating revenue from Manila. These funds are assigned directly in a top-down fashion contributing significantly to an increase in corruption, but little in terms of development in the region. Indeed, the highest policy and lawmaking body for the region (the 21-member Regional Legislative Assembly) has been accused of, 'caring more about pork barrel than about policy' (Gutierrez and Danguilan-Vitug, 1999, p. 199). The insertion of an extra bureaucratic tier has in fact reduced the efficacy of health and education services while increasing discontent (Salvaña Bautista, 2010). The local government and the ARMM continue as patronage sources by providing employment; their financing is dependent upon government transfers (either as a percentage of their Internal Revenue Allotment (IRA) or as Congressional appropriations). These structures spend most of their allocation to personnel salaries and Maintenance and Other Operating Expenses

(MOOE) and hardly for any development projects. The national government uses these local government structures as conduits for national-funded development projects, but much is lost because of corruption, mismanagement, and bureaucratic incapacity (Makinano and Lubang, 2001, p. 4).

Indeed, although as a result of the human insecurity and underdevelopment prevalent in Muslim Mindanao, government welfare agencies and foreign development groups have started to prioritize the region as a recipient of massive amounts of aid, especially following devolution and the approval of the 1991 Local Government Code (LGC), the creation of the ARMM and the successful Government–MNLF peace agreement in 1996. This has led to the capture of local state power becoming more attractive for the *datu* elites. Vellema *et al.* (2011) have noted that beyond using local political office as an avenue to extract payments from illegal businesses in the region, significant amounts in IRAs that went with the LGC became opened up for misuse. 'Political office enabled the clans to access the networks, links, and resources that could expand the capital and scope of their underground businesses and illegal operations. Political power could also but tress the protection of their enterprises and enable them to extort taxes from competitors and other entrants to the underground economy' (Vellema *et al.*, 2011, p. 312).

After the 1996 Peace Agreement with the Moro National Liberation Fund, the Southern Philippines Council for Peace and Development (SPCPD) was created to formulate a development agenda for the SZOPAD. This new structure did not supersede the ARMM but rather acted as parallel body and as a 'practice-governance run' for the MNLF's supposed transformation into a regional political party. In its three years of existence (1996–99), the SPCPD suffered from inherent weaknesses. It did not have a robust mandate to formulate a development agenda; it had minimal allocation from Congress relative to its geographic scope, funded as it were under the Office of the President; it had no control over the disposition of its resources which was dictated by the national government. Like the ARMM, it was an employment agency for former MNLF members (Mercado, 2000; Cook and Collier, 2006, p. 37).

When the MNLF claimed electoral victory and assumed control over ARMM in 1996, the institution was adjudged 'corrupt and mismanaged' (Bertrand, 2000, p. 37), 'wasteful and a poor performer' (Gutierrez and Danguilan-Vitug, 1999), and exhibited similar tendencies to 'centralize' fiscal power in the hands of the executive (governor) (*ibid.*, p. 193). Development aid delivery was deemed a failure under ARMM due to poor fiscal resources, internal power wrangling, corruption, weak human resource capacity, and a convoluted regional decision-making process involving multiple government stakeholders (for example, Regional Development Councils, National Economic Development Authority, Mindanao Economic Development Council, Office of the Presidential Adviser for Mindanao) (Mercado, 2000).

Following the 2001 Tripoli Peace Agreement with the MILF, a new framework was also created to address the rehabilitation and development concerns of MILF-controlled areas. The Bangsamoro Development Agency (BDA), an NGO attached to the MILF, became another player in the increasingly labyrinthine development game in Mindanao. As an NGO, the BDA could enter into contractual arrangements with national government line agencies, the ARMM and international funders in carrying out projects in areas under its influence. While the BDA appears to have a more robust standing, greater fiscal flexibility (direct access to international monies) and narrow geographic target than SCPCD, MILF's capacity to manage development projects remains a nagging concern.

According to Mara Stankovitch (1999, p. ix), 'hardly anyone in Mindanao is satisfied with developments since the peace agreement. Those who welcomed the agreement have been disappointed; those who were cautious have had their doubts confirmed; and those who opposed it have had their prejudices reinforced'. The autonomous region formula has been unable to satisfy Muslim aspirations precisely because it was seen as a creature of the powers in Manila, and also because it was not able to address the underlying causes of Muslim grievances. Indeed, for Lara Jr and Champain (2009, p. 12), 'whereas the original discourse of social exclusion was synonymous with the anti-statist political line advanced by the Moro separatists ... the current discourse of exclusion is being wielded ... against the rebel-separatists themselves. Their grievance – economic and political exclusion ... Their target – the Misuari-led ARMM, the current ARMM administration, and the MOA-AD'. Thus, having reached agreement with the MNLF (which subsequently lost a degree of influence among disaffected Muslims), the Philippine government has been forced to engage another Muslim armed opposition group, the MILF which has demanded an independent Islamic state.

Meanwhile, promotion of development activities also occurs at the macro level with concessions to large financial interests and a focus on plantation, logging, and mineral extraction activities. Aid in Mindanao tends to be of a bilateral nature and focused on large-scale macro projects of which the ARMM attracts the smallest share (Gardiola, 2005, p. 9). Even with the Comprehensive Agrarian Reform Program (CARP), large portions of agricultural landholdings have yet to be redistributed to potential beneficiaries; 'or where they have been redistributed, the nexus of control over most plantations remain in the hands of former landowners or investors' (ICCO and AFRIM, 2008, p. 34). The NCIP allocates little budget or priority for the delineation of ancestral lands and socioeconomic activities. This explains the policies of direct application and one Certificate of Ancestral Domain Title (CADT) per province per year, which in turn puts ancestral domains at the mercy of companies that may offer assistance in the processing of CADT applications in exchange for the acceptance by the community of their extractive activities like mining operations. Indeed, the State can be seen as having acquired more leverage and resources to enforce control over various overlapping and competing tenurial instruments, which in the long run weaken property claims if not undermine the IP's power to govern, own, and control their domains.

> For the IPs land is not only a means for productive activities but more importantly for the foundation of their political and sociocultural existence. With no budget appropriation from the national government, it would be difficult to uphold and ensure the socioeconomic development of the IPs even if they shall have formulated an ADSDPP [Ancestral Domain Sustainable Development Protection Plan]. This situation makes them susceptible to the temptation of selling, mortgaging or leasing their lands to investors. (*ibid.*, p. 32)

A failure fully to integrate development and security policies has further characterized policies issuing from Manila and undermined their efficacy in Mindanao. These range from a Reconstruction and Development (RAD) Program in Muslim Mindanao launched in 1973, through the 1996 FPA itself, to 2000's National Peace and Development Plan (NPDP), and the 'all-out war' and 'all-out peace' initiatives of Presidents Estrada and Arroyo respectively. The first of these failed in part not only because of the macro focus as detailed above but also because RAD proved impossible to conduct in isolation in what was effectively a war zone. The FPA omitted many key development issues, including reparations, economic redistribution, affirmative action, and conflicting land claims as 'too explosive' to tackle, and perhaps in the hope that rapid national economic development would provide adequate livelihoods for all through a trickle down process and obviate the need to address these underlying problems. The FPA did provide for the injection of funds for 'massive socioeconomic development' in the newly defined SZOPAD in order to address the clamor for compensatory justice for the Muslims, but by the time the peace agreement was signed, all government funds for the next budgetary cycle had already been allocated (Concepciòn *et al.*, 2003, p. 12). The NPDP, as the name suggests, was supposed to take a holistic or total approach, but policy priority was still overwhelmingly military, with the development phase to follow sequentially after the military objectives and phases of clear, hold, and consolidate. In other words, the NPDP was predicated on a total military victory – one which was never achieved – before moving on to development phase, and 'in such a scenario, conflict will never abate as poverty and oppression of the people will continue – thus swelling the ranks of the rebels' (Adriano, 2007, p. 117).

President Joseph 'Erap' Estrada's 'all-out war' policy following the takeover of a town hall in Lanaodel Norte by the MILF in March 2000 involved a military offensive against MILF camps. The camps themselves were, however, in fact communities run by the MILF and included many civilians and civilian buildings such as mosques and *madrasahs* as well as the homes of the people. The government declared a military victory over the MILF, but the increased suffering potentially generated more support for the *jihad,* the latter subsequently declared. After succeeding the ousted Estrada in January 2001, former Vice President, and new President Gloria Macapagal Arroyo (GMA), declared a counter policy of 'all-out peace' and sent emissaries to talk to the MILF. Yet again, regardless of the official policy title, Arroyo actually continued the earlier policies of prioritizing a security solution before sequentially moving on to the issue of poverty, taking the stance of 'no development without peace'. Talking to the country in her 2008 State of the Nation Address, Arroyo laid blame for the failure to eradicate poverty in Mindanao on the conflict itself (Dearn, 2009). 'It is perhaps a truism therefore that 'policy and its intentions alone do not produce outcomes' (ICCO and AFRIM, 2008, p. 35).

ODA projects, bilateral and multilateral, despite showing some promise have also encountered problems related to central government policy-making and administration. A UN multi-donor program called 'ACT (Action for Conflict Transformation) for Peace' committed US$500 million in support of the 1996 FPA with the MNLF (Cragin and Chalk, 2003, p. 17). A similar effort under World Bank (Multi-Donor Trust Fund for Mindanao) was created after the 2001 Tripoli Peace Agreement with the MILF. The USAID expenditure program in the Philippines almost doubled from US$47.4 million in 2001 to US$82.8 million in 2007 – an estimated 60 per cent of which went to Mindanao (Tuminez, 2008). Similarly, Japan committed US$400 million special aid program for Mindanao in 2002. These ODA-funded projects covered education, livelihood, microfinance, and small-scale community-based infrastructure improvements in contrast to the large-scale infrastructure projects of the previous decades, and also involved NGOs.

In reality, the full amounts pledged by international donors were never actualized, partly because of the lack of 'national government counterpart funding'. The national government did not live up to its commitment to match the foreign aid infusion (Cook and Collier, 2006, p. 62). The implementation of the projects also fell victim to local government incapacity, weak accountability mechanism, and ill-match between donor program requirements and actual needs on the ground. Accountability for ODA is an attendant concern. The MNLF leadership contends that it was not informed of the status of pledges by external donors nor was the national government transparent with regards to the availability of monies for infrastructure investments. The national government's support for the Philippine military's expanded civic action and reconstruction activities (through the newly-created National Development Support Command) has also raised concerns about the 'militarization of aid' and its connection to counter-insurgency (Soriano, 2006, p. 20). US and Australian ODA is tied to broader strategic goals of securing favorable security arrangements (for example, status of forces agreement) with the national government (Cook and Collier, 2006), not a genuine desire for a long-term solution of the conflict.

Finally, the Human Security Act (HSA) (otherwise known as Republic Act No. 9372: An Act to Secure the State and Protect our People from Terrorism), passed by the Philippine Senate in February 2007, despite the promise of the title, singularly failed to bring together the different strands of security and development. While some of its champions in the Philippine Senate may have claimed that the Act was intended to add a new dimension to human security, and to recognize the linkage between human rights and national security, it had very little to do with human security per se, but was rather a purely top-down anti-terrorism empowerment of the instruments of the state designed, according to different commentators, to respond to US calls for enact anti-terror measures in the wake of the 9/11 attacks in 2001, and/or to shore up the scandal-ridden GMA administration (Eadie, 2011, pp. 28–9). Furthermore, Eadie argues that the HSA was designed to be at one and the same time a sop to the United States and unworkable in practice, and that it has never been used in court, successfully or otherwise, to prosecute those suspected of terrorist activity in the Philippines (*ibid.*, p. 24).

Thus, as pointed out by Merlie B. Mendoza (2010, p. 84), 'clearly the experience in the Southern Philippines has shown that most of the traditional development interventions introduced by the Government and by International Donor Institutions and NGO shave either been wanting or have failed', with people still living in poverty, conflict and fear, even after hundreds of millions of dollars in assistance poured into the area and decades of programs upon programs being introduced. The military approach has likewise failed repeatedly. It seems that top-down economic and security approaches which aim only at conflict management or at best resolution, but are unable to transform the conflictual nature of relationships as they do not address fundamental human security and BHN concerns of some of the most vulnerable sections of society are doomed to repeat this cycle of governance and policy failure.

Conclusion

Political proposals and/or security operations operating in isolation or as preconditions for the implementation of measure to alleviate poverty in Mindanao have failed to defuse the situation there as they fail to address the root causes of discontent and hence the conflict itself. Indeed, there is evidence that they merely serve to increase hardship, discontent, and to radicalize the most dissatisfied elements. Top-down economic initiatives have also done little to reduce resentment of Manila's rule of the region as what little they have achieved appears to have benefited those already relatively well off – international and national investors and corporations, Christian settlers, and Muslim elites. Again, this is unlikely to satisfy the most vulnerable strata of society, and indeed may further antagonize them as both wealth and expectancy gaps grow. Indeed, Marides Gardiola (2005, p. 10) has pointed to instances where development initiatives have even exacerbated the causes of conflict by breeding divisions among communities when there are only a limited number of potential beneficiaries.

What is needed is a holistic and comprehensive action plan which addresses the needs of the most vulnerable, in terms of both human security and development, while also giving them ownership in the process by building projects from the bottom up rather than imposing from Manila or even at the regional level. Again Mendoza reasons that:

> The underlying framework for interventions in areas of conflict must be that of human security, which espouses the protection of the vital core of all human lives in a way that enhances human freedoms and human fulfillment – the freedom from FEAR, freedom from WANT and freedom from HUMILIATION. It must be understood, particularly by those charged with national security, that human security enhances & ensures internal state security. (2010, p. 87)

In May 2010, populist president Benigno 'Noynoy' Aquino was elected (taking office June 30) with one of his main campaign pledges to restart peace talks with the MILF and bring an end to the violence. Slowly, but surely, the two sides do seem to be drawing together, withdrawing from state-centric bargaining positions, to focus instead on mutual interests. On 23 September 2010, Mohagher Iqbal, spokesman and Chairman of the MILF Peace Panel conducting peace talks with the Philippine Government said that the MILF will aim for the creation of a sub-state entity likened to a US State rather than full independence from the Philippines. The Muslim sub-state would not exercise power over national defense, foreign affairs, currency and coinage, or postal services, which would remain the prerogatives of the central government. Igbal further added that the sub-state would not have its own armed forces but instead would maintain internal security (Teves, 2010). The government side responded positively, and despite ongoing tensions and occasional clashes, a comprehensive peace treaty was finally brokered in 2012 which apparently covered many of the issues raised in this chapter, and with which both sides expressed satisfaction and optimism. The highlights of the October agreement include:

> The Parties agree that the status quo is unacceptable and that the Bangsamoro shall be established to replace the Autonomous Region in Muslim Mindanao (ARMM.) The Bangsamoro is the new autonomous

> political entitle (NPE) referred to in the Decision Points of Principles as of April 2012 ...
>
> The Parties recognize Bangsamoro identity. Those who at the time of conquest and colonization were considered natives or original inhabitants of Mindanao and the Sulu archipelago and its adjacent islands including Palawan, and their descendants whether of mixed or of full blood shall have the right to identify themselves as Bangsamoro ... The Bangsamoro shall be governed by a Basic Law ... The Basic Law shall reflect the Bangsamoro system of life and meet internationally accepted standards of governance. It shall be formulated by the Bangsamoro people and ratified by the qualified voters within its territory ...
>
> The Parties agree that wealth creation (or revenue generation and sourcing) is important for the operation of the Bangsamoro. Consistent with the Bangsamoro Basic Law, the Bangsamoro will have the power to create its own source of revenue and to levy taxes, fees, and charges, subject to limitations as may be mutually agreed upon by the Parties ...
>
> The Bangsamoro shall have a just and equitable share in the revenues generated through the exploration, development, or utilization of natural resources obtaining in all the areas/territories, land or water, covered by and within the jurisdiction of the Bangsamoro, in accordance with the formula agreed upon by the Parties ...
>
> The Parties agree that sustainable development is crucial in protecting and improving the equality of life of the Bangsamoro people.
>
> To this end, the Bangsamoro shall develop a comprehensive framework for sustainable development through the proper conservation, utilization and development of natural resources ... (Framework Agreement, 2012)

It is interesting to note that all of these identity, development, and community clauses come before the traditional bugbears of security, political rights, and zero-sum considerations of the extent of territory. Clearly an interest-based and comprehensive approach to good governance covering all elements of human security and development appears to have had more success than previous top-down models. Hence, when announcing the deal on 7 October 2012, President Aquino noted that, 'this framework agreement paves the way for a final and enduring peace in Mindanao', and MILF Vice Chairman Ghazali Jaafar was quoted as saying, 'We are very happy. We thank the president for this'. It is too early to assess whether this latest peace accord will finally bring to an end the long running conflict between the Moro people and the national government in Manila (as President

Aquino noted, there are still many details to be hammered out), but at least, thanks to the new approach, the initial signs are good, and it is hoped that the agreement could be implemented on the ground by the end of President Aquino's term in 2016 (BBC, 2012).

This challenging case study has expanded the parameters of the concept of spillover from human to state insecurity introduced in Chapter 4. It has also highlighted the dangers of top-down policy approaches when attempting to undo the negative effects of bad governance. Finally, it has highlighted the importance of economic considerations, and the close relationship between underdevelopment and insecurity. Chapter 6 not only further explores this relationship but also challenges the assumptions of positive and negative reinforcement between these variables through analysis of the challenging case study of the Lao People's Democratic Republic.

References

Abinales, P. N. (2010) *Orthodoxy and History in the Muslim-Mindanao Narrative* (Manila: Ateneo de Manila Press).

Adriano, F. D. (2007) 'A Review of the Government's Mindanao Peace and Development Paradigms', Mindanao Studies Conference Davao City, *Mindanao Studies Consortium Foundation*.

BBC (2012) 'News Asia: Philippines and Muslim Rebels Agree Peace Deal', *BBC*, 7 October 2012, http://www.bbc.co.uk/news/world-asia-19860907.

Bertrand, J. (2000) 'Peace and Conflict in the Southern Philippines: Why the 1996 Peace Agreement Is Fragile', *Pacific Affairs*, 73(1), 37–54.

Collier, P. (2007) *The Bottom Billion* (New York: Oxford University Press).

Concepciòn, S., Digal, L., Guiam, R., De La Rosa, R. and Stankovitch, M. (2003) 'Breaking the Links between Economics and Conflict in Mindanao: Discussion Paper', *Clapham Road: Business and Conflict Programme, International Alert.*

Cook, M. and Collier, K. (2006) *Mindanao: A Gamble Worth Taking* (Sydney: Lowy Institute for International Policy).

Cragin, K. and Chalk, P. (2003) *Terrorism & Development: Using Social and Economic Development to Inhibit a Resurgence of Terrorism* (Santa Monica: Rand).

Dearn, M. (2009) 'Mindanao: Poverty on the Frontlines', *Open Democracy*, June 4, http://www.opendemocracy.net/article/email/mindanao-poverty-on-the-frontline.

Ducanes, G. (2005) *Macroeconomic Effects of Conflict: Notes for the Macroeconomic Presentation*, http://hdn.org.ph/wp-content/uploads/2005_PHDR/2005%20Geoffrey_Ducanes.pdf.

Eadie, P. E. (2011) 'Legislating for Terrorism: The Philippines' Human Security Act 2007', *Journal of Terrorism Research*, 2(3), 24–33.

Fisher, R., Ury, W. and Patton, B. (1991) *Getting to Yes* (New York: Penguin.)

Framework Agreement (2012) *Framework Agreement on the Bangsamoro*, http://pcdspo.gov.ph/downloads/2012/10/GPH-MILF-Framework-Agreement-10062012.pdf, 12 March 2013.

Gardiola, M. (2005) *Putting the Money Where the Mouth Is – ODA in Mindanao: A View from the Communities*, http://hdn.org.ph/wp-content/uploads/2005_PHDR/2005%20Marides_Gardiola.pdf.

Garrido, M. (2003) 'The Evolution of Philippine Muslim Insurgency', *Asia Times,* 6 March 2012, http://www. atimes.com/atimes/Southeast_Asia/EC06Ae03.html.

George, T. J. S. (1980) *Revolt in Mindanao: The Rise of Islam in Philippine Politics* (Kuala Lumpur: Oxford University Press).

Gutierrez, E. and Danguilan-Vitug, M. (1999) 'ARMM after the Peace Agreement' in K. Gaerlan and M. Stankovitch (eds), *Rebels, Warlords and Ulama: A Reader on Muslim Separatism and the War in Southern Philippines* (Quezon City: Institute for Popular Democracy).

Human Development Network (HDN) (2005) *Philippine Human Development Report 2005: Peace, Human Security and Human Development in the Philippines*, 2nd edn (Manila: HDN).

Hurights, O. (2008) 'Mindanao Conflict: In Search of Peace and Human Rights', *Focus*, December 2008, 54, http://www.hurights.or.jp/archives/focus/section2/2008/12/mindanao-conflict-in-search-of-peace-and-human-rights.html.

Interchurch Organisation for Development Cooperation (ICCO) and Alternate Forum for Research in Mindanao (AFRIM) (2008) *Building Unities and Strengthening Cooperation towards Peace and Development in Mindanao* (Davao City: AFRIM).

IRIN Asia (2010) 'Mindanao Conflict Fuels Trafficking', *IRIN*, 31 March 2010, http://www.irinnews.org/report.aspx?ReportId=88631.

Judd, M. (2005) 'The Mindanao Conflict in the Philippines: Roots, Costs, and Potential Peace Dividend', *Social Development Papers: Conflict Prevention & Reconstruction*, 24, http://internal-displacement.org/8025708F004CE90B/(httpDocuments)/8A4B6AFE92D9BB82802570B700599DA1/$file/WP24_Web.pdf.

Lara Jr., F. and Champain, P. (2009) *Inclusive Peace in Muslim Mindanao: Revisiting the Dynamics of Conflict and Exclusion* (London: International Alert).

Makinano, M. and Lubang, A. (2001) *Disarmament, Demobilization and Reintegration: The Mindanao Experience,* http://www. international.gc.ca/arms-armes/isrop-prisi/research-recherche/intl_security-securite_int/makinano_lubang2001/index.aspx?view=d.

Mendoza, M. B. (2010) 'Humanitarianism in Complex Areas' in M. B. Mendoza and V. M. Taylor (eds), *Challenges to Human Security in Complex Situations: The Case of Conflict in the Southern Philippines* (Kuala Lumpur: ADRRN (Asian Disaster Reduction and Response Network)).

Mercado, E. (2000) *Peace and Development: The MNLF and the SPCPD Experience,* http://www.mindanao.com/kalinaw/peaceproc/pa-imp-mercado.htm.

National Statistical Coordination Board (NSCB) (2005) *Gross Regional Domestic Product: Per Capita*, http://www.nscb.gov.ph/grdp/2005/2005concap.asp.

NSCB (2010) *Philippine Statistical Yearbook* (Makati: NSCB).

Quimpo, N. G. (2001) 'Options in the Pursuit of a Just, Comprehensive, and Stable Peace in the Southern Philippines', *Asian Survey*, 41(2), 271–89.

Rasul, A. (2003) 'Poverty and Armed Conflict in Mindanao' in A. Rasul (ed.), *The Road to Peace and Reconciliation: Muslim Perspective on the Mindanao Conflict* (Makati City: AIM Policy Center, Asian Institute of Management).

Rodil, R. B. (2010) 'Achieving Peace and Justice in Mindanao through the Tri-people Approach', *Mindanao Horizons,* 1(2), 25–46.

Salamat, H. (2002) *Referendum: Peaceful, Civilized, Diplomatic and Democratic Means of Solving the Mindanao Conflict* (Mindanao: Agency for Youth Affairs).

Salvaña Bautista, Pauline Angela. (2010) Interviewed by author in Manila, Philippines, 30 July 2010.

Santos Jr, S. M. (2005) 'Evolution of the Armed Conflict on the Conflict on the Moro Front', http://hdn.org.ph/wp-content/uploads/2005_PHDR/2005%20Evolution_Moro_Conflict.

Soriano, C. R. (2006) 'The Challenges of Relief and Rehabilitation Assistance in an Ongoing Conflict', *Kasarinlan*, 21(1), 4–33.

Stankovitch, M. (1999) 'Introduction' in K. Gaerlan and M. Stankovitch (eds) *Rebels, Warlords and Ulama: A Reader on Muslim Separatism and the War in Southern Philippines* (Quezon City: Institute for Popular Democracy).

Transparency Accountability Governance (TAG) (2012) *About TAG: Overview*, http://www.tag.org.ph/about_tag/default.htm.

Tan, S. K. (2000) *Understanding the Mindanao Conflict: Mindanao at the Crossroad*, http://bugsnbytes.tripod.com/bb_newsletter_0004_02.html.

Teodoro, G. (2009) 'Teodoro Discuss Mindanao Conflict with Ateneo Students', *Political arena.com*, 1 September 2009, http://ph. politicalarena.com/gilbert-teodoro/news/teodoro-discuss-mindanao-conflict-with-ateneo-students.

Teves, O. (2010) 'Philippine Muslim Rebels Drop Independence Demand', *Associated Press/UT San Diego*, 23 September 2010, http://www. utsandiego.com/news/2010/sep/23/philippine-muslim-rebels-drop-independence-demand.

Tuazon, B. M. (ed.) (2008) *The Moro Reader History and Contemporary Struggles of the Bangsamoro People* (Quezon City: CenPEG Books).

Tuminez, A. (2008) 'Rebellion, Terrorism, Peace: America's Unfinished Business with Muslims in the Philippines', *Brown Journal of World Affairs*, 5(1), 211–23.

United States Agency for International Development (USAID) (2009) *Country Assistance Strategy – Philippines: 2009–2013*, http://pdf.usaid. gov/pdf_docs/PDACN452.pdf.

Vellema, S., Borras Jr, S. M. and Lara Jr, F. (2011) 'The Agrarian Roots of Contemporary Violent Conflict in Mindanao, Southern Philippines', *Journal of Agrarian Change*, 11(3), 298–320.

6
Human Insecurity and Underdevelopment in Laos

Introduction

Anticipated post-Cold War peace dividends and supposed universal economic benefits from globalization have not materialized. The number of people in the world exposed to extreme poverty has remained high, despite widening rapid economic growth in East Asia. Even within this rapidly developing region, some countries are missing out on the 'economic miracle' phenomenon. These countries do not receive the degree of attention devoted to deserving cases in other parts of the world, precisely because they exist in a region seen as a developmental success story. The Lao PDR is one such case where, although development exists, it is happening at a slower pace, with very uneven distribution, and significant negative effects (Pholsena and Banomyong, 2006; Baird and Shoemaker, 2007).

The government in Vientiane has shown great determination to graduate from the UNDP list of least-developed countries by 2020. The World Bank (2013) notes that Laos is on track to achieve this goal, and credits reforms for having reduced poverty and stimulated growth, with economic expansion averaging over 7 per cent per annum since 2001, and gross national income (GNI) per capita moving up from a lower economy status to a lower-middle income economy. Hydroelectric exports are a key element in this development strategy. Indeed, 'natural resources – forestry, agricultural land, hydropower, and minerals – comprise more than half of the total wealth of Lao PDR' (World Bank, 2013).

Opinions are, however, divided on the degree of development success experience in Lao PDR, and the future prospects of the Lao economy. Laos remains one of the world's LDCs, with significant areas still inaccessible by road. Despite steady economic growth in the past decade, with

---

A version of this chapter was previously published with Kearrin Simms (2011) as 'Human Security and Human Development in the Lao PDR: Freedom from Fear and Freedom from Want', *Asian Survey* 51(2), April, pp. 333–55.

GNI per capita rising to US$2600, food insecurity remains widespread and alarmingly high in rural areas (WFP). While macro-economic projects are blossoming, in 2012 subsistence agriculture still accounted for 30 per cent of GDP and 75 per cent of total employment, and it is in rural areas where human development challenges are most severe (CIA, 2013). Progress has been made on MDG targets, but shortfalls persist in alleviating malnutrition and ameliorating infant and maternal health; significant disparities remain between urban and rural areas as well as among ethnic groups (UNFPA, 2010). An increasing Gini coefficient, which has now reached 36.7, indicates that the benefits of development are not being realized equally and disparities are widening (AUSAID, 2012, p. 3). Indeed, some feel that Laos has started to enter an economic nightmare scenario (Doussantousse, 2010; Bird and Hill, 2010).

Furthermore, the building of hydroelectric dams has generated fear and hostility both within the country and beyond its borders. The year 2012 saw the breaking of ground for the latest of these projects, a hugely controversial dam being constructed on the Lower Mekong River near Xayaburi, which is opposed by Vietnam and Cambodia at least until further impact assessments have been conducted. The fear is that this dam would threaten fish stocks, rice production, and the livelihoods of the tens of millions of people who live downstream. There are already four dams on the Upper Mekong in China, but Xayaburi would be the first on the lower part of the river, with at least 10 more being proposed (BBC, 2012). State-run media sources claimed that Laos would not press ahead with construction until environmental issues were resolved, but activists and international reporters secured video footage and photographs of apparent construction work.

The controversial Xayaburi Dam was eventually given an official go-ahead, despite the opposition. A formal ceremony marking the start of full construction at Xayaburi was held on Wednesday, 7 November 2012. The National Assembly in Vientiane, convening from December 5–20, apparently threw its support behind the project. According to state media, members of the National Assembly were invited to 'debate' whether to adopt the Xayaburi Dam project. Not a single lawmaker spoke out against the government decision to build the dam, with one speaker commending the government for 'convincing' neighboring countries and environmentalists that the dam will 'not have any adverse impact on humans or the environment' (RFA, 2012).

Both domestic institutions and international donors and actors have failed to provide a safe haven for the most vulnerable sections of the Lao populations, with severe challenges in terms of both freedom from fear and freedom from want. Indeed, Laos remains one of the poorest countries in the world, with a life expectancy of just 56.29 years. Here, it must be noted that further problems exist with aggregate data in this particular case study. Records are incomplete, collection of data is difficult, and much of what is collected is of uncertain quality. In particular, as the Lao PDR has no life registry, all population and mortality data are only estimates based on surveys and census. Given data collection shortcomings, the figure of 56.29 is a best estimate based on the aggregate data collected, and, despite the apparent accuracy of the figure, it is not intended to imply true scientific precision.

This chapter explores some of the reasons for such underdevelopment in Laos, with a particular focus on how insecurity undermines economic well-being and poses a threat to further development projects. It also addresses the consequences of underdevelopment for human security in terms of shortening lifespans and undermining quality of life. Thus, in some ways, the Lao PDR faces the classic post-conflict society double jeopardy of insecurity and underdevelopment, whereby underdevelopment undermines human security and insecurity threatens development.

This chapter, however, further challenges the simplistic assumption of human development and human security as mutually reinforcing processes. Human security in the Lao PDR is additionally threatened by the forces of development. Consequently, successful development strategies within Laos will require a response to both the human development and human security insufficiencies that currently exist. A purely development-focused approach is unlikely to bolster human security, whereas focusing exclusively on protecting the population of around 6.5 million will do little to fulfill human needs. Hence, in the Lao PDR, the government and the international community can substantially improve the lives of the most vulnerable only by focusing simultaneously on protecting individuals from immediate threats and taking responsibility for the provision of havens within which their well-being can flourish.

Lao PDR embodies some of the key conundrums associate with human insecurity and underdevelopment. It is perhaps the clearest case study of the negative impact conflict and its aftermath can have upon development, and also demonstrates the horrific toll underdevelopment can exact on the lives of the most vulnerable. It clearly demonstrates not only the shortcomings of national and international institutions when providing good governance but also the perils of focusing on top-down governance, aggregate development measurements, and focusing on efficiency rather than providing safe havens.

Paris (2001, p. 88) has called attention to the dangers of definitions of human security which are 'extraordinarily expansive and vague, encompassing everything from physical security to psychological well-being, which provides policymakers with little guidance in the prioritization of competing policy goals and academics little sense of what, exactly, is to be studied'. In response, it has been argued that the key to transforming human security from a disparate theory into a functional tool of analysis is prioritizing its components in a structured format (Alkire, 2004). This chapter demonstrates the necessity of a combined focus on freedom from fear (protection of persons) and freedom from want (provision of human needs) in a structured format prescribing policies which prioritize the provision of safe havens for the most vulnerable sections of society (Krause, 2004).

The Lao PDR is a small, mountainous, landlocked country with the lowest population density in Southeast Asia and an estimated total population of just 6,677,534 (Pholsena and Banomyong, 2006; CIA, 2009). These geographic and demographic considerations, as explained below, contribute to the areas of extreme poverty and underdevelopment in the country. Furthermore, however, Laos is also the most bombed country in history (Kingshill, 1991; Cave *et al.*, 2006, p. 23), with heavy ERW contamination, and, to a considerable extent as a result of these factors, ranks 138 out of 187 countries on the 2011 UNDP HDI (UNDP, 2011). The state contains 16 provinces and one municipality and can be further demarcated into 139 districts of which 25 have been identified as 'poor' and 22 as 'very poor' (NSEDP, 2006). Very poor villages are those with an incidence of poverty exceeding 70 per cent while the total average incidence of poverty in the total 72 poor and very poor districts is 55 per cent (NCCR, 2008).

In total, the 47 poorest districts account for approximately 1.2 million people, or over one-sixth of the Lao population (NSEDP, 2006). As will be explored within this chapter, there is a close correlation between the poorest districts and those which were most bombed. As is common in LDCs, development within these districts is inhibited by inadequate public infrastructure, lack of medical facilities, scarce employment opportunities, vulnerability to natural disasters, food insecurity, illegal activities such as human trafficking and drug use, and limited access to education. Human security is further endangered by corrupt officials who sell villagers' land, the lack of negotiation skills among the most vulnerable residents, and the abuse from external agents from Vietnam and China. The latter are accused of illegal acquiring land, withholding payment for wage-labor, and misuse of agricultural chemicals thereby polluting forests and water sources (Baird and Shoemaker, 2008).

While unemployment remains low, (national average 2.5 per cent), in the youngest population in Asia (median age just 21), it is rising. This is particularly the case among the young, where it is double the national average. There is also significant underemployment, and as a result, there is an increased migration to urban areas and over borders – 60,000 per year fail to find full employment and join these ranks (International Organization for Migration – IOM). The estimated 33 per cent of the total population still living under 1.25 dollars a day, and many living close to it, are concentrated in districts located in the remote and mountainous north and in the Southeast along the border with Vietnam (AUSAID, 2012, p. 3).

Not surprisingly, Lao PDR is one of the LDCs described in Chapter 2 as having experienced grave episodes of violence and instability, and is perhaps the best (or worst depending on perspective) example of the phenomenon in East Asia. The negative reinforcement of insecurity and underdevelopment has certainly continued long after the official cessation of hostilities. In particular, Laos has faced overwhelming post-bellum threats to life and well-being in the form of an unparalleled ERW legacy.

ERW include UXO, landmines, and abandoned explosive ordnance (AXO). Lao PDR experiences many of the negative effects of ERW listed in Chapter 2. These include physical harm, amputation and death, psychological trauma, food insecurity, infrastructure limitations, and increased rebuilding costs. ERW in Laos are obstacles to the use of land for agriculture, grazing, housing, resettlement, and commerce, and they are deterring public and private investment and economic development through increased uncertainty, higher costs, and delays resulting from their suspected presence. Not only do they harm productive members of Lao society, including children trying to salvage them for scrap metal, but they are also serving as a poverty multiplier due to the individual and community costs of dealing with casualties in the country.

Yet Lao PDR is experiencing a third side to the insecurity-underdevelopment conundrum whereby the forces of development are themselves posing a further threat to the human security of the most vulnerable sections of society. These can negatively impact on local populations through the development of mega projects such as hydroelectric dams forcing people to move. Relocation of communities can create new or increased exposure to disease, increased challenges to food security, and exposure to contaminated water sources, and can exacerbate the ills of modernization and urbanization such as drug addiction and traffic accidents. In addition, an increased demand for resources from dangerous environments, such as mineral mining or harvesting scrap metal from ERW, often places economically vulnerable people in harm's way. Thus, assuming a constant positive mutual reinforcement between development and human security is as flawed in policy terms as is treating either process in isolation.

Hence, this chapter demonstrates the need for an integrated approach to dealing with human security and development, using evidence from the Lao case study. The next two sections address the more conventional perspectives of human security in the Lao PDR, considering in turn the threats posed to human security by underdevelopment and the threats to development from insecurity. The final analytical section looks at the negative impact of development upon human security in Laos.

Threats to human security from underdevelopment in the Lao PDR

Underdevelopment is a source of many human security challenges in the Lao PDR. When the Pathet Lao gained control of Laos in 1975 they inherited a state ravaged by the effects of warfare. No longer sustained by the millions of dollars of US aid given to the royal government during the war, in 1975 Laos was one of the ten poorest countries in the world (Warner, 1996). Geographically, the Lao PDR is the only country in Southeast Asia faced with Collier's 'poverty trap' of lacking direct access to the sea (Collier, 2007). Being landlocked has presented a challenge for Lao residents' ability to participate in transnational trade since the 16th century (Pholsena and Banomyong, 2006).

Laos' status as a landlocked state has become the focus of ongoing development proposals for the country to become 'land-linked' or a crossroads for trade (Rigg, 1997; Evans, 1998; Pholsena and Banomyong, 2006). Other observers have, however, pointed out that this reconfiguration might also boost increases in diseases including HIV/AIDS, bolster human and drug trafficking, and speed environmental destruction (Serdán, 2008; Warr, 2008). Indeed, many of the human security challenges faced by the Lao PDR appear to derive from international involvement. The French promoted the production of opium in Laos as a means to extract wealth during the colonial period. In some parts of the country only Vietnamese operations – not local communities – have logging rights, and 'the roads are like the straw in a glass, sipping natural resources and people' (Vandergeest, 2003; Doussantousse, 2010). In other words rather than promoting the well-being of local communities, such infrastructure development can in fact leave a region poorer in terms of natural and human resources.

As is common in both post-conflict countries and LDCs, the Lao government has been economically weak and dependent on outside support (Del Castillo, 2008). Since 1990, financial aid from bilateral donors and multilateral funding organizations has amounted to more than US$250 million per year or about US$40 per inhabitant. This is the highest per capita level in Southeast Asia (Evans, 2002; Pholsena and Banomyong, 2006). Such international aid, although necessary, limits the state's autonomy and control over its own future (Thomas-Slayter, 2003). Viliam Phraxayavong (2009) has been particularly critical about the motivations behind and the effects of foreign development aid to Laos, suggesting that aid limits the state's autonomy to pursue its own development aspirations, and promotes corruption, as cultural practices in Laos may lead to aid being seen as 'free' money. Meanwhile, government officials are reluctant to oppose the wishes of international donors, particularly if the officials wish to send their children on educational scholarships to America, Australia, or China (Doussantousse, 2010).

Public infrastructure, food security, communicable diseases, assistance to remote rural communities, and sustainable use of the environment are all ongoing development concerns (Pholsena and Banomyong, 2006). Road networks are limited and poorly constructed; local roads account for 70 per cent of the total network. Just 4 per cent of roads are paved and some 40 per cent of the people live more than six kilometers from the nearest road – an important development issue because the lack of roads means lower rates of school attendance and higher rates of sickness (Pholsena and Banomyong, 2006; Warr, 2008). Even in the capital, Vientiane, where the road network may be considered of a reasonable standard for an LDC, there are concerns that government and international non-governmental organizations are promoting unsustainable use of luxury cars as status symbols, while the city still lacks a sewer system (Askew *et al.*, 2007).

Food security remains a serious concern for the Lao PDR. Two-thirds of rural households are at risk of food shortages should certain livelihood shocks occur. Examples of relevant livelihood shocks provided by the WFP include droughts, floods, and problems of land access due to UXO (the most common subset of ERW) contamination (WFP, 2007, p. 21; GOL and the UN, 2008). Forty to fifty per cent (estimates vary) of children under the age of five continue to be affected by chronic malnutrition, and this figure has remained largely unchanged for over a decade. In the 25 most food-deficient districts, annual rice consumption deficits for some households average more than four months. Although often viewed as a 'subsistence' farming society, 80 per cent of Lao households have no rice fields and many farmers can cover only a small proportion of their food requirements from their own production (WFP, 2007).

Limited alternatives, particularly in remote rural areas, have led the Lao PDR to evolve into one of the largest opium producers in the world, and therefore to become a target of both criminal networks and international policing initiatives. Worryingly from a human security perspective, the majority of drug production is consumed locally. Indeed, in recent years Laos has passed from being a net exporter to a net importer of drugs, as amphetamines replace opium among modern addicts. The number of households involved in cultivation of opium has substantially decreased due to eradication programs, but the figures remain high in some of the more remote areas (UNODC, 2006, p. 40). Furthermore, villagers often have to sell poppy harvests in order to pay for items such as hand tractors. Thus, a declining market and eradication programs can actually contribute to insecurity among the rural poor. At the same time, growers and occasional users are subject to harsh measures to reduce supply and are vulnerable to human trafficking as a result of their desperation quickly to find alternative forms of income (Cohen, 2009).

Although the Lao economy is slowly growing, unemployment remains high, in particular among youth in urban centers. In rural areas, the lack of opportunities, poor living conditions, and dearth of available land have all helped push people to leave, resulting in large-scale unregulated migration to neighboring countries (Serdán, 2008). This in turn has resulted in a potential increased threat of human trafficking because of corruption and weak law enforcement. Laos, together with neighboring Thailand, Cambodia, and Myanmar, lies along the main human trafficking routes. The lack of a legal agreement between Thailand and Laos on migration makes it hard to distinguish between legal immigrants, illegal immigrants, and those whom have been trafficked. There are an estimated 200,000 illegal Lao workers in Thailand, but the numbers do not identify those being exploited (UNDP, 2006).

The assumed relationship between the spread of HIV and human trafficking was supported by a United Nations Children's Fund (UNICEF) report on trafficking in Laos. Investigators found that 'the overwhelming majority of trafficking victims surveyed (60 per cent) are girls' aged between 12 and 18. Many victims (35 per cent) end up in forced prostitution (UNICEF, 2003, p. 8). The prevalence of HIV/AIDS remains low, however, because of the Lao PDR's geographic isolation. At the same time, expanding road networks and increasing migration mean there is a significant threat that morbidity of the disease will increase (GOL and the UN, 2008). In China (700,000), Vietnam (290,000), and Cambodia (75,000), the estimated numbers of people infected with HIV/AIDS are significantly higher than in Laos (5,500) while in Thailand the figure is more than 600,000 (CIA, 2009).

Malaria and other communicable diseases such as tuberculosis and cholera continue to afflict the Lao population and its development; morbidity from malaria still affects 48 of every 1,000 people (Serdán, 2008). The proportion of the population using bed nets against mosquitoes increased from 25 per cent in 1999 to 60 per cent in 2002, leading to a marked reduction in deaths. Nevertheless, 76 per cent of Lao living in malarial areas still uses no preventive or treatment measures. Those living in remote regions along streams and without proper sanitation remain vulnerable. People moving from the highlands to lowlands may be unaware of the disease risks from mosquitoes that do not live at higher altitudes. Although potable water is accessible in the capital and in some other urban centers, people in rural areas lack safe water and live in poor sanitary conditions. They tend to store standing water, which attracts mosquitoes (GOL and the UN, 2008).

Life expectancy remains an important issue, with an under-five mortality rate of 61 deaths per 1,000 live births, and a maternal mortality rate of 403 deaths per 1,000 live births (UNICEF, 2011). These rates remain among the worst in the world. Many women and children continue to die because of lack of basic medication or malnourishment and infections; few births are attended by skilled personnel (*ibid.*). Direct causes of death relate to malnutrition, diarrhea, malaria, and communicable diseases. Indirect causes include a lack of adequate facilities and medicines, food insecurity, and ignorance of existing health care options.

As part of the government's poverty reduction efforts, health centers have been built in and around remote areas; however, their numbers and degree of geographical penetration remain limited. The United Nations Population Fund (UNFPA) and the Ministry of Health acknowledge that services remain poor. Taken together, the inadequate numbers of trained staff, scarcity of medicines, and delays imposed by long distances and poor infrastructure tend to discourage the use of health facilities. Language, ethnic, and gender barriers between patients and health workers may also spur avoidance of modern health care even when it is available (*ibid.*). Failures of the Lao government to address the needs of the country's numerous ethnic communities arguably stem from prejudice by the dominant Lao ethnicity as from lack of capability (Rehbein, 2007). And some traditional ethnic groups prefer to have babies delivered in their own communities rather than going to neighboring towns with health centers.

Thus, as a result of underdevelopment, the most vulnerable sectors of the population in the Lao PDR face not only shorter lives but often also lives in fear of imminent death or incapacity, in abject poverty, or in want of BHN. In other words, underdevelopment has a clear negative impact on the human security of Laos. The next section identifies the extent to which a vicious circle is operating in the Lao PDR, with insecurity undermining both economic well-being and development projects aimed at raising people out of poverty.

Threats to development from insecurity in Lao PDR

As noted above, Laos holds the dubious distinction of being the most bombed country in history (Kingshill, 1991). As part of their support to the Royal Lao Government and to serve their own interests fighting against the North Vietnamese and the spread of communism, the United States conducted an extensive bombing campaign over Laos during the Second Indochina War (Warner, 1996). Under the guise of 'armed reconnaissance missions', the United States flew 580,944 bombing missions over Laos, dropping over 2,000,000 tons of munitions. This equated to one planeload of bombs every eight minutes for nine years and at a cost of 2,190,000 USD per day (UNDP, 2001). According to a 2008 report by Landmine Monitor, four million large bombs, defoliants, herbicides, and more than 270 million sub-munitions were dropped over Laos. The most prolific form of UXO remaining in Laos today are air delivered sub-munitions including BLU-3, 7, 18, 24/66, 26/36/59, 42/54, 43, 44, 45, 61, 63, 66, 73, and Mk 118 (Handicap International, 2004, p. 13).

While there is no accepted figure for the direct casualties of US bombing, the intensity of the attacks coupled with eyewitness accounts suggest civilian casualty levels were appallingly high (Cave *et al.*, 2006). Of the survivors, many became refugees: between 1962 and 1971, 600,000 Lao (from a total population of just three million) fled their country (Paul, 1971). The living conditions of those who remained in their home villages were often deplorable, as frequent bombardments forced many residents to move into makeshift underground shelters or to flee into the jungle to live as 'almost hunter-gatherers' (Zasloff, 1970).

Now, more than 35 years since the cessation of this conflict, there remains a close correlation between Laos' poorest districts and those of which were most bombed. An estimated failure rate for the munitions dropped during the conflict of between 10 and 30 per cent (Cave *et al.*, 2006) left Laos also the world's most UXO-contaminated country (NRA, 2008). Fifteen of Laos' seventeen provinces are contaminated by UXO, with a quarter of all villages severely contaminated (UNDP, 2008; NCCR, 2008) (see Figure 6.1 below). UXO can be found everywhere in Laos, from hillsides to rice fields, in schoolyards, in rivers, along roads and footpaths, and even in the center of provincial towns. Since regulated clearance began in 1996, over 186 different types of UXO have been found (Landmine Monitor, 2008). UXO restricts access to usable land; increases the cost and time of development initiatives; inhibits access to shops, schools, and medical facilities; disrupts potential earnings from tourism, mining, and hydroelectric projects; and causes significant human casualties.

Aside from the humanitarian effects of UXO contamination, UXO is one of the primary factors limiting social and economic development in Laos. A strong correlation exists between the prevalence of poverty and UXO contamination (compare Figure 6.1 with Figure 6.2 below). UXO contamination is considered an ongoing development concern in all UNDP development assistance frameworks and humanitarian development frameworks for Laos. Likewise, the government's National Socio-Economic Development Plan for 2006–10 recognizes UXO as a significant inhibitor to development that affects, in particular, already poor and vulnerable groups (Cave *et al.*, 2006). While Laos' population is slowly becoming more urbanized, population growth continues to create the need for more safe land. Given the high levels of subsistence farming noted above, the inhibitory effect of UXO on land access is a significant livelihood constraint for many people.

Within Laos' 47 poorest districts, the amount of contaminated land with potential agricultural use is some 200,000 hectares. At current clearance rates, it will take approximately 50 years to clear, at considerable cost (Griffin *et al.*, 2008). Livestock are at risk of UXO accidents, and even access to water and fuel is impaired by UXO contamination (Kett and Mannion, 2004). As can be seen in the following comments by Cooperative Orthotic Prosthetic Enterprise (COPE) employee Jo Pereira and two residents from Nakai District in the heavily contaminated Khammouane Province, Yai Saengchan and Pommachanh Sisomsouk, the widespread effects of UXO commonly mentioned within professional literature are reflected in the opinions of both UXO sector operators and those living in contaminated landscapes:

> UXO affects poverty, it affects disability, it affects infrastructure; it pretty much just affects everything that people are trying to do here. (Pereira, 2009)

> It [farming] is also very hard because of the bombs. There are lots of bombs here and people are scared of the bombs. When we plant rice we must be careful and we cannot grow enough food. (Saengchan, 2009)

> UXO is the biggest problem. We do have other problems but UXO is the biggest. (Sisomsouk, 2009)

Figure 6.1 Map of UXO-contaminated areas in Laos

Source: UXO Lao Bombing Data, 2001, Map of UXO impact and bombing data 1965–75, Vientiane, Phoenix Clearance Limited.

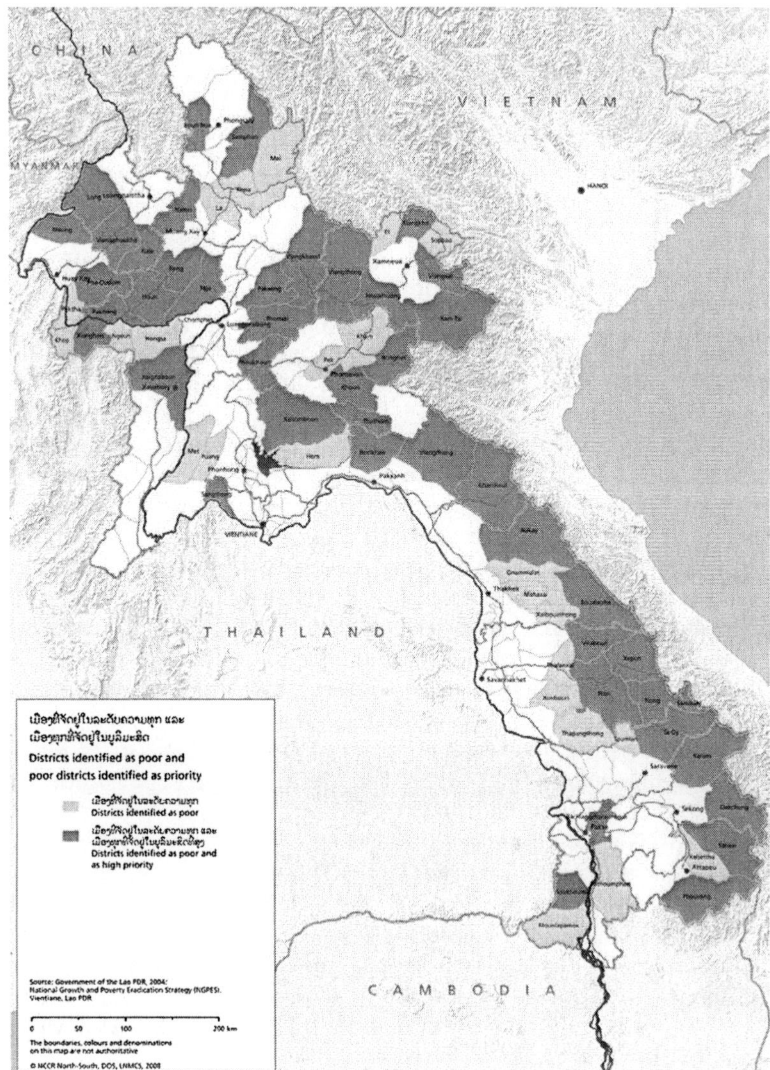

Figure 6.2 Map of Laos' 47 poorest districts

Source: Swiss National Centre of Competence in Research (NCCR) (2008).

Indeed, all Nakai residents interviewed highlighted UXO as the biggest problem that they faced. In addition to restricting land access, the presence of UXO has resulted in the overuse of non-contaminated land and reduced agricultural yields because of environmental degradation (UNIDIR, 2008).

Such restrictions on development because of UXO have been labeled by the World Bank as 'negative investment' because of the many ways they detract from Laos' development by adding to the costs and time needed for development initiatives (World Bank, 2008). A recent estimate by the Ministry of Transport of the excessive cost to civilian infrastructure resulting from UXO contamination was up to US$5000 per hectare.

Aside from the employment and development limitations for UXO survivors and UXO-contaminated communities, the costs of medical treatment or funerals for UXO casualties can push poor families deeper into poverty and destitution (Cave *et al.*, 2006). As Tim Horner (2009), former senior technical advisor to the National Regulatory Authority for the UXO Sector in the Lao PDR explains, 'The people hit hardest by UXO are often the poorest. Having to pay for treatment basically takes people from just being able to cope to being poverty stricken'.

One of the most common methods used by rural villagers to pay for medical treatment is selling livestock, yet this practice also often leads to labor shortages and the removal of family assets that could have been used to cope with future financial hardship. According to the National Socio-Economic Development Plan, the average cost of treatment for UXO injuries can be as much as half the annual income of a rural family. It is in this sense that UXO contamination has been labeled a 'poverty multiplier' (Handicap International, 2004, p. 26). On a broader scale, treatment and care of UXO survivors can be a burden for entire communities and a significant additional expenditure for Laos' overtaxed medical system (UNDP, 2008).

Thus, the poor internal security of the Lao PDR has a history of restricting the development of the country and the economic opportunities and well-being of its citizens. Poor human security continues to pose a major development challenge; creates a number of economic burdens upon individuals, communities, and the state; and operates as a disincentive for future investment and development projects. At every level of analysis, the negative reinforcement tendencies of underdevelopment and insecurity in Laos appear to function across the board. There is, however, another reason bolstering the need to avoid studying either phenomenon in isolation: development itself is undermining human security in Laos. This will be addressed in the next section.

Threats to human security from development in Laos

The government of Laos (GOL) has focused primarily on macro-economic and international development projects and policy goals rather than on providing safe havens for the most vulnerable of its citizens. Hence, Laos participates actively in sub-regional, regional, and international cooperation frameworks, particularly those connected with the ASEAN and involving economic cooperation. These include the ASEAN Free Trade

Area (AFTA); the Cambodia, Laos, Vietnam (CLV) Development Triangle Area; Cambodia-Lao-Myanmar-Vietnam (CLMV); and the Greater Mekong Sub-Regional (GMS) cooperation institutions. Likewise, the long-mooted high-speed rail line between China and Laos is, according to 2012 reports, now back on track.

Throughout 2012, the GOL accelerated its efforts to achieve the 'ambitious target' of joining the WTO by the end of the year (WTO, 2012a). The Protocol of Accession to the WTO was signed on October 26, after a final meeting between Laos' chief negotiator, Industry and Commerce Minister Nam Viyaketh, and WTO Director-General Pascal Lamy. Copies were submitted to the National Assembly for ratification, over 15 years after Laos first applied to join the WTO (WTO, 2012b). The National Assembly duly ratified the membership package on December 6, paving the way for the country's entrance to the 157-member organization 30 days later, in early 2013 (AFP, 2012).

Although the Lao PDR has maintained substantial economic development for over a decade, it remains categorized by the UN as an LDC. Development has improved some living conditions, such as better education and decreased mother and child mortality. But it has also hurt some of the most vulnerable people, spurring increases in traffic accidents, human trafficking, forced migration, and AIDS morbidity, as well as demand for scrap metal that raises the risk of being harmed by UXO.

The scrap metal trade

Even though UXO is one of the most significant restraints to human development in Laos, it has also become an economic resource through a well-established scrap metal trade (Moyes, 2005). Paradoxically, this trade is responsible both for increasing casualty rates across Laos and for boosting cash incomes for the poor. Essentially, gleaning scrap metal from UXO has in some ways, as detailed above, inhibited development due to the impact of casualties, while at the same time becoming an economic asset of the Lao population, as well as for Vietnamese middlemen who prey upon the trade (Robson, 2008). People use war scrap for everyday items such as pots, buckets, and belt buckles, as well as for small boats – and even prostheses.

The collection and sale of scrap metal has become one of the most extensive enterprises in Laos. As development, trade, and the availability of consumer goods increases, former subsistence economies are becoming increasingly cash driven. In many areas the sale of scrap metal is the only means for people to participate in a monetary economy (UNDP, 2008). Furthermore, regional and global rises in the demand for steel, coupled with increased availability of cheap metal detectors and expanding road networks, are nourishing the scrap metal trade. In recent years, the numbers of scrap metal collectors, dealers, and foundries have all increased (MAG, 2008).

While contributing substantially to rural livelihoods, the scrap metal trade is also the most common way in which people voluntarily expose themselves to UXO risks. The demand for scrap is likely the primary reason why UXO casualty rates in Laos are now increasing after years of steady decline. As John Dingley (2009), UNDP Senior Technical Advisor to UXO Lao states, 'the scrap metal trade is a major problem for the creation of casualties, but it is also a big enabler of cash into rural households'. Scrap metal collectors search for scrap and sell their findings to local dealers, who in turn sell the metal to scrap foundries where it is melted down and converted into rebar used in construction (MAG, 2008).

People engage in the scrap metal trade for a variety of reasons; however, the most common and influential is need of money (Vosburgh, 2006). Indeed, with ongoing construction booms in border countries such as China, the sale of scrap metal connects some of Laos' poorest people to international trade markets (Moyes, 2005). The scrap metal trade prospers with diverse levels of involvement; some people leave other forms of employment to search for scrap metal, while for others, participation merely involves selling items found while farming (Robson, 2008). Some people may stay away from their homes for several days to search for scrap; others may join scrap metal collection labor gangs (Moyes, 2005).

Broadly speaking, distinctions may be made between those who search for scrap and those who merely discover it by chance, as well as between those who avoid UXO when discovered and those who actively try to dismantle it (GICHD, 2007). In the case of the latter, many scrap metal dealers and foundries will not take items they identify as UXO. Still, some scrap collectors will attempt to salvage the material, which means that the poorest individuals in the scrap metal trade face the greatest levels of risk (UNDP, 2008).

In the context of poverty and geographical isolation, scrap metal collection is often regarded as a security activity in the sense that it generates an extra income to complement subsistence farming (GICHD, 2007). Intentional risk-taking by those engaged in the scrap metal trade is generally based on a rational decision-making process that evaluates the costs and benefits of pursuing other options. Indeed, previous studies have shown that where other options have more perceived advantages, such as high-value cash crops or well-paid employment in the private sector, people will generally abandon the scrap metal trade (Durham, 2007).

Such viable alternatives have proven extremely difficult to create. Even when other sources of income are available, the sheer amount of scrap metal means that the trade generally provides the most substantial returns on time and labor invested (Moyes, 2005). Furthermore, scrap metal collection is one of the few activities where buyers will come into the village to collect the product. Where other types of financing are non-existent, some scrap metal dealers have even been willing to provide metal detectors in lieu of payment (GICHD, 2007).

When labeling the scrap metal trade a high-risk activity, it must be remembered that in heavily UXO-contaminated areas, it is likely that the limited available farmland may also be contaminated. Growing crops is therefore also potentially risky. In a 2007 study by the Geneva International Center for Humanitarian Demining (GICHD), rural Lao villagers said they could find up to 30 kilograms of scrap metal per year just by conducting their regular farming activities. In times of food shortage, illness, or other livelihood shocks, any additional income helps buffer the family; scrap metal collection is often perceived as a risk worth pursuing.

That said, although scrap metal collection may be more prevalent among Laos' poorest people, it is not solely a subsistence activity. In many areas the sale of war scrap is increasingly being used to generate income for an expanding market of consumer goods, or for social events such as weddings. Being a finite resource may lead to an increase in scrap metal collection. Likewise, as safe scrap becomes harder to find, people are likely to take greater risks with UXO (Moyes, 2005).

The resettlement question

Resettlement is another escalating development and human security issue facing Laos, involving some of the most vulnerable populations in the country. It is a source of contention over political motivations, unequal distribution of the burdens and rewards of development, and discrimination issues. It has been argued by some that prevailing development initiatives have increasingly conceptualized ethnic minorities as backward and problematic, and that resettlement policies are politically motivated, targeting the Hmong minority because of their involvement in the Second Indochina War, known in the West as the Vietnam War (Serdán, 2008). According to numerous public statements by Amnesty International, resettlement of Hmong refugees returning from Thailand to Laos continues to involve mistreatment by the Lao state, including imprisonment, torture, and a lack of provision of basic resources (Amnesty International, 2007, 2008).

Inequalities experienced by many ethnic minorities may, however, be the result of geographic isolation as much as discrimination: similar discrepancies exist between urban and rural populations, and between uplanders and lowlanders (Serdán, 2008). In largely rural-upland Houaphan Province, for example, the number of people living under the national poverty standard is the highest in the Lao PDR at 74.6 per cent, while in Vientiane Municipality, the figure is just 12.2 per cent (UNDG, 2006). Indeed, one of the biggest challenges to development in Laos is accessing remote communities (World Bank, 2008). Currently, the government response is to relocate them to more accessible areas, although this strategy has resulted in further human security difficulties.

Resettlement policies aimed at moving rural communities closer to existing health facilities, economic markets, and public infrastructure have instead, in many cases, decreased land availability and led to increased food shortages. In theory, government policies are aimed at inducing villagers to migrate in order to better access government services, generating possible mitigation of health related risks and offering the chance for improved livelihoods. In reality, migration can exacerbate already tenuous livelihoods in the original upland or highland villages and increase residents' exposure to human security threats such as new diseases, trafficking, and exploitation (GOL and the UN, 2008, p. 44).

Displacement to lower land areas and deforestation can diminish the amount of non-timber forest products, hunting, and fishing available thereby decreasing the nutritional intake and threatening the human security of displaced persons. A 2006 GOL and UNDP-sponsored study backed up previous reports that relocated communities in Laos experience several months of rice shortages and are prone to getting new illnesses such as malaria (Goudineau, 1997; UNDP, 2006). The arrival of government services may be delayed until several months after the relocation, imposing a tremendous burden on families who have to sell livestock and belongings to cover their basic needs (Serdán, 2008). Perhaps even more problematic are the negative effects relocation has had on human security and development, even when communities are moved within their own districts.

Although poor villagers from remote rural areas are sometimes resettled to boost human security and human development, officials also clear land and relocate villagers to make way for large infrastructure projects such as hydroelectric dams. The World Bank supported construction of the Nam Theun II Dam in Khammouane Province, prompting the resettlement of more than 6,000 villagers and affecting around 100,000 people living downstream. Such projects are poignant examples of how macro-scale development initiatives may jeopardize the human development and human security of small rural communities. Indeed in Khammouane's Nakai District, the implications of Nam Theun II-related resettlement programs were mentioned by many residents as the second biggest inhibitor to their food security after UXO contamination. As residents put it:

> Before people planted the rice by themselves. Then Nam Theun II came to this area and made the dam. Then Nam Theun II gave the people new land but they did not give them enough. They only gave them 0.6 hectares. (Khamphong, 2009)

> People here plant rice for food. But there is not enough food because there is not enough area to plant the rice because Nam Theun II did not give local people enough land. (Somsak, 2009)

> Before Nam Theun II Dam started, local people had farms on the flat land and planted rice there. Now it is covered by the water and local people

> moved to the mountain. If they move to the mountain there is more area if local people wanted to cut down the trees. But Nam Theun II said, no, you don't have to cut the trees, and they gave the local people a small area ... but it is too small. (Sisomsouk, 2009)

Hydroelectric projects such as the Nam Theun II Dam also have the potential to cause vast environmental destruction: in recent years, forest resources near the dam have declined considerably. Land reforms, displacement, and resettlement policies have all decreased the land available to farmers. The agricultural output of rice has dropped, leading to the need to import it and other staples (Serdán, 2008, p. 5). In many instances, opium eradication programs have also undermined food security as eradication has taken place prior to the provision of alternative crops or other forms of income generation (WFP, 2007).

Other consequences of development

The increasing movements of Lao workers to Thailand, the creation of large infrastructure projects attracting foreign workers, higher volumes of tourists, and the construction of new roads boosting the number of drivers have combined to trigger a rise in the incidence of HIV/AIDS. Development has fueled a new sexual economy in the traditionally isolated farming communities of Luang Namtha Province (ADB, 2010; Doussantousse *et al.*, 2011). Sex workers face ballooning exposure rates and are at high risk because they may be ignorant of protection options. Men working abroad often acquire the HIV virus and return infected, passing it on to their wives. This perpetuating cycle is particularly prevalent in the Lao-Thai border areas in the southern parts of Laos, and in the capital, Vientiane (Serdán, 2008).

Likewise, drug addiction and drug trafficking patterns are changing as the Lao PDR develops. Various types of illicit and intravenous drugs are increasingly used among the Lao population, in particular by youth. The increased openness of the country to trade and communication networks has exposed it to trafficking from neighboring Thailand, Myanmar, and China. Development and resettlement have contributed to urbanization, and young people living in urban and border areas appear to be susceptible to such drugs, rather than opium (Laugen, 2004). Rising urban unemployment exacerbates the human security threat to the youth of the Lao PDR.

Finally, as a result of development and the explosion of roads and private vehicle ownership (with many new drivers ignorant of road regulations), road accidents have registered an increase from 3,407 cases in 1997 to 9,788 in 2003. Police data estimate that in 2006, there were more than 4,600 traffic accidents in Vientiane, an increase of 19 per cent from 2005. Considering the capital's population of only 690,000, the per capita death rate in Vientiane City from traffic accidents can be estimated at around 70 per 100,000, one of the highest in Asia (Serdán, 2008, p. 20). In fact, road traffic accidents now rank alongside or even slightly ahead of malaria and UXO as causal agents of physical harm in Laos, ahead of maternal mortality and only significantly behind child mortality. Traffic accidents may, however, be considered less of a human security or development concern because they do not affect food security or development projects, and do not have the same psychosocial effects on communities or foster the same feelings of injustice for survivors.

Conclusion: freedom from fear and want in the Lao PDR

Despite rapid development and increased human security in other countries in the region, Laos remains a remarkably poor country. For its most vulnerable citizens, life is filled with hardship, is tenuous, and short. In part, this situation stems from classic post-conflict society double jeopardy, whereby underdevelopment undermines human security and insecurity threatens development. Human security in the Lao PDR is also, however, threatened by the forces of development.

Narrow definitions of human security tend to focus on the physical threats to individuals and prescribe a responsibility to protect them from danger. As such, these approaches fail to address the problems faced in the Lao PDR, with its multiple developmental challenges constituting threats to lives and well-being. Indeed, people are unlikely to turn away from practices such as scrap metal collection that increase their exposure to harm, unless they have sufficient alternative sources of income. Moreover, high infant mortality dwarfs the threat to human security posed by all other contributing factors.

Likewise, many examinations of development and official development assistance take a macro approach, focusing on statistical data and measurements of aggregate well-being and improvement while missing the impact of underdevelopment on the most vulnerable sectors of society. Focusing solely on development issues is also insufficient because not only does insecurity hinder development but also development can boost existing or generate new threats to human security. It is not that processes of development are inescapably detrimental to human security in Laos; rather, evaluations and policies relating to these two interrelated concepts require an understanding that goes beyond their commonly portrayed symbiosis.

The experience of the Lao PDR demonstrates the dangers of taking top-down aggregate-data improvement approaches to development and security: these are likely to overlook the impact of action and inaction upon the most vulnerable sectors, and upon minorities who may be excluded from collective goods as a result of either political or geographic marginalization. This case study generates several implications for what should be studied and prioritized in terms of policy prescription, namely that (1) the human security paradigm is a vital contribution to the theory and practice of providing safe havens, (2) the freedom from fear and want of the most vulnerable should be pursued simultaneously, (3) simultaneous provision of development and human security procedures can be managed as long as the concept is not broadened too far along political and psychological lines, and (4) the focus should always be on individual human beings rather than collective entities.

References

Asian Development Bank (ADB) (2010) *Build It and They Will Come: Lessons from the Northern Economic Corridor, Mitigating HIV and Other Diseases* (Manila: ADB).

Agence France-Presse (AFP) (2012) 'Laos Ratifies WTO Membership', 7 December 2012, http://www.google.com/hostednews/afp/article/ALeqM5iuWBelJ3aRyQeVyjyojck-amfr8w?docId=CNG.5a0075054a86241b1b38bbf239bbe196.731.

Alkire, S. (2004) 'A Vital Core that Must Be Treated with the Same Gravitas as Traditional Security Threats', *Security Dialogue*, 35(3), 359–60.

Amnesty International (2007) *Lao People's Democratic Republic ThaoMoua and Pa FueKhang: Hmong Imprisoned After Unfair Trial*, http://www.unhcr.org/refworld/publisher,AMNESTY,,LAO,4678dcaf2,0.html.

Amnesty International (2008) *Thailand: The New Thai Government Must Stand up for Human Rights of Refugees*, http://www.amnesty.org/en/library/asset/ASA39/004/2008/en/f6ad1652-0d56-11dd-a114-e974a1f25b3e/asa390042008eng.html.

Askew, M., Logan, W. S. and Long, C. (2007) *Vientiane: Transformations of a Lao Landscape* (London: Routledge).

Australian Government Overseas Aid Program (AUSAID) (2012) 'Lao People's Democratic Republic Annual Program Performance Report 2011', June 2012, http://www.ausaid.gov.au/Publications/Pages/lao-pdr-appr-2011.aspx.

Baird, I. G. and Shoemaker, B. (2007) 'Unsettling Experiences: Internal Resettlement and International Aid Agencies in Laos', *Development and Change*, 38(5), 865–88.

Baird, I. G. and Shoemaker, B. (2008) *People, Livelihoods, and Development in the Xekong River Basin, Laos* (Bangkok: White Lotus Press).

BBC News Asia (2012) 'Team Visits Controversial Laos Dam', *BBC*, http://www.bbc.co.uk/news/world-asia-18993032.

Bird, K. and Hill, H. (2010) 'Tiny, Poor, Land-locked, Indebted, but Growing: Lessons for Late Reforming Transition Economies from Laos', *Oxford Development Studies*, 38(2), 117–43.

Cave, R., Lawson, A. and Sherriff, A. (2006) *Cluster Munitions in Albania and Lao PDR: The Humanitarian and Socioeconomic Impact* (Geneva: UNIDIR).

Central Intelligence Agency (CIA) (2009) *CIA World Factbook*, https://www.cia.gov/library/publications/the-world-factbook/geos/la.html.

CIA (2013) 'The World Factbook – Laos', https://www.cia.gov/library/publications/the-world-factbook/geos/la.html.

Cohen, P. T. (2009) 'The Post-Opium Scenario and Rubber in Northern Laos: Alternative Western and Chinese Models of Development', *International Journal of Drug Policy*, 20(5), 424–30.

Collier, P. (2008) *The Bottom Billion* (Oxford and New York: Oxford University Press).

Del Castillo, G. (2008) *Rebuilding War-Torn States* (Oxford and New York: Oxford University Press).

Dingley, J. (2009) Interviewed by Kearrin Simms in Vientiane, Laos, 15 June 2009.

Doussantousse, S. (2010) Lead Researcher for Social Environment Research Consultants (SERC), [online conversation], Vientiane, Laos, 25 July 2010.

Doussantousse, S., Sakounnavong, B. and Patterson, I. (2011) 'An Expanding Sexual Economy along National Route 3 in Luang Namtha Province, Lao PDR', *Culture, Health & Sexuality*, 13, S279–91.

Durham, J. (2007) 'Needs Assessment in Lao PDR', *Journal of Mine Action*, 11(1), http://maic.jmu.edu/journal/11.1/notes/durham/durham.htm.

Evans, G. (1998) *The Politics of Ritual and Remembrance: Laos Since 1975* (Honolulu: University of Hawaii Press).

Evans, G. (2002) *A Short History of Laos: The Land in Between* (Crows Nest: Allen and Ulwin).

Geneva International Centre for Humanitarian Demining (GICHD) (2007) *Lao PDR Risk Management and Mitigation Mode* (Geneva: GICHD).

Government of Lao PDR (GOL) and the UN (2008) *Millennium Development Goals Progress Report Lao PDR* (Vientiane: UN), http://www.unlao.org/Blog/file.axd?file=2009%2f4%2fLAOMDGPR08Archivecopy.pdf.

Goudineau, Y. (ed.) (1997) *Resettlement and Social Characteristics of New Villages. Basic Needs for Resettled Communities in the Lao PDR, an OSTOM Survey* (Vientiane: UNDP).

Griffin, R., Keeley, R. and Sayyasouk, P. (2008) *UXO Sector Evaluation Lao PDR; June–July 2008, Final Report*, http://www.undplao.org/whatwedo/projectnews/UXO/UXO%20Sector%20Evaluation%20Lao%20PDR%20Aug%202008.pdf.

Handicap International (2004) *Life after the Bomb: A Psychosocial Study of Child Survivors of UXO Accidents in Lao PDR* (Vientiane: Handicap International).

Horner, T. (2009) Interviewed by Kearrin Simms in Vientiane, Laos, 2 June 2009.

International Organization for Migration (IOM) 'Where We Work: Lao PDR', http://www.iom.int/cms/en/sites/iom/home/where-we-work/asia-and-the-pacific/lao-pdr.html, date accessed 15 March 2013.

Kingshill, K. P. (1991) 'Present-Day Effects of United States Bombing of Laos during the Vietnam War: Can Injured Laotians Recover under the Federal Tort Claims Act', *Loyola of Los Angeles International and Comparative Law Journal*, 13, 133–78.

Kett, M. E. and Mannion, S. J. (2004) 'Managing the Health Effects of Explosive Remnants of War', *The Journal of the Royal Society for the Promotion of Health*, 124(6), 262–7.

Khamphong, T. (2009) Interviewed by Kearrin Simms, Nakai, Laos, 24 June 2009.

Krause, K. (2004) 'The Key to a Powerful Agenda, if Properly Delimited', *Security Dialogue*, 35(3), 367–8.

Landmine Monitor (2008) *Landmine Monitor Report; Lao People's Democratic Republic*, http://www.the-monitor.org/index.php/publications/display?url=lm/2008/countries/lao.html#1971062807.

Laugen, J. (2004) 'Annex 7: Drugs and Human Trafficking' in NORPLAN and EcoLao', *Cumulative Impact Analysis and Nam Theun 2 Contributions, Final Report*, http://www-wds.worldbank.org/external/default/WDSContentServer/WDSP/IB/2005/09/15/000011823_20050915115516/Rendered/PDF/E385v120Cumul1t0Analysis11Dec02004010.pdf.

Mines Advisory Group (MAG) (2008) *LAO PDR: Safer scrap*, http://www.maginternational.org/news/lao-pdr-safer-scrap/.

Moyes, R. (2005) *A Study of Scrap Metal Collection in Lao PDR* (Geneva: GICHD).

Swiss National Centre of Competence in Research (NCCR) (2008) *Socio-economic Atlas of the Lao PDR: An Analysis based on the 2005 Population and Housing Census* (Bern: NCCR).

National Socio-Economic Development Plan (NSEDP) (2006) *National Socio-Economic Development Plan 2006–2010* (Vientiane: NSEDP).

National Regulatory Authority for UXO/Mine Action Sector in Lao PDR (NRA) (2008) *UXO Sector Annual Report*, http://www.nra.gov.la/resources/Annual%20Reports/UXO%20Annual%20Report%202008_English.pdf.

Paris, R. (2001) 'Human Security: Paradigm Shift or Hot Air?'*International Security*, 26, 87–102.

Paul, R. A. (1971) 'Laos: Anatomy of an American Involvement', *Foreign Affairs*, 49(3), 533–47.

Pereira, J. (2009) *Effect of UXO Contamination* [conversation], Vientiane, Laos, 18 June 2009.

Pholsena, V. and Banomyong, R. (2006) *Laos: From Buffer State to Crossroads?* (Bangkok: Mekong Press).

Phraxayavong, V. (2009) *History of Aid to Laos: Motivations and Impacts* (Bangkok: Mekong Press).

Rehbein, B. (2007) *Globalisation, Culture and Society in Laos* (London: Routledge).

Radio Free Asia (RFA) (2012) 'Lawmakers Back Mekong Dam', 7 December 2012, http://www.rfa.org/english/news/laos/lawmakers-12072012173200.html.

Rigg, J. (1997) 'Uneven Development and the (Re-)engagement of Laos', in C. Dixon and D. Drakakis-Smith (eds), 1998, *Uneven Development in South East Asia* (Aldershot: Ashgate).

Robson, A. (2008) 'Laos Reaps a Deadly Harvest', *Le Monde Diplomatique* [Diplomatic World], http://mondediplo.com/2008/06/09Laos.

Saengchan, Y. (2009) Interviewed by Kearrin SimmsNakai, Laos, 24 June 2009.

Serdán, G. G. (2008) *Lao PDR Human Security Profile: Draft March 2008* (Bern: Swisspeace), https://sites.google.com/site/agguerreroserdan/LaoPDRHumanSecurityProfile_Final.pdf.

Sisomsouk, P. (2009) Interviewed by Kearrin Simms Nakai, Laos, 26 June 2009.

Somsak, B. (2009) Interviewed by Kearrin Simms Nakai, Laos, 24 June 2009.

Thomas-Slayter, B. P. (2003) *Southern Exposure: International Development and the Global South in the Twenty First Century* (Bloomfield: Kumarain Press).

United Nations Children's Fund (UNICEF) (2003) *Broken Promises Shattered Dreams: A Profile of Child Trafficking in the Lao PDR*, http://www.unicef.org/media/files/BrokenPromisesFULLREPORT.pdf.

UNICEF (2011) *Country Statistics 2011*, http://www.unicef.org/infobycountry/laopdr_statistics.html.

United Nations Development Group (UNDG) (2006) *United Nations Common Country Assessment: Lao PDR*, http://www.undg.org/archive_docs/1715-Lao_PDR_CCA_-_CCA.pdf.

United Nations Development Programme (UNDP) (2001) *National Human Development Report Lao PDR 2001: Advancing Rural Development*, http://hdr.undp.org/es/informes/nacional/asiapacifico/lao/Lao_2001_en.pdf.

UNDP (2006) *National Human Development Report: International Trade and Human Development: Lao PDR*, http://www.undplao.org/whatwedo/bgresource/humandev/UNDP-NHDR06c.pdf.

UNDP (2008) *Hazardous Ground: Cluster Munitions and UXO in the Lao PDR* (Vientiane: UNDP).

UNDP (2011) *Human Development Report* (New York: Oxford University Press).

United Nations Population Fund (UNFPA) (2010) 'Lao PDR, UNFPA Priorities', http://countryoffice.unfpa.org/lao/2010/05/20/2129/unfpa_priorities_2007-2011/.

United Nations Institute for Disarmament Research (UNIDIR) (2008) *The Humanitarian Impact of Cluster Munitions* (Geneva: UNIDIR).

United Nations Office on Drugs and Crime (UNODC) (2006) *Opium Poppy Cultivation in the Golden Triangle: Lao PDR, Myanmar, Thailand* (Vienna: UNODC), http://www.unodc.org/pdf/research/Golden_triangle_2006.pdf.

UXO Lao Bombing Data (2001) *Map of UXO Impact and Bombing Data 1965–75* (Vientiane: Phoenix Clearance Limited).

Vandergeest, P. (2003) 'Land to Some Tillers: Development-induced Displacement in Laos', *International Social Science Journal*, 55(175), 47–56.

Vosburgh, A. (2006) 'Mine-Risk Education and the Amateur Scrap Metal Hunter', *Journal of Mine Action*, 10(2), http://www.maic.jmu.edu/JOURNAL/10.2/focus/vosburgh/vosburgh.htm.

Warner, R. (1996) *Shooting at the Moon; The Story of America's Clandestine War in Laos* (South Royalton: Steerforth Press).

Warr, P. (2008) 'How Road Improvement Reduces Poverty: The Case of Laos', *Agricultural Economics*, 39(3), 269–79.

World Food Programme (WFP) (2007) *World Food Programme Lao PDR: Annual Report 2007* (Vientiane: WFP). http://www.wfp.org/sites/default/files/WFP%20Lao%20PDR%202007%20Annual%20Report.pdf.

World Food Programme (WFP) (2013) *Laos Overview*, http://www.wfp.org/countries/lao-pdr.

World Bank (2008) *Lao PDR Economic Monitor* (Vientiane: The World Bank), http://siteresources.worldbank.org/INTLAOPRD/Resources/293582-1096519010070/534072-1229571730280/LaoEconomicMonitor_Nov2008_final.pdf.

World Bank (2013) *Lao PDR Overview*, http://www.worldbank.org/en/country/lao/overview.

World Trade Organization (WTO) (2012a) 'Accessions: Lao People's Democratic Republic', http://www.wto.org/english/thewto_e/acc_e/a1_laos_e.htm.

World Trade Organization (WTO) (2012b) 'General Council accepts Laos' Membership, Only Ratification Left', 26 October 2012, http://www.wto.org/english/news_e/news12_e/acc_lao_26oct12_e.htm.

Zasloff, J. J. (1970) 'Laos: The Forgotten War Widens', *Asian Survey*, 10(1), 65–72.

7

Transforming Conflictual Relationships in Myanmar/Burma

Introduction

While most national armies defend their country from exterior threats, Myanmar's military forces, officially known as the *Tatmadaw*, have been fighting a long, drawn out internal war against political dissenters and armed ethnic nationalists. Myanmar is currently going through an important political transition which may lead to genuine stability and development after decades of unrest, but many internal and external commentators have dismissed government reforms, elections, and constitutions as shams. Furthermore, it is unclear the extent to which, even if the current political transformations prove substantive and enduring, the human security and development of the most vulnerable sections of society in Myanmar will be improved.

Chapter 2 introduced the concept of a security continuum, whereby human insecurity spillovers can undermine national security considerations, and also how the human security of the most vulnerable sections of society can be sacrificed on the altar of national security policymaking. This was further developed in Chapter 4 with regard to North Korea. Indeed, intra-state conflicts or conflicts involving non-state actors have increased sharply since the end of the Cold War, and members of the international community have likewise started to focus on people within states rather than states in terms of security. Therefore, the referential object of security has been shifted from the state to the people, and the subject category of threats to security expanded to include sub-state actors, transnational actors and forces and the environment. This chapter provides further illustration of the complex relationship between traditional and non-traditional security concepts, by examining closely the consequences of military rule

---

Having acknowledged the controversy regarding the use of Burma or Myanmar, from this point on Myanmar only is used consistent with its recognition by the UN. This chapter benefited from significant research assistance from Suyoun Jang.

and national security prioritization in Myanmar. The key questions included who or what needs securing, and from whom and what should it be secured (Baldwin, 1997, pp. 13–18).

While human security has become increasingly mainstream, non-traditional security threats have not had the same level of acceptance within some Southeast Asian states. In Southeast Asia, as a result of the sub-region's colonial experience and post-colonial state-building, security threats have generally been identified from the perspective of the state (Nishikawa, 2009, p. 217). To a certain extent, therefore, the concept of human security contrasts with the region's values and practices. Of all Southeast Asian countries, the 'state' has been most central in the security discourse, and most controversial in Myanmar. Since independence from Britain in 1948, Myanmar has experienced a complex set of conflicts between governments and people. For Martin Smith (2007, p. 3), the country stands out as 'a pre-eminent example of a post-colonial state subsumed in what development analysis describes as a "conflict trap"'.

Facing diverse challenges, including ethnic insurgencies and remnants of colonial experience, successive governments have adopted state-centric national security policies with an emphasis on national sovereignty, territorial integrity, and the national unity of diverse ethnic nationalities (Tin, 1998, p. 392). Alternative conceptions of security have been rejected or viewed as a threat by the Government. Moreover, because the country has primarily been ruled by a military junta seeking regime survival, the distinction between the security interests of state, regime, and military have been blurred. Consequently, the human security of the most vulnerable sections of society in Myanmar has been ignored, sacrificed, or directly threatened.

State-centricity has not only bedeviled security considerations but has also impacted detrimentally upon government, opposition, and even international, policymaking, and negotiating stances. The Government of Myanmar has prioritized the security of the state at a macro, nationwide level, and development models as well as the position of the government in negotiations with internal opposition groups and the international community have been wedded to concepts of national sovereignty, territorial integrity, and central planning. Likewise, the main opposition grouping, the National League for Democracy (NLD), has historically emphasized the need for a wholesale change in governance practices, with human rights and democracy replacing a security emphasis, while rejecting more incremental reforms. Hence, until recently the NLD boycotted elections as they were not full and free, and supported sanctions and embargoes, and discouraged tourists from visiting and contributing to the local economy. Finally, Western members of the international community have tied international assistance to government performance in Myanmar, and have even considered humanitarian intervention to rectify the perceived failure of central governance policymaking and implementation.

These prioritizations have led to a number of unfortunate consequences: first, centralized planning and policymaking by the Government has jeopardized the human security of the most vulnerable sections of society in Myanmar, even if it is justified by those in power in terms of macro security and development agendas. Second, opposition leaders have been accused of being blind to the suffering of minorities who do not form the base of their constituency against the Government. Indeed, the NLD's charismatic leader, Aung San Suu Kyi, has been severely criticized for having a 'blind spot' when it comes to the suffering of the Rohingya Muslims detailed later in this chapter (Taylor and Wright, 2013). Third, by engaging in positional negotiations, government, opposition, and international participants from the West are unlikely to be able to get beyond conflict management, or at best conflict resolution, without approaching a true transformation of the conflictual relationships which undermine both development and human security in Myanmar.

It is against this background that the people of Myanmar carry on their day-to-day lives, and their well-being is marred by such fallouts as displacement, forced labor, child soldiering, human trafficking, and injury from landmines. Furthermore, constant instability has not been conducive to sustained development. Economic hardship and dissatisfaction with the Government have led to numerous riots and organized demonstrations over the years. The inability or disinclination of the government to deal with the central challenges to human security and development in Myanmar, particularly after the impact of Cyclone Nargis, has led commentators such as Gareth Evans and Madeleine Albright to consider an 'aid invasion'. The most common international response to internal conditions in Myanmar, however, has been the imposition of sanctions targeted at the release of pro-democracy activists such as Aung San Suu Kyi and forcing genuine political reform. This chapter also considers, therefore, whether in prioritizing political rights in Myanmar the international community may in fact have further jeopardized the entitlement rights of the most vulnerable sections of society. In doing so, it contrasts the policies of Western and Asian international actors in general, and Canada and Japan in particular (identified in this volume as two of the most important state proponents and propagators of the human security paradigm), and addresses the important subsidiary themes of the human rights spectrum, also introduced in Chapter 2.

In arguing that Myanmar's state-centric national security approach has endangered the most vulnerable sections of domestic society, this chapter first examines the historical background of national security policy prioritization. It then provides an analysis of human security and development within Myanmar and highlights the distressing conditions for millions of people who still suffer from low levels of human security and live below the poverty line. This is followed by a comparative analysis of the impact of Western and Asian models of engagement and interaction with Myanmar's

Government. This chapter concludes with an overview of hopes and aspirations for a better human security environment in the country in years to come.

National security prioritization in Myanmar

In Myanmar, the state has been the principal referential element of security since it gained independence from Britain. The government, historically, has regarded elements of its population as a threat to national sovereignty and security, and a priority has been placed upon state-centric security and the justification of the government's right to rule on behalf of all of the people (ICG, 2001). Such a strong emphasis on national security is based upon both security concerns over diverse ethnic nationalities associated with multiple ethnic insurgencies and historical experience with colonialism (Callahan, 2003; Tin, 2010, p. 124).

Myanmar has over 100 ethnic groups, languages and dialects, and therefore embodies one of the richest sources of ethnic diversity in the world. Such diversity is attributed to the country's geographical location on a strategic crossroads, where it has acted as a buffer between the neighboring powers of India, China, and Thailand. There is no reliable data on Myanmar's ethnic minorities but according to the military regime that has ruled Myanmar since 1962, there are 135 different ethnicities (Smith, 1994). Of these peoples, the Shan (9 per cent of the population of 54 million) and Karen (7 per cent) are the largest minority groups, with the Rakhine, Mon, Chin, and Kayah collectively comprising around 10 per cent of the population (CIA, 2012). The remaining ethnic minorities comprise around 5 per cent of the total population. The Myanmar ethnic majority, Bamar or Burman (68 per cent), dominates the military forces and government.

During the British colonial era, colonial government distinguished between Ministerial Burma or lower land of Myanmar and Frontier Areas along territorial and racial lines. While Ministerial Burma, dominated by the Burman majority, was brought under full colonial rule, the Frontier Areas, where most ethnic minorities lived, were subjected to a form of indirect rule through princely leaders (Holliday, 2007, p. 384). This divide-and-rule policy created 'two Burmas' in the administrative and security arms of the state and resulted in political, economic, and social boundaries that continue to divide the country today (Callahan, 2003, p. 16).

The territorial and ethnic division was deepened during the Japanese occupation. After seizing Burma from Britain in 1942, Japan created the first national indigenous army, the Burma Independence Army (BIA), which was staffed only by ethnic-majority Burman in former Ministerial Burma (Callahan, 2003, p. 46). Later, the BIA was replaced by the newly formed Burma Defence Army (BDA) which consisted of a selected small group of soldiers and officers of the BIA. Simultaneously, during World War II, the Allied

Forces, predominantly the military forces of Britain and the United States, recruited ethnic minorities in the former Frontier Areas into anti-Japanese and anti-BDA guerilla units and promised them political independence from the Burman majority after the war ended (*ibid.*, p. 67). This segregation was reflected in 1947 Panglong Agreement and the first Constitution of independent Burma, which recognized the autonomy of some of the hill peoples.

With many of the ethnic minorities forming insurgent armies and rebelling against the state demanding secession, the government was unable to cope effectively with these threats to national unity and security, and was beginning to fall apart politically (Ganesan, 2007, p. 22). This was the critical trigger for a military coup in 1962, and the military junta has wielded strong political power ever since. The new regime initiated a wide range of state-building programs and suppressed ethnic minority groups which in turn waged guerilla warfare against the government for four decades (Callahan, 2003, p. 209). Although in recent years the national authorities have agreed to a truce with rebels of the Shan ethnic group, and ordered the military to stop operations against ethnic Kachin rebels, such accords are tenuous at best (as demonstrated by the January 2013 airstrikes and renewed government offensives against the Kachin), and serve to reinforce the limitations of conflict management or resolution (peace treaties) when underlying conflictual relationships are not addressed. Indeed hostilities are, at best, potentially only on hold with (in addition to the Shan and the Kachin) the Karen, the Karenni, the Chin, the United Wa State Army, the Mon, and the Mongla (BBC, 2012b).

Conflict management refers to the long-term management of intractable conflicts: an ongoing process that may never reach a resolution. The term conveys the idea that even if resolution is impossible, conflicts and disputes can be managed constructively, and the worst manifestations avoided by the managing agent. Strategic and coercive tools such as defense and deterrence can form part of the arsenal of the conflict manager. For much of the ongoing conflict with ethnic separatist groups, the Government of Myanmar has relied on management techniques, using a coercive war-fighting approach to what they perceive to be acts of terrorism. There are, however, significant limitations with 'managing' such asymmetric conflict situations.

In the aftermath of the terrorist attacks of 9/11, US Secretary of Defense Donald Rumsfeld (2002) admitted that there is no way to defend against terrorist acts, 'because a terrorist can attack at any place at any time using any technique, and it's physically impossible to defend it every time at every place against every technique'. What Rumsfeld instead argued for was 'to take the battle to those people who are determined to try to kill large numbers of human beings'. But this also involves major problems when dealing with the proponents of asymmetric warfare. Terrorists (or ethnic separatists) may hide within wider populations, who may largely be innocent of harboring the insurgents, let alone of actively supporting them. Under such conditions, repressive counter-measures such as preemptive strikes, preventative actions, or military invasions of host communities, are like as not to alienate the local people, and perhaps others who share a culture, religion, or border. Such tactics can thereby end up fostering rather than undermining the inclination to resort to asymmetric warfare.

This is also the main problem with deterrence – how is it possible to identify the targets who must be threatened with massive retaliation, especially if they are citizens of one's own country? Terrorism and other forms of asymmetric war-fighting are often the recourse of the socio-economically, militarily, and politically weak, disenfranchised and desperate. By emphasizing one's power-political superiority, it may be that potential asymmetric war-fighters will deem they have nothing left to lose, thus traditional rational modeling no longer applies.

Conflict resolution on the other hand looks to bring about an agreed and formally recognized end to a conflict, usually through some process of dispute resolution, sometimes involving external actors and third parties, culminating in a public declaration. A managed conflict always has an ever present liability to reignite, but even one apparently ended or resolved by a formal agreement of some sort, is still liable to recur in the future when one or more parties to the accord finds themselves dissatisfied with the outcome. Hence, numerous processes of mediation and arbitration, as well as other alternative dispute resolution mechanisms have been put in place, peace plans and framework agreements have been signed, but the conflicts between the Government of Myanmar and many of its ethnic minorities persist.

State-centric liberal economic approaches to the resolution of conflict have also merely exacerbated many of the existing problems in Myanmar. Neoliberal growth models advocate further economic development, integration, and modernization as a panacea for making the world a better place, for making everybody better off, and for reducing both material incentives and metaphysical desires for waging war, thereby 'resolving' conflict. The Government of Myanmar has repeatedly emphasized a desire to develop its way out of conflict, and exploit the abundant natural resources of the country. But these measures have faced significant challenges. Support for liberal economic and political transition within communities is only generated by the general optimism that ultimately all will benefit; the hope that even if this is not the case, then at least the majority will do so; and the common belief held by most, that they will form part of this majority. Despite liberal optimism, economic development is not a universal win-win: some societies, some groups, and some individuals are always likely to lose out, at least in relative terms if not in absolute terms. In Myanmar, much of the abundant natural resources are to be found in areas predominantly inhabited (if not actively controlled) by minorities, yet the benefits of national development programs fall disproportionately to the Burman majority (or rather to the minority elite of the majority) and the costs fall disproportionately upon the vulnerable groups in the border regions.

The Government of Myanmar, regardless of which party is in power, can only truly secure peace with its truculent border regions (and thereby also national security) if the conflictual relationship between the parties is transformed. This is where it is important to return to the concept of human security. As previously noted in Chapter 2, and particularly apt in this case study, fear on an individual level, for example, caused by violence from other individuals or even the state, may lead a group of victims to take refuge in a neighboring country, impacting upon its human security condition, but in addition, those refugees may regroup, recruit, and rejuvenate to strengthen their capacity to undermine the security of those who forced them to flee in the first place. Also, want on an individual level such as lack of food or energy – especially if it is spread unevenly across the nation – may undermine national cohesion and weaken national strength, increasing national insecurity. Thus, to a great extent, fear on an individual level in Myanmar's border regions has percolated up to fear on a national level with human insecurity becoming a source of insecurity for states.

In terms of conflict transformation, British operations during the Malayan Emergency, when the term 'Hearts and Minds' was coined in relation to counter-insurgency strategy, have been held up as an exemplary model. While the degree to which hearts and minds strategies were pursued exclusively by government forces may be debated, certainly the successful transformation of the conflictual relationships appears to have endured. An essential element of the British campaign in Malaya was the attempt to break the link between the Chinese squatter community and the 'bandits'. 'It was apparent that unless these squatters were brought under normal administrative control only the insurgents could benefit' (Osborne 1970. pp. 74–5). Therefore, the resettlement of these communities was to be given top priority. After physically breaking the link between squatters and insurgents, it was then intended to break the emotional links between them by offering the squatters a better life in the resettlement areas than that which they previously enjoyed, or could hope to enjoy under Communist rule. 'New Villages', after fulfilling the objective of providing security for the community from the guerrillas, were to be supplied with essential services such as schools and clinics.

In addition, inhabitants were to be given permanent title to land, were eventually offered Malayan citizenship, and were even given the right to bear arms in the Home Guard in defense of their new communities. Part of the appeal of the guerrillas was that they were fighting a nationalist war against an imperialist power and for the rights of the stateless. The Hearts and Minds approach, however, brought a promise that Malaya should in due course become a fully self-governing nation with a common form of citizenship for all. With both the antagonists claiming that they would give the people what they most desired, it was left to the people to decide which was most likely to give it to them quickest, and once that decision was made, then any support for the other side would only delay the fulfillment by prolonging the struggle. How convincing the government was, was directly related to its performance in other areas. As Richard Stubbs (1989, p. 184) has noted, 'propaganda could not by itself win the war; it was only as effective as the other elements in the government's strategy'. Perhaps, the single most influential area concerning government credibility and insurgent weakness was food security, or 'freedom from want'.

Thus, if the Government of Myanmar were to take anything from the Period of Emergency in Malaya, it should be that national security objectives when dealing with insurgency, can best, and perhaps only be achieved, by transforming the conflictual relationship between the central authorities and those who would rebel against them. This is done through reducing the impetus to rebel by demonstrating that the government is in the best position to provide what all sections of society desire and need – freedom from fear and freedom from want. In particular, when it comes to the most vulnerable sections of Burmese society, those found in the volatile border regions, the focus should be on providing safe havens. Unfortunately, the military backed regimes in Myanmar have found it difficult to detach themselves from a top-down national security focus either when in dealing with separatist insurgents or with pro-democracy demonstrators.

After a crackdown on a nation-wide pro-democracy movement in 1988, the junta has repeatedly acted with hostility way toward those seen as obstacles to its state-rebuilding project with its aim of centralizing and concentrating state power and resources in the hands of the military regime (Flink, 2009, p. 2). This fixation on regime survival has, however, isolated the military regime, alienating them from their population and fuelling dissent against the military regime. A vicious cycle of national security prioritization undermines human security, leads to ever more forceful expressions of dissent, and ever more severe clamp-downs in the name of national unity. In a like manner to North Korea's pursuit of *Juche* detailed in Chapter 4, Myanmar's leadership also looked to follow a self-sufficient path, whereby they were not beholden to external forces. The pursuit of isolationism resulted in low levels of infrastructure development and service provision. Consequently, while most of the post-colonial Southeast Asian countries experienced economic growth after decade-long civil warfare following independence, such developments did not occur in Myanmar (Ganesan, 2007, p. 23).

Thus, Myanmar's historical experience with colonialism and internal insurgencies has produced a military regime that is obsessed with domestic order, self-sufficiency, central control, and state security. In other words, Myanmar's security perception has been pre-occupied with domestic threats from variety of ethnic insurgencies characterized as violent challenges to the state sovereignty, paranoia about external intervention, and a conviction that domestic opposition groups are in some way agents of external powers, or at the very least disloyal threats to domestic order. The Government of Myanmar has crystallized this world view in a number of policy platforms such as 'Three Main National Causes',[1] 'People's Desire',[2] and 'Political Objectives'[3] (Myanmar Archives, 2012). The consequences for the human security of both the most vulnerable sections of the populace and for the citizenry as a whole have been severe. To a great extent, human security challenges in Myanmar are a direct or indirect consequence of central government policy prioritization and governance failure. The next section addresses human security challenges in Myanmar in more detail.

Human security challenges in Myanmar

Considering that state sovereignty means not only the authority over territory and citizens but also the responsibility for their well-being, the Myanmar Government has failed in its responsibility to protect and provide for the people of Myanmar, adopting a state-centric national security policy approach focusing on sovereignty, territorial integrity, and national unity (Foot, 2005). Moreover, the conceptualization and scope of national security in Myanmar have been determined by a small elite group (Tin, 2010). As a result, there are many prevailing and potential threats to security, safety, and well-being of the people in Myanmar. Human security has become a popular political cause and there is a growing recognition that real security must serve people, not enslave them (Zaw, 2000).

As addressed in Chapter 2, the concept of human security encompasses both 'freedom from fear' and 'freedom from want'. While proponents of the narrow freedom from fear concept focus on physical violent threats to individuals (ICISS, 2001; HSC, 2005), proponents of the broad concept of human security, inclusive of freedom from want, argue that the threat agenda should be widened to include hunger, disease, and natural disasters because these kill far more people than war, genocide, and terrorism combined (UNDP, 1994; CHS, 2003). In the case of Myanmar, both aspects of human security have been threatened under the military regime for more than half a century. Myanmar is ranked 181 out of 232 countries in the Human Security Index and 180 out of 182 countries in the HDI (HIS, 2011; UNDP, 2011).

Freedom from fear

The people of Myanmar have been fighting against the military junta for peace and security since its independence. In response, the military government has consistently suppressed them and pursued a policy of state-building with the aim to resist calls for devolution (ICG, 2001, pp. i–ii). In line with its state-building paradigm, the government pursued a 'Four Cuts' policy aiming at cutting off armed ethnic nationalities groups from food, money, intelligence, and recruits (Flink, 2001, p. 48). This strategy was based on the assumption that 'the best way to destroy these groups is to destroy the ability of the civilians to support them' (Karen Human Rights Group, 2000, p. 15). This differed significantly from the Hearts and Minds approach of destroying the empathy of civilians for insurgents, and thus their *desire* to support such groups. Instead, it was implemented by systematic repression of the civilian population until they no longer had the capacity to support the opposition. Moreover, the military regime delineated regions and forced hundreds of villages to move to army-controlled sites. Consequently, this led thousands of civilian deaths and the destruction of food, crops, and more than 3,700 villages since 1996 (IDMC, 2009, p. 5).

As a result of government offenses against armed ethnic minority groups near Myanmar's borders with Thailand and China, there are now more than 500,000 IDPs, and more than 140,000 international refugees (CIA, 2012). Even when the government is not actively targeting minority groups, their general neglect of communities outside that of the state norm, or fear of the threat they pose to the nation-building project, has led to severe challenges to the human security of the most vulnerable. Perhaps, the clearest example of this is to be found in the plight of the Muslim Rohingya minority. Since June 1012, more than 100,000 have been displaced in by violence in Burma's Rakhine state between ethnic Rakhine Buddhists and Rohingyas, mostly from the Muslim Rohingya minority. Dozens have been killed, thousands of homes burnt, and many of the displaced remain in squalid camps, boats, or on islands or hilltops, in need of urgent aid (BBC, 2012c). The authorities regard the Rohingya as illegal immigrants, but there is also widespread animosity toward them and other minority Muslim groups, such as the Kamans, who do have citizenship, among the majority Buddhist population of Myanmar as a whole. Neighboring Bangladesh, also a conflict-affected, poverty-stricken country already hosts several hundred thousand refugees from Myanmar, and says it cannot take any more. Meanwhile, the Thai foreign ministry is investigating claims that refugees from Rakhine state have been intercepted by the Thai navy and police, with deals then being done to sell the people to traffickers to use as forced labor or to hold for ransom (BBC, 2013).

Refugees and IDPs are, in fact, particularly vulnerable to further exploitation, whether in terms of human trafficking, forced and child labor, or becoming victims of criminal gangs and other predators. They are also denied many of the BHN that form the foundations of broader definitions of human security. Refugees and IDPs from Myanmar form a resource reservoir for women, children, and men trafficked for the purpose of forced labor and commercial sexual exploitation. Women and children are trafficked to East and Southeast Asia for commercial sexual exploitation, domestic servitude, and forced labor; children are subjected to conditions of forced labor in Thailand as hawkers and beggars; but Myanmar's internal trafficking remains the most serious concern. The military continues to engage in the unlawful conscription of child soldiers, and continues to be the main perpetrator of forced labor inside Myanmar (CIA, 2012). Smith (2007, p. 2) refers to an 'inter-linking spiral of humanitarian emergencies' including 'refugees, internally-displaced persons, illicit narcotics production and the spread of such preventable diseases as HIV/AIDS and Malaria'.

At the same time, in line with its state-building campaign, the junta has expanded the armed forces. In the wake of the 1988 pro-democracy movement, the national armed forces grew from 186,000 to more than 330,000–370,000 in the early 1990s and reached 500,000 by the end of the century (Steinberg, 2001, p. 78). The Government of Myanmar has also increased military expenditure from between 25 and 40 per cent of the national budget in 1970s to 50 per cent in the 1990s (*ibid.*, pp. 77–8). Again the policy prioritization of the regime is seen to revolve around conflict management, deterrence, and national/regime security rather than conflict transformation, winning the people over, and human security.

In 2007, the Government of Myanmar drew the attention of the international community when monks, along with the general public, protested to the military junta about the rising cost of fuel (Thawnghmung and Myoe, 2008, p. 15). The world media widely reported the military crackdown on public dissent, with the International Crises Group (ICG) (2008) reporting 13 deaths along with several thousand arrests of political protestors as a result of military action against the public. The ICG estimates that many more have since been arrested in house raids and others have died whilst in detention (*ibid.*). The chants of the protesters closely mirrored the central concepts of human security demanding freedom from fear and freedom from want.

At the time of the junta's actions against the population, the President of the UN Security Council condemned the use of violence against peaceful demonstrations in Myanmar (UNSC, 2007). The UN's Human Rights Council also expressed concern over abuses including extrajudicial executions, torture, and the repression of ethnic and religious minorities and urged the Myanmar Government to exercise utmost restraint and to desist from further violence against peaceful protesters (UN News Center, 2007). The junta responded to international pleas and demands for restraint by expelling the UN's most senior representative in November. The junta's refusal to acknowledge international concerns for the security of the people living within Myanmar displayed their long-running disregard for international pressure (ICG, 2008). So grave did conditions become that East Timor President Jose Ramos-Horta and the Burma Lawyers' Council announced that they were ready to go to the ICC to charge Senior General Than Shwe with human rights abuses and violations of international law.

Things deteriorated still further after the protests, triggered by fuel price rises but sustained by general discontent with governance failings and repression, had been crushed. Myanmar was hit by a devastating tropical cyclone. As a result of the failure of the government response to the crisis, as well as the obstacles put in the path of international humanitarian responses, the international community was stimulated to launch a sustained and vocal criticism of governance failures in Myanmar. Madeleine Albright (2008), the former US Secretary of State thought the government to be criminally neglectful in its response to Cyclone Nargis, US Defense Secretary, Robert Gates considered intervention, Gareth Evans, president of the ICG 2000–09 and a former foreign minister of Australia reflected on whether it was 'time for an aid invasion' (Evans, 2008), and French Foreign Minister, Bernard Kouchner, proposed that the R2P be invoked to legitimize the forcible delivery of humanitarian assistance (Bellamy and Davis, 2009, p. 548).

Freedom from want

The Government of Myanmar has not only failed in its responsibility to protect people from fear but it has also failed in its responsibility to provide for the well-being of the vast majority of the people of Myanmar. Myanmar is a developing nation with significant humanitarian need and a considerable portion of its population living in extreme poverty. This, to a great extent, is a consequence of military regime's state-building project for regime security. As previously mentioned, the Four Cuts policy had devastating direct impacts on the human security of the most vulnerable sections of society, but military prioritization has also had significant indirect impact on the ability of the regime to provide freedom from want. The expansion of the military and large expenditures on defense have restricted the ability of the state to deal effectively with social issues including poverty, education, health, sanitation, water, food security, transport, and infrastructure.

Myanmar suffers from major deficiencies in most basic services due to the regime's priority of military expenditure over social development. For example, as of 2009, the Government spent just 0.2 per cent of GDP on health care (UNDP, 2011). This figure is the lowest level in Southeast Asia. Indeed, globally the national health system is ranked 190th out of 191 (Mullany *et al.*, 2008. p. 45). In addition to the low level of public health spending, the escalating cost of private health care may interrupt access to health services (Oehlers, 2005). Therefore, despite marked increases in the number of public health care personnel as well as health facilities, infant and maternal mortality rates have not shown significant improvement. Furthermore the military elite have, to a considerable extent, been insulated from many of the challenges to human security as a result of independent systems of welfare, health, and education, which have created an exclusive social order of privilege for military (Callahan, 2003, p. 211). Not surprisingly then, improvement in the public systems of provision and distribution has not featured as a high priority of the state and the regime has been rather reluctant to recognize problems.

Those resources which have been earmarked for infrastructure development have been distorted by central security and development considerations, and diverted into projects such as the construction of the new, isolated (and thus more secure) capital of Naypyidaw, and to macro-development projects such as gas pipelines and hydroelectric dams, which can in fact have severe negative consequences for the human security of the most vulnerable sections of society. In November 2012, monks and local villagers protested against a US$1 billion copper mine expansion, a joint project between the Burmese military and Chinese weapons manufacturer Norinco, which will lead to forced eviction from their land. At least 50 people were injured and 23 hospitalized after suffering burns, when police hurled devices described as 'phosphorous bombs' into protestors' camps, and fired on them with flare guns (The Telegraph, 2012).

In Myanmar, per capita income has increased more than four times from US$364 in 1980 to US$1535 by 2011 and average GDP growth rate is 9.46 per cent since the 1988 movement (World Bank, 2011). Yet there are a number of caveats related to this performance. First, Myanmar has been starting from a very low base – indeed one of the poorest countries in the world. Second, many of the measured increases have not been distributed evenly, but rather have merely served to concentrate further wealth in the hands of the elite. For instance, in 2010–11, 'the transfer of state assets – especially real estate – to military families under the guise of a privatization policy further widened the gap between the economic elite and the public' (CIA 2012). Despite impressive development in its economic sector, 31.8 per cent of the population is still in poverty and 17 per cent undernourished (UNDP, 2011).

Again, it is important, therefore to look at what progress, if any, has been achieved at the level of the most vulnerable sections of society. While the Myanmar Government-produced MDG reports of 2005 and 2006 suggest progress in a number of areas, it has performed poorly across most of the MDG targets (GoUM, 2005, 2006; Ware, 2011). In part, this reflects the macroeconomic, state-centric development focus of the Government. Burma's poor investment climate, including weak rule of law, hampers the inflow of foreign investment to all areas of the economy with the exception of those extractive industries favored by the government such as gas, power generation, timber, and mining, which do not benefit the population at large (CIA, 2012). The development of these sectors has in many cases posed additional challenges to the human security of the most vulnerable sections of society, whether through relocation, forced labor, or environmental degradation.

Failure of the Government of Myanmar's economic policies significantly to raise the standard of living of the vast majority of the population is also linked, however, to their contribution to inflationary forces rather than actual GDP growth. While there have been substantial price rises, especially in terms of essentials such as fuel and food, wages in both public and private sectors have fallen behind the inflation of commodity prices (Tin, 2007, pp. 178–9). Cross-border movement of people from Myanmar is not only triggered by the fear of violent attack detailed above but also due to a lack of economic security. The bulk of Myanmar's economic migrants can be found in the labor forces of neighboring countries, including Thailand and Malaysia, and even China. Although most of them work under harsh conditions, such as low pay, long hours, and poor work safety, they cannot claim legal protection because of their illegal status (*ibid.*, p. 179).

Thus, while prioritizing a national unity and security project, the Government of Myanmar has not only failed in its domestic governance obligations to its citizens in general but also in particular toward the most vulnerable sections of society such as women, children, and ethnic and religious minorities. International actors have also, however, had their efforts to protect and provide undermined by state-centric policy prioritization and an emphasis on political rights over basic entitlement rights. The next section contrasts different international policies of engagement toward Myanmar.

International engagement

Japan and Canada have been the most important international promoters of the idea of human security in the policy domain. These middle powers were the first to put the concept into practice in order to shape parts of a newly emerging international structure following the end of the Cold War, and continue in the vanguard of such efforts (Bosold and Werthes, 2005, p. 85). The limited, individual human rights-based conceptualization of human security has been regarded as a Western legacy, stemming from liberalism (Rothschild, 1995, pp. 60–1), and is thereby challenged by claims of cultural specificity by some Asian Actors (Acharya, 2001, p. 1). On the other hand, inclusive approaches to security and development, often with a strong economic emphasis, have often been associated with Asian policymaking. Indeed, the region has been described as being suffused with a remarkable 'econophoria', wherein all governance problems, whether domestic or international, are seen as surmountable through development and growth – an outlook which has emerged alongside the dynamic economic success stories of most states in the region (Buzan and Segal, 1998, p. 107). Because of their different or even opposing understandings of human security, as well as their geopolitical operating environments, recent investigations have therefore identified policy divergence between Japan and Canada as existing along an East-West axis, and indeed, the two countries can be seen as the primary champions of the relative perspectives.

Identifying the different understandings of human security, representing 'East versus West', may have important consequences for development experiences of countries like Myanmar. As noted above, Myanmar has traditionally been dominated by the national security paradigm, the principles of absolute sovereignty, and non-interference in domestic affairs, and thus can regard humanitarian assistance or intervention as, potentially, illegitimate interference. Thus, the extent to which Asian solutions to Asian problems can be pursued with regard to human security may turn out to be of vital importance for peace-building and development in Myanmar.

The Canadian human security perspective and Myanmar

Canada was the first state to embrace human security as a guiding focus for development and peace-building activities, and it has prioritized the promotion of human security in the post-Cold War period as part of its active international involvement (Bernard, 2006, pp. 233–4). Canada helped give the new diplomatic paradigm traction by identifying the notion of human security as a main theme of its foreign policy and encouraging other countries to join in pushing the idea of a people-centered foreign policy.

Canada's foreign policy identity self-imaging has long been as a 'helpful fixer', 'honest broker', and 'international do-gooder' (Bosold, 2007, pp. 175–200). As a major contributor to UN Peacekeeping Operations in the former Yugoslavia, Rwanda, Somalia, and other conflict areas, the Canadian government advocates the need to protect civilians in armed-conflict situations within state borders and has stressed the need to rethink the notion of humanitarian intervention (Axworthy, 1997, p. 183). Thus, the Canadian conceptualization of human security is closely associated with crisis prevention and conflict-management tools. In addition, Canada has emphasized the humanitarian aspect of its foreign relations. It was not, however, until toward the end of the 1990s that the Canadian government narrowly defined human security.

Canada's Foreign Affairs Minister Lloyd Axworthy, generally regarded as a promoter of the narrow definition, previously called for the extension of the security framework and explicitly located human security within the context of the UNDP's conceptualization, linking the concept to human rights and human development (*ibid.,* p. 184). According to his two statements in 1997 and 1999, the key challenges for human security are much more than mere military threats and include the abuse of human rights, disease, environmental degradation, population growth, and the widening gap between rich and poor (DFAIT, 1995, ch. 6).

The Lysoen declaration, which Canada helped draft, however, argues that while the fundamental values of human security are freedom from fear, freedom from want, and equal opportunities, the core value of a human security conception is freedom from 'pervasive threats to people's rights, their safety or their lives'. In other words, what the declaration has identified as a freedom from fear (DFAIT, 1999). It lists ten areas in which such normative prioritization is required: anti-personnel and mines, small arms, children in armed conflict, ICC proceedings, exploitation of children, safety of humanitarian personnel, conflict prevention, transnational organized crime, and resources for development (*ibid.*). All but the last may be seen as areas in which a narrow definition trumps that of a broader approach.

The narrowing of focus was in part due to the constraints of a new regime of fiscal austerity with significant budget cuts in the related fields of foreign affairs, ODA, and the military in the 1990s and 2000s (Bosold, 2007). While the number of missions abroad grew during that period, the percentage of Canadian development aid has been cut from 0.46 per cent at the beginning of the 1990s to 0.24 per cent of the national budget in 2002 and 2003 (*ibid.)*. In addition, the military budget which is needed to train and deploy peacekeepers decreased by 23 per cent between 1993 and 1998 (*ibid.)*. It seems, therefore, that to an extent Canada has made a virtue out of necessity. The UNDP approach was rejected as an unwieldy policy instrument which emphasized the threats associated with underdevelopment while largely ignoring the continuing human insecurity resulting from violent conflict, and for Canada the concept of human security has increasingly centered on the human costs of violent conflict (DFAIT, 1999).

Two policy initiatives reflect Canada's rethinking on human security: the Convention on the Prohibition of the Use, Stockpiling, Production and Transfer of Anti-Personal Landmines (Ottawa Convention), and the creation of the ICC. In addition to these legal framework, Axworthy sought to institutionalize and multi-lateralize the human security agenda by creating the Human Security Network (HSN) which is a coalition of like-minded governments interested in promoting people-centered human security strategies in foreign policy (Small, 2001, pp. 231–5). Axworthy also called for addressing human security issues through humanitarian-inspired intervention by saying that human security 'is going to have to be reconciled with the principle of non-intervention in the internal affairs of states', and that the concept of national sovereignty 'cannot be absolute' (Hubert and Bonser, 2001, p. 112–13). This stance led Canada to create the ICISS and help formulate the commission's final report, *The Responsibility to Protect*. There has, therefore, been a high level of continuity in Canada's foreign policy since the beginning of the 1990s, when the country adopted the new security framework. For Canada, human security is narrowly defined as associating with conflict-related threats and hence its foreign policy mainly focuses on working to keep people safe from violence or threats of violence. In this sense, 'vigorous action' including coercive measures, such as sanctions and military force, is allowed in pursuit of the human security agenda.

Canada's policy on Myanmar has directly reflected a narrow human security perspective on the severe problems that the military government has created for its people. Foremost among the concerns, therefore, is the appalling mistreatment of the people of Myanmar, who are deprived of fundamental human rights and denied a voice in the way they governed, with a primary focus on refugees and internally displaced persons in the border regions (DFAIT, 2012). In this regard, although the Canadian government suspended ODA to Myanmar in 1988, Ottawa has been working in conjunction with the international community to strengthen democratic forces and civil society, as well as addressing the humanitarian needs of those who have sought refuge outside of Myanmar. It has provided US$12.4 million for the past five years and renewed funding amount to US$15.9 million over the next five years to support refugees (Government of Canada, 2012). Furthermore, since 2006, Canada has accepted more than 5,000 refugees from Myanmar and provided hundreds of millions of dollars for its reconstruction.

At the national level, however, Canada has imposed tough sanctions against Myanmar in order to exert pressure on the military junta. Since 1988, in addition to banning the export of arms to Myanmar, Canada has placed sever limitations on the export of all other goods, including those needed for humanitarian purposes. In 2003, Ottawa excluded Myanmar from Canada's LDC list, and also imposed restrictive measures targeting senior members of the regime in response to the continued harassment and imprisonment of Aung San Suu Kyi and members of her political party. More recently in 2007, when the military regime cracked down on the protesters triggered by an up to 500 per cent increase in the price of fuel, the Canadian government issued a statement condemning the excessive use of force by the government of Myanmar and urged them to respect human rights and fundamental freedoms of the people. Furthermore, it imposed the toughest sanctions in the world under the 2007 Special Economic Measures Regulations (Burma Regulations) in order to respond to the gravity of the human rights and humanitarian situation in Myanmar (Government of Canada, 2007). While, in 2012, it eased its economic sanctions and most prohibitions of the Burma Regulation were suspended, the Canadian government continues to closely monitor the situation in Myanmar and urge the authorities to release all remaining political prisoners and to work with ethnic minorities to find sustainable solutions to conflict.

The Japanese human security perspective and Myanmar

In contrast to the Canadian approach, Japan broadly defined human security embracing both freedom from fear and freedom from want. Japan's broad or holistic human security initiatives have their roots in the country's post-war pacifism and adherence to anti-militarist norms. Economic prioritization was strengthened by the rejection of the use of military force incorporated in Article 9 of the 1946 Pacifist Constitution, which restricted Japanese military activities to self-defense only. Given internal and external structural constraints on the use of force, ODA and other forms of international assistance, including foreign direct investment and loans came to be seen as one of the few areas of autonomous Japanese foreign policy formation. These elements will be developed in more detail in Chapter 10, which addresses Japan's role in the historical development of a broad human security paradigm, and the strategic use of international assistance. In this section, Japanese engagement with Southeast Asia in general, and with Myanmar in particular, will be explored in terms of the consequences of a broad approach to human security.

Anti-military, pro-economic norms have become characteristic of Japanese foreign and security policy, and this is particularly apparent when we consider Japanese policy toward Southeast Asia. The recognition of the centrality of the concept of human security in Japan is related to both the Asian financial crisis and the desire to play a bigger role in international society under the concept of proactive pacifism. The crisis had a devastating impact on Asia's economy, increasing poverty and political instability, and underscoring the crucial need for social safety nets for the poor and for a new understanding of security, focusing on Asian peoples rather than states. Prime Minister Keizo Obuchi committed to help Asian countries overcome crises and to assist socially vulnerable people, and emphasized his perception of human security as being people- rather than state-centric, comprising 'a comprehensive view of all threats to human survival, life and dignity' and as one of the three areas on which Asia should focus for a 'century of peace and prosperity' (Obuchi, 1998). He also contributed 500 million yen (US$4.2 million) for the establishment of the human security fund under the UN (later renamed the United Nations Trust Fund for Human Security – UNTFHS), as an expression of Japan's commitment to promoting the paradigm and supporting related projects by UN agencies. Together, these initiatives laid the foundation for human security as the main pillar of Japan's foreign policy agenda. With the fusion of human security and ODA, Japanese aid policy has been transformed into a vehicle for transporting the human security idea.

From 2003, the concept was prioritized in Japan's policy through revision of the ODA charter. The revised ODA charter states the 'objectives of Japan's ODA are to contribute to the peace and development of the international community and thereby to help ensure Japan's own security and prosperity' (MOFA, 2003). The document then proceeds to explain that human security is one of the 'basic policies' of ODA and the first 'priority issue'. In other words, ODA policies reflect the concept of human security. The document clearly states that Japan will implement ODA to protect and empower people. In addition, subsequent policy papers implementing ODA in accordance with the charter note that it should be made up of 'assistance that puts people at the center of concerns and that effectively reaches the people' (MOFA, 2005).

While Canada has used sanctions as a strategy for change and looked to coerce the Government of Myanmar into adhering to international good governance norms, Japan has advocated increased political and economic cooperation with the military (and successor) regimes in Myanmar which is in line with Japan's broad interpretation of human security. Indeed, among the donors and development actors, Japan alone has sustained a continuous dialogue with the Myanmar government, and consistently featured as the largest aid donor to Myanmar. As can be seen in Figure 7.1, Japan provided more than half of the total ODA to Myanmar until the early 2000's, and Table 7.1 also shows that Japan has long been the largest donor.

Japanese economic assistance to Myanmar began in the form of war reparations in 1955, and has continued virtually uninterrupted until the present, despite unacceptable behavior by successive Myanmar administrations. Since the start of the military government in 1962, Myanmar has relied heavily on Japanese foreign aid (Oishi and Furuoka, 2003, p. 898). Japan's ODA to Myanmar increased rapidly from the latter half of the 1970s, when the military government relaxed its strict neutralist foreign policy and opened up to more ODA in order to overcome the country's economic and political crisis of the mid-1970s. The onset of the second military administration in 1988 undermined this favorable relationship, and Japan suspended its ODA on account of the junta's poor human rights record and delay in democratization. Tokyo did, however, recognize the military regime, and resumed economic assistance to the government of Myanmar the very next year (although the amount of aid at that time was small).

While Japan's continued aid provision – seemingly unconditional regardless of how badly the government of Myanmar treated its people – was

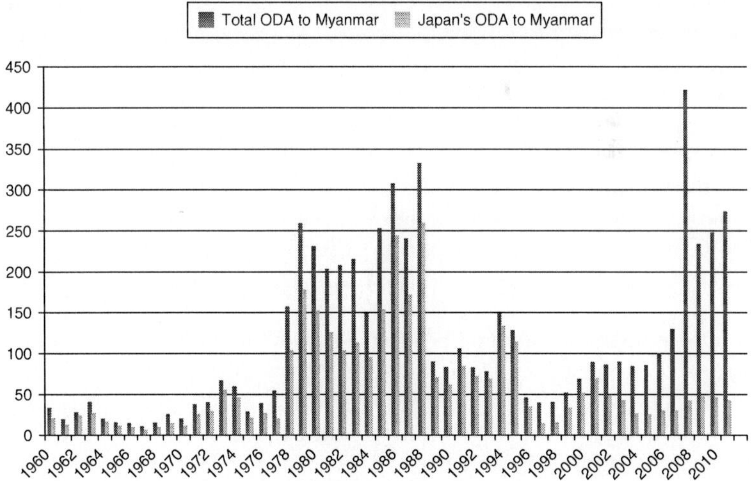

Figure 7.1 ODA disbursements to Myanmar: OECD DAC versus Japan (net disbursements, US$ million)

Source: Query Wizard for International Development Statistics, http://stats.oecd.org/qwids/.

Table 7.1 Top five donors to Myanmar (net disbursements, US$ million)

Year	1	2	3	4	5	Total
1961–1970	Japan 147.74	United States 33.84	Germany 16.03	Canada 6.97	Australia 5.36	214.22
1971–1980	Japan 662.97	Germany 134.27	Australia 44.22	United Kingdom 34.26	Denmark 27.54	975.60
1981–1990	Japan 1,400.6	Germany 347.7	Australia 76.77	France 59.31	US 59	2,083.21
1991–2000	Japan 625.29	France 29,48	Germany 18.82	Australia 12.84	Norway 12.81	792.32
2001–2010	Japan 413.58	United Kingdom 252.89	United States 187.48	Australia 160.98	Norway 114.01	1,570.39

Source: OECD, International Development Statistics (2012).

criticized in the West, Japan did not change its policy to bring it closer to that of the Western countries' sanction-oriented approach. Rather the Japanese government began expanding grants to Myanmar in the form of 'Grant Assistance for Grassroots Human Security Projects (GGP)' which was launched to promote human security and support small-scale project directly benefiting the grassroots level (Akimoto, 2004). This was despite the fact, and perhaps because of it, that Myanmar's human security and development conditions worsened dramatically following the coup, and the military's atrocities against minorities involved in insurgencies were even more dreadful they had been under the previous regime. Tokyo's reasoning was that resumption of economic assistance was necessary to protect people and to ensure the survival and dignity of individuals as human beings.

The continuation of Japan's aid to Myanmar, therefore, amounts to what is known as 'positive engagement' whereby unconditional assistance is given in the hope that gradual positive changes in internal governance will be achieved. Some critics argue, however, that in terms of total ODA, and when compared to large infrastructure projects also supported by Tokyo, Japan's 'human security' aid to refugees and Burmese minorities was very limited, implying that it is in the former area that Japanese prioritization can truly be found (Akimoto, 2004). Furthermore, Japanese aid projects and activities have been highly restricted and controlled by the military junta. Therefore, only a few aid projects reached peripheral areas and democratization-oriented projects in particular have been greatly curtailed.

Implications

We can conclude from this section that Canadian human security policy in Myanmar is clearly based on freedom from fear largely focusing on helping refugees and internally displaced people as well as imposing sanctions against the military junta threatening human security. Whereas Japan has applied limited sanctions, the ODA remained the most essential tool employed by Japanese government in its association with the military regime. While the effects of each human security policy are difficult to measure as many factors have to be taken into consideration, Canada and Japan have pursued distinctive policies on the basis of their different understandings of human security. Canada has emphasized the freedom from pervasive threats, such as physical violence in conflicts and the protection of people's rights, safety, and lives. Ottawa has called for the international community to address these issues and defend human security objectives through coercive measures including sanctions and even military force if necessary. Tokyo, however, has associated its foreign policies, particularly its development policies, with the pursuit of human security. Japan's economic development aid policies, manifested in the development assistance, traditionally incorporated both aspects of freedom from fear and freedom from want.

In terms of the entitlement rights model illustrated in Chapter 2, Canada's approach to promoting human security in Myanmar has focused on the core spheres of entitlement to freedom from fear of imminent and arbitrary death, and freedom from fear of being left to die. At the same time, however, great emphasis has been placed on the final sphere; that of the political rights associated with liberal concepts of freedom, equality, and justice. Indeed, it seems that this fifth sphere of rights has been prioritized in Ottawa's dealings with Myanmar, even to the exclusion of support for the other spheres. Hence, sanctions have been adhered to even in the face of human suffering in Myanmar, with the justification that aid will not resume until political rights are granted to the people.

Meanwhile, Tokyo has clearly prioritized economic assistance geared toward the third and fourth sphere of entitlement rights, promoting freedom from want of BHN, and freedom from want of a good life, in the hope that this will also impact on the first two spheres, and regardless of progress toward the provision of political rights. In fact, it could be argued that Tokyo's unconditional support lessened any incentive the Government of Myanmar might have to make significant changes in governance.

Fortunately, recent developments within Myanmar suggest that the two approaches may now be able to be pursued simultaneously allowing a mutual reinforcement of the elements of human security protection and development. Relaxation of restrictions on opponents has not only allowed the NLD and their leader, Aung San Suu Kyi, to stand in and win elections but it has also been sufficient for the opposition to end their boycott of the political process. In 2011, Aung San Suu Kyi made it clear that the NLD were shifting their positional stance to one of more cautious support for responsible international investment, tourism, and the lifting of sanctions (Aung San Suu Kyi, 2011). Furthermore, in 2012, President Thein Sein signed a law allowing peaceful demonstrations for the first time. ASEAN nations have already indicated a willingness to push for sanctions to be lifted (BBC, 2012a), and the EU also agreed to suspend restrictive measures, including sanctions, against Myanmar for one year with only the embargo on arms and equipment which can be used for internal repression remaining in force (Council of the EU, 2012). Furthermore, ahead of a first-ever presidential visit to Myanmar, the United States formally lifted a decade-old ban on most imports from the country in recognition of and to support the continued progress toward reform (BBC, 2012d). During this visit, President Barak Obama encouraged ongoing reform and called on the country to embrace the democratic system of governance in which the military takes orders from civilians and human rights are respected (Baker, 2012).

These development hopefully will open up the way for a more comprehensive approach to peace-building and development in Myanmar more in line with Japan's model, but the developments themselves may only have come about because of a hardline approach pursued by the international community under Western influence and leadership that had more in common with Canada's position. It may be of no coincidence that policy shift by Myanmar's leadership came in the wake of ASEAN caving in to Western pressure and abandoning its non-interventionary tradition with regard to Myanmar, and that it accelerated as NATO fought the first R2P engagement in Libya. This has also coincided with Chinese efforts to be recognized as a responsible global citizen, and pressure from the Union of Myanmar's only remaining ally of note on the government to reform its governance practices.

Future prospects

Despite elections in November 2010 resulting in a nominally civilian government being installed, and then the NLD winning 43 out of 45 seats in landmark parliamentary by-elections in April 2012, there are ongoing concerns that the constitution remains rigged for continued military rule, continued fraud, and the marginalization of many ethnic minorities. As the overwhelming vehicle for opposition political movements, there is a danger that the NLD will pander solely to majority Burman interests, neglecting the most vulnerable, and potentially storing up future discontent. For true conflict transformation to take place in Myanmar, those who govern need to be concerned with the human security and development of all sections of the population. There is also a danger that the NLD is overly dependent on Aung San Suu Kyi, who has had some health issues in recent months.

From late 2011, hundreds of political prisoners have been released, but several hundred remain behind bars. President Obama avoided the new capital of Nay Pyi Taw, with President Thein Sein instead traveling to Yangoon to meet him, where the US President also met with Aung San Suu Kyi. Obama also delivered a speech at Rangoon University, a cornerstone of the mass protests of 1988. Phil Robertson, from Human Rights Watch in Bangkok, expressed concern, however, that the Government of Myanmar, having achieved the prestige of a US presidential visit, may end up backsliding on their commitments to release all political prisoners (BBC, 2012e).

As detailed above, progress toward reconciliation with ethnic minorities has been very limited, and although there are encouraging signs of economic growth, Myanmar still has a long way to go before it can claim to provide safe havens free from want and fear for the most vulnerable of its citizens. Devolution and decentralization of power and governance are probably required along with the tentative political and economic reforms and stuttering peace processes. Indeed, 'in areas of political coexistence, the international community has far greater opportunity to support and strengthen the work of local or national community organizations and NGOs in the service, development, humanitarian, and peacebuilding sectors' (Callahan, 2007, p. 52). The Government of Myanmar must be encouraged to rein in the military campaigns against minorities and prohibit and prevent security forces from utilizing forced labor, extra-judicial killings, sexual violence, and indiscriminate attacks on civilians. The opposition needs to embrace the issues of vulnerability among all of the Burmese people, including the most marginalized. The international community needs to support progress where it is being made, but also to continue to hold those who govern to account.

There does seem to be a mood of guarded optimism for the future among most, if not all the key players. Bolstered by internal reforms and international support, it is hoped that Myanmar's transformation will prove to be substantive, irreversible, and above all, positive. Care must be taken, however, that development projects and reforms are not only beneficial to the majority but also do not endanger vulnerable minorities. MNCs must be strictly regulated in their dealings with Myanmar adhering to the highest standards of corporate social responsibility, rather than being blinded by the resource riches to be had in the country. Aung San Suu Kyi and the NLD's greatest concern with regard to market opening is that irresponsible development and tourism operations by unscrupulous international agencies will actually undermine the human security of the most vulnerable and also impact negatively upon the environment of Myanmar (Aung San Suu Kyi, 2011). Furthermore, as Sean Turnell (2008, p. 972) has warned, we must be wary of a potential 'resource curse' in Myanmar whereby 'resource windfalls can undermine good governance, democracy, the rule of law'.

Notes

1. Three Main National Causes include "non-disintegration of the union," "non-disintegration of national solidarity" and "perpetuation of sovereignty" (Myanmar Archive 2012).
2. People's desires are to oppose those relying on external elements," "oppose those trying to jeopardize stability of the state and progress of the nation," "oppose foreign nations interfering in internal affairs of the State" and "crush all internal and external destructive elements as the common enemy" (Myanmar Archive 2012).
3. Political objectives are "stability of the State, community peace and tranquility, prevalence of law and order," "national reconsolidation," "emergence of a new enduring State constitution" and "building of a new modern developed nation in accord with a new State constitution" (Myanmar Archive 2012).

References

Acharya, A. (2001) 'Human Security: East versus West', *Institute of Defence and Strategic Studies (IDSS) Working Paper Series*, 17.

Akimoto, Y. (2004) '*A Yen to Help the Junta*', *The Irrawaddy* 12(9), October 2004, http://www2.irrawaddy.org/article.php?art_id=4128.

Albright, M. (2008) 'End of Intervention', *The New York Times*, 11 June 2008, http://www.nytimes.com/2008/06/11/opinion/11albright.html.

Aung San Suu Kyi (2011) Interviewed by author, National League for Democracy Headquarters, Yangon, Myanmar, 26 July 2011.

Axworthy, L. (1997) 'Canada and Human Security: The Need for Leadership', *International Journal*, 52(2), 183–96.

Baker, P. (2012) 'Obama, in an Emerging Myanmar, Vows Support', *The New York Times*, 18 November 2012, http://www.nytimes.com/2012/11/19/world/asia/obama-heads-to-myanmar-as-it-promises-more-reforms.html?pagewanted=all.

Baldwin, D. A. (1997) 'The Concept of Security', *Review of International Studies*, 23, 5–26.

BBC (2012a) 'ASEAN Calls for Burma Sanctions to be Lifted', BBC, 3 April 2012, http://www.bbc.co.uk/news/world-asia-17599929.

BBC (2012b) 'Burma's Ethnic Conflicts See Slow Progress to Resolution', BBC, 26 May 2012, http://www.bbc.co.uk/news/world-asia-pacific-18189153.

BBC (2012c) 'Burma Violence: 20,000 Displaced in Rakhine State', BBC, 28 October 2012, http://www.bbc.co.uk/news/world-asia-20114326.

BBC (2012d) 'US Lifts Burma Imports Ban Ahead of Obama Visit', BBC, 16 November 2012, http://www.bbc.co.uk/news/world-asia-20373019.

BBC (2012e) 'Barack Obama and the perils of embracing Burma', BBC, 18 November 2012, http://www.bbc.co.uk/news/world-asia-20354355.

BBC (2013) 'Burmese Refugees Sold on by Thai Officials', BBC, 23 January 2013, http://www.bbc.co.uk/news/world-asia-21161745.

Bellamy, A. J. and Davis, S. E. (2009) 'The Responsibility to Protect in the Asia-Pacific Region', *Security Dialogue*, 40(6), 547–74.

Bernard, P. Jr. (2006) 'Canada and Human Security: From the Axworthy Doctrine to Middle Power Internationalism', *The American Review of Canadian Studies*, Summer 2006.

Bosold, D. and Sascha W. (2005) 'Human Security in Practice: Canadian and Japanese Experiences', *International Politics and Society*, 1, 84–101.

Bosold, D. (2007) 'The Politics of Self-Righteousness: Canada's Foreign Policy and the Human Security Agenda' in Klaus-Dieter Ertler and Paulina Mickiewicz (eds), *Transcultural Perspectives on Canada* (Brno: Masaryk University Press), pp. 175–200.

Buzan, B. and Segal, G. (1998) 'Rethinking East Asian Security' in M. T. Klare and Y. Chandrani (eds), *World Security: Challenges for a New Century* (New York: St. Martin's Press).

Callahan, M. P. (2003) *Making Enemies: War and State Building in Burma* (Ithaca: Cornell University Press).

Callahan, M. P. (2007) 'Political Authority in Burma's Ethnic Minority States: Devolution, Occupation, and Coexistence', *Policy Studies*, vol. 31 (Washington: East-West Center).

Commission on Human Security (CHS) (2003) *Human Security Now* (New York: CHS).

Central Intelligence Agency (CIA) (2012) *The World Factbook, Burma,* https://www.cia.gov/library/publications/the-world-factbook/geos/bm.html.

Council of the EU (Council of the European Union) (2012) 'Burma/Myanmar: EU Sanctions Suspended', Brussels, 14 May 2012, http://www.consilium.europa.eu/uedocs/cms_Data/docs/pressdata/EN/foraff/130188.pdf.

Department of Foreign Affairs and International Trade (DFAIT) (1995) 'Canada in the World: Canadian Foreign Policy Review' (Ottawa: DFAIT), Ch. 6, http://www.dfait-maeci.gc.ca/foreign_policy/cnd-world/chap6-en.asp.

DFAIT (1999) 'A Perspective on Human Security: Chairman's Summary', Lysøen, Norway, 20 May 1999, http://www3.sympatico.ca/ideabank/ksk/News/990520_dfait.html.

DFAIT (2012) 'Canada's Policy on Burma', http://www.international.gc.ca/sanctions/burma-birmanie.aspx?lang=eng.

Evans, G. (2008) 'Time for an Aid Invasion?', *The Age,* 19 May 2008, http://www.theage.com.au/news/opinion/time-for-an-aid-invasion/2008/05/18/1211049061508.html.

Flink, C. (2009) *Living Silence in Burma: Surviving Under Military Rule,* 2nd ed. (Chiang Mai: Silkworm Books; London and New York: Zed Books).

Foot, R. (2005) 'Human Rights and Counterterrorism in Global Governance: Reputation and Resistance', *Global Governance,* 11(3), 291–310.

Ganesan, N. (2007) 'State-society Relations in Southeast Asia' in N. Ganesan and K. Y. Hlaing (eds), *Myanmar: State, Society, and Ethnicity* (Singapore: Institute of Southeast Asian Studies).

Government of Canada (2007) 'Special Economic Measures Act', http://canadagazette.gc.ca/archives/p2/2007/2007-12-26/html/sor-dors285-eng.html.

Government of Canada (2012) 'Canada-Burma Relations', http://www.canadainternational.gc.ca/thailand-thailande/bilateral_relations_bilaterales/canada-burma-birmanie.aspx?view=d.

Government of Union Myanmar (GoUM) (2006) *Millennium Development Goals Report 2006* (Nay Oyi Taw: GoUM).

GoUM (2005) *Millennium Development Goals Report for Myanmar* (Nay Oyi Taw: GoUM).

Holliday, I. (2007) 'National Unity Struggles in Myanmar: A Degenerate Case of Governance for Harmony in Asia', *Asian Survey,* 47(3), 374–92.

Human Security Center (HSC) (2005) *Human Security Report 2005: War and Peace in the 21st Century* (New York and Oxford: Oxford University Press).

Human Security Index (HSI) (2010) *HIS Version 2,* http://www.humansecurityindex.org/.

Hubert, D. and Bonser, M. (2001) 'Humanitarian Military Intervention' in R. McRae and D. Hubert (eds), *Human Security and the New Diplomacy* (Montreal and Kingston: McGill-Queen's University Press).

International Crisis Group (ICG) (2008) *Burma/Myanmar: After the Crackdown,* http://www.crisisgroup.org/~/media/Files/asia/south-east-asia/burma-myanmar/144_burma_myanmar___after_the_crackdown.ashx.

ICG (2001) *Myanmar: The Military Regime's View of the World* (Bangkok and Brussels: ICG).

International Commission on Intervention and State Sovereignty (ICISS) (2001) *The Responsibility to Protect: The Report of the International Commission on Intervention and State Sovereignty* (Ottawa: International Development Research Centre).

Internal Displacement Monitoring Centre (IDMC) (2009) *Myanmar: Conflicts and Human Rights Violations Continue to Cause Displacement* (Geneva: IDMC).

Karen Human Rights Group (2000) *Suffering in Silence: The Human Rights Nightmare of the Karen People of Burma* (Parkland: Universal Publishers).

Ministry of Foreign Affairs (MOFA) (2003) 'Japan's Official Development Assistance Charter', http://www.mofa.go.jp/region/n-america/us/q&a/oda/3.html.

MOFA (2005) *Japan's Medium-term Policy on Official Development Assistance* (Tokyo: MOFA).

Mullany, L. C., Lee, C. I, *et al.* (2008) 'The MOM Project: Delivering Maternal Health Services among Internally Displaced Populations in Eastern Burma', *Reproductive Health Matters,* May 2008, 16(31), 44–56.

Myanmar Archives (2012) *The New Light of Myanmar,* http://www.myanmararchives.com/newspapers/?dir=/The-New-Light-of-Myanmar.

Nishikawa, Y. (2009) 'Human Security in Southeast Asia: Viable Solution or Empty Slogan?' *Security Dialogue,* 40(2), 213–36.

Obuchi, K. (1998) 'Toward the Creation of a Bright Future for Asia', Policy Speech at the Institute for International Relations Lecture Program, Hanoi, Vietnam, 16 December 1998, http://www.mofa.go.jp/region/asia-paci/asean/pmv9812/policyspeech.html.

Oehlers, A. (2005) 'Public Health in Burma: Anatomy of a Crisis', *Journal of Contemporary Asia,* 35(2), 195–206.

Oishi, M. and Furuoka, F. (2003) 'Can Japan Aid be an Effective Tool of Influence?: Case Studies of Cambodia and Burma', *Asian Survey,* 43(6).

Osborne, M. (1970) *Region of Revolt: Focus on Southeast Asia* (Sydney: Pergamon Press).

Rothschild, E. (1995) 'What is Security?' *Daedalus: Journal of the American Academy of Arts and Sciences,* 124(3), The Quest for World Order (Summer, 1995), 53–98.

Rumsfeld, D. H. (2002) *Defense Department Town Hall Meeting With Secretary of Defense Donald H. Rumsfeld,* Transcript and Question and Answer Period, 7 March 2002, http://www.defenselink.mil/speeches/2002/s20020307-secdef.html.

Small, M. (2001) 'The Human Security Network' in R. McRae and D. Hubert (eds), *Human Security and the New Diplomacy* (Montreal and Kingston: McGill-Queen's University Press).

Smith, M. (1994) *Ethnic Groups in Burma: Development, Democracy and Human Rights* (London: Anti-Slavery International).

Smith, M. (2007) 'State of Strife: The Dynamics of Ethnic Conflict in Burma', *Policy Studies,* vol. 36 (Washington: East-West Center).

Steinberg, D. I. (2001) *Burma: The State of Myanmar* (Washington, DC: Georgetown University Press).

Stubbs, R. (1989) *Hearts and Minds in Guerrilla Warfare* (Toronto: Oxford University Press).

Taylor, J. and Wright, O. (2013) 'Burma's Rohingya Muslims: Aung San Suu Kyi's Blind Spot', *The Independent,* 31 January 2013, http://www.independent.co.uk/news/world/asia/burmas-rohingya-muslims-aung-san-suu-kyis-blind-spot-8061619.html.

Thawnghmung, A. M. and Myoe, M. A. (2008) 'Myanmar in 2007: A Turning Point in the "Roadmap"?' *Asian Survey*, 48(1) (January/February 2008), 13–19.

The Telegraph (2012) 'Burma Copper Mine Protest Broken up by Riot Police', 29 November 2012, http://www.telegraph.co.uk/news/worldnews/asia/burmamyanmar/9711747/Burma-copper-mine-protest-broken-up-by-riot-police.html.

Tin, M. M. T. (2010) 'Tatmadaw and Myanmar's Security Challenges' in S. M. Tang and P. E. Lam (eds), *Asia Pacific Countries' Security Outlook and Its Implications for the Defense Sector* (Tokyo: The Institute for Defense Studies).

Tin, M. M. T. (2007) 'Mapping the Contours of Human Security Challenges in Myanmar' in N. Ganesan and K. Y. Hlaing (eds), *Myanmar: State, Society, and Ethnicity* (Singapore: Institute of Southeast Asian Studies).

Tin, M. M. T. (1998) 'Myanmar: Preoccupation with Regime Survival, National Unity, and Stability' in M. Alagappa (ed.), *Asian Security Practice: Material and Ideational Influences* (Stanford: Stanford University Press).

Turnell, S. (2008) 'Burma's Insatiable State', *Asian Survey*, 48(6), 958–76.

UNDP (2011) *Human Development Report 2011: Sustainability and Equity: A Better Future for All* (New York: Oxford University Press).

UN News Center (2007) *UN Human Rights Council Calls on Myanmar to Release Detainees, Political Prisoners'*, http://www.un.org/apps/news/story.asp?NewsID=24124&Cr=myanmar&Cr1.

United Nations Security Council (UNSC) (2007) Presidential Statement, Security Council, SC/9139, 5757th Meeting, http://www.un.org/News/Press/docs/2007/sc9139.doc.htm.

Ware, A. (2011) 'The MDGs in Myanmar: Relevant or Redundant?', *Journal of the Asia Pacific*, 16(4), 579–96.

World Bank (2011) *Data*, http://data.worldbank.org/indicator.

Zaw, A. (2000) 'Human Security in Burma', *The Irrawaddy*, 8(10), http://www2.irrawaddy.org/print_article.php?art_id=2060.

8
Rebuilding Human Security in Timor-Leste

Introduction

Having been colonized by Portugal in the 16th century, Timor-Leste had to wait until 1975 to declare its independence, only to be invaded, occupied, and re-colonized by Indonesia almost immediately thereafter. The ensuing liberation struggle left 102,800 dead (approximately 18,600 killings and 84,200 'excess' deaths from hunger and illness). The chronic challenges to human security promoted international solidarity, especially after the end of the Cold War, and, ultimately, in 1999, a UN-sponsored act of self-determination (Silva and Ball, 2006, pp. 1–2). Following a large vote in favor of independence despite intimidation of voters by pro-Indonesian militias, Indonesia relinquished control of the territory. Although Indonesia accepted the result of the referendum, the militias did not, going on a murderous rampage which was finally ended by an international peacekeeping force followed by a UN mission. Timor-Leste became the first new sovereign state of the 21st century on 20 May 2002, but with ongoing UN and other international security support continuing for another decade.

A great deal of progress has been made in the state-building project, but Timor-Leste continues to suffer from the legacies of conflict and colonialism. In part, these legacies are similar to those found in many conflict-affected states, and as discussed in Chapter 2 – low economic growth due to low investment, disrupted infrastructure, macro-economic instability, low political legitimacy and corruption, a small donor presence focused mainly on humanitarian aid, limited civil society organization, eroded community and national spirit, internally displaced populations and refugees, the problems

Officially the Democratic Republic of Timor-Leste, and acknowledged as such or by the shortened form Timor-Leste by the international community as represented by the United Nations. Commonly known in English, however, as East Timor. From this point on Timor-Leste will be used except when other sources are referenced, or the adjective 'East Timorese' is used of re-integration of demobilized combatants, and psychological effects of war trauma and communities fragmented by hostility. Other problematic legacies, however, are not conflict related, but apply rather to colonial overhangs from periods of Portuguese and Indonesian governance, and even from the UN administration period, including linguistic, economic, and demographic structural impediments.

Much has in fact been done to reduce the threats to life and limb from violence, and compared to the messy outcome of many other 'humanitarian' interventions, by the UN and other members of the international community, Timor-Leste is a relative success story. 'An impoverished, war-torn country has, in 13 years, become a fairly stable small state with promising economic growth prospects' (BBC, 2012). Timor-Leste is widely regarded as a benchmark for UN peacekeeping efforts and for progress along narrow human security dimensions (UN Foundation, 2002). Indeed, for Markus Benzing (2005, p. 297), Timor-Leste is particularly noteworthy as it is 'the most radical 'state-building' exercise the United Nations has engaged in to date, in the most literal sense of the word, as the United Nations acted as midwife for a new state'.

Yet in terms of broader definitions of human security, Timor-Leste does not only have a long way to go with regard to countering freedom from want but international and domestic administrations may also be storing up security threats for the future. While a tremendous UN and international presence has increased human security on the political side of the equation, it has achieved little in terms of economic or food security and has even undermined these elements through inflationary pressures and local market distortion. Norm diffusion led to the involvement of the international community in a global governance mission, but conditions on the ground have revealed that one size does not fit all when it comes to post-conflict development.

This chapter addresses the continued obstacles to the provision of human security and development in Timor-Leste. The OECD DAC has carried out substantial work related to the Paris Declaration on aid effectiveness and its relevance and application in fragile contexts such as Timor-Leste. The findings of the committee are that 'business as usual' does not work and may in fact go against the principle of 'do no harm'. The theme of 'adaptation' to context is critical. At the Fourth High Level Forum on Aid Effectiveness in Busan, South Korea, participants agreed to a 'New Deal for Engagement in Fragile States', which proposed far-reaching peace-building and state-building goals while at the same time placing fragile states at the helm of their development goals. Building upon previous declarations for good international engagement in fragile states, the New Deal articulates the vision and principles of the Millennium Declaration acknowledging that fragile states require special assistance in developing strong government institutions (Busan, 2012). And this is certainly the focus the international community has taken toward Timor-Leste. Yet the huge international presence necessary to build strong government institutions has contributed an additional layer of development challenges in the country.

Since the actions of UN midwifery that brought East Timorese state into being, large volumes of international aid and development assistance have been poured into the country and much of the internal security apparatus has been provided by external forces. Yet Timor-Leste remains a fragile and underdeveloped state. The OECD's *Principles for Good International Engagement in Fragile States and Institutions* highlights the need for international engagement to be concerted and sustained, with a focus on first, supporting the legitimacy and accountability of states by addressing issues of democratic governance, human rights, civil society engagement and peace-building; second, strengthening the capability of states to fulfill their core functions as a pre-requisite to tackling poverty effectively (OECD, 2007). The principles acknowledge that there may be 'tensions and trade-offs between objectives, particularly in the short-term, which must be addressed when reaching consensus on strategy and priorities. For example, international objectives in some fragile states may need to focus on peace-building in the short-term, to lay the foundations for progress against the MDGs in the longer-term'(*ibid.*). Yet this focus, in the case of Timor-Leste, has left efforts at providing freedom from want, particularly for the poorest sections of society, lagging drastically behind the provision of havens of safety, free from fear. The next two sections contrast successful peace-building and state-building efforts, with the limitations of human development in Timor-Leste.

Peace-building, state-building, and freedom from fear

To a certain extent, Timor-Leste was lucky in that it came of age just as Indonesia democratized and its military was leaving the national stage. The post-Soeharto civilian political leadership of Indonesia quickly turned its back on the former province and got on with the business of internal reform, repealing the 1976 integration law in October 1999 and leaving the territory to the UN (Della-Giacoma, 2012a). Nevertheless, the birth of the new nation was a traumatic one. The UN played a vital role in Timor-Leste's independence by organizing the 1999 referendum which ended Indonesia's 24-year occupation, and sending in the peacekeepers to put an end to the militia-inspired violence which followed. The first task, therefore, was to put an end to the killings and provide safe havens to allow the people to return home.

Peace-building

Order was fairly swiftly restored by several battalions of Australian and New Zealand troops later reinforced by UN peacekeepers. On their arrival, however, late in 1999, the UN and NGO aid workers found that 75 per cent of the entire population of 800,000 had been displaced, nearly 70 per cent of all houses had been destroyed, and many people had been killed (Macaulay, 2003, p. 40). Subsequently, a huge input of funds and training of personnel, from agencies of the UN, various national governments, and aid organizations, enabled both the building of some aspects and the rebuilding of other parts of the security infrastructure so that the East Timorese could take over their own administration on 20 May 2002. UN peacekeeping troops returned in 2006 in the guise of the Australian-led International Stabilisation Force (ISF) after a failed military coup led to social and political instability. Significant outbreaks of violence recurred during the build-up to, and after elections in 2007. President José Ramos-Horta was critically injured in an assassination attempt on 11 February 2008, and Prime Minister Xanana Gusmão also attacked in a failed coup, again leading to the Australian government immediately sending reinforcements to Timor-Leste to keep order.

The objectives of the international community listed above (to put an end to the killings and general state of insecurity, thereby allowing people to return home) appear, however, to be drawing close to a successful conclusion in Timor-Leste. In 2012, the year in which only the tenth anniversary of new-founded independence was celebrated, Timor-Leste was able to hold three sets of free and fair elections (two presidential and one parliamentary) without significant disruption beyond stone-throwing incidents, appearing to consign its recent fractious and violent past to the pages of history, and allowing the withdrawal of UN peacekeepers to proceed as scheduled in December (Della-Giacoma, 2012b). This was in stark contrast to the violence surrounding the elections of 2007. Furthermore, although international forces are drawing down, Timor-Leste is not being abandoned to its fates. While Australian military forces left with the UN peacekeepers after their six-year stabilization mission, Canberra has committed to continued training and support for the police force.

State-building

Strong state- and institution-building has been the primary focus of the international community and has created a permanent legacy. Indeed for Hideaki Asahi (2012, pp. 3–4), in the Timorese context, peace-building is tantamount to state-building, with reference to top-down, state-centric processes with a structural focus on putting in place the central- and national-level institutions of the state, as well as nation-building reflecting a unique recent historical trajectory. Timor-Leste lacked experience of self-rule, effective government institutions, and laws, regulations, and other normative codes of control to bind or unite local communities and citizens. Thus, the first task of the international community was to foster the growth of such indigenous governance structures. Accordingly, therefore, Kamalesh Sharma, Special Representative of the Secretary General (SRSG) of the UNMISET, the UN's first peace-building mission after the independence of Timor-Leste, immediately identified the need to 'Start from Scratch' (*ibid.*,

p. 4). In recent years, efforts by international and national administrators have also been strikingly successful in the field of state-building.

The 2006 crisis highlighted the inadequate development of state institutions for Timor-Leste following the withdrawal of international security agents in the post-transition period. 'Despite the timely warnings and suggestions from some commentators, the international actors – which provided financial support and policy and human resource expertise – and the Timorese authorities both failed to address the internal dimension of the security threat posed by rivalries among political groups' (Sahin, 2007, p. 254). Furthermore, following the 2006 troubles, in response to the invitation from the then Senior Minister and Minister of Foreign Affairs José Ramos-Horta, the Independent Special Commission of Inquiry for Timor-Leste was formed by the United Nations High Commissioner for Human Rights at the request of the Secretary-General. The commission began its work in July and released its report in mid-October, acknowledging the fragility of state institutions and the weakness of the rule of law as underlying factors that contributed to the crisis (*ibid.*, p. 263). In response, UN Security Council Resolution 1704 approved the establishment of a multidimensional, integrated mission (UNMIT). This time the official mandate specifically included 'enhancing a culture of democratic governance'.

Despite the ongoing instability, multiple successful elections were held in 2007. Ramos-Horta won the presidential polls on May 9 as an independent, against the FRETILIN (Frente Revolucionária de Timor-Leste Independente) candidate, Francisco 'Lu-Olo'Guterres, and on 30 June, parliamentary elections brought former President Xanana Gusmão to power, this time as prime minister. 'The significance of the 2007 elections was that FRETILIN, which had ruled with a strong parliamentary majority for five years, was comprehensively replaced by Gusmão and his political allies in Parliament' (Arnold, 2009, p. 434).

The 2008 assassination attempt and failed coup showed, however, that there was still some way to go to achieve the desired democratic culture, and reflected a state of continued fragility in East Timorese due process and rule of law. But Damien Kingsbury also sees the events as having broken a critical stalemate in Timor-Leste's political life, and which therefore could be seen as having many more positive than negative consequences. For him, the death of coup leader, Major Alfredo Reinado, allowed the government to begin its program of relocating IDPs back to their homes free from the fear of insecurity generated by the 'petitioners' (2006 army deserters or those illegitimately sacked by the authorities depending on one's perspective); it undermined the bargaining position of lawless forces; it distanced both the prime minister and the president from the taint of association with Reinado which had dogged them until that point; and it enhanced their legitimacy, particularly that of Ramos-Horta who was in a very real sense 'blooded' (Kingsbury, 2009, pp. 360–1).

For Matthew Arnold (2009, p. 449), that the incidents of February 2008 did not devolve violently out of control as happened in April and May 2006 is the best sign that Timor-Leste was in fact stabilizing, and it is 'notable that after the cantonment of the petitioners in February 2008 and the surrender of the mutineers in April, the political tensions surrounding them calmed, and there has been no further violence directly related to them'. The government was mostly able to complete the relocation of IDPs and closing down their camps. Paying families up to US$4,000 to return to their places of origin, equivalent of around eight years' average income, represented a significant incentive to most of the IDPs. Likewise, without Reinado's shadow over the proceedings, there was eventually progress in resolving the claims of the Petitioners, even if not through returning them to the military, but with their acceptance of what appeared to be a generous pay-out offer of US$8,000 each to rebuild their lives (Kingsbury, 2009, pp. 361–2). Thus, by the end of 2008, Timor-Leste was showing real signs of internal stabilization, reflected in the Australian Defence Force drawing down 100 of its 700 personnel contribution to the ISF sent to quell the troubles of 2006 (*ibid.*, p. 367).

From 2009 to 2012 and the end of the UN mission, the national institutions of Timor-Leste assumed control with increasing confidence. Policing operations were gradually handed over to the Timorese Police Force (Policia Nacional de Timor-Leste, PNTL), until with the final drawdown of UN and Australian forces, only some limited external logistical and training support will be required. The East Timorese armed defense forces (FALINTIL-Forças Defesa de Timor-Leste, F-FDTL) have successfully been brought under civilian government control, and now owe their allegiance to the democratically elected government, regardless of the party or parties which emerge victorious in elections. In a relatively short period of time since regaining independence, Timor-Leste has actually developed a comparatively good record of democratic competition and has firmly established many of the conditions for a working representative democracy.

Indeed, it is to be hoped that the 2012 elections which produced a stable government generally accepted as legitimate, even by those who lost, will provide a necessary condition for Timor-Leste's transition from what has been called a 'flawed democracy' into an established, consolidated democracy. Its party system, while underdeveloped, is already more coherent than that of many conflict-affected developing states (Shoesmith, 2012, pp. 33, 49). As noted by former President (and losing presidential candidate in 2012) Ramos-Horta in a recent interview forum, 'Reconciliation is always a long, drawn-out process in any country. But our collective effort is bearing fruit. Our social and political atmosphere has been remarkedly free of tension in the last few years' (Ramos-Horta, 2012, p. 106). Kingsbury (2012a) supports this optimism by pointing to the extent that the people of Timor-Leste have embraced the idea that they can determine their own affairs and are committed to regularizing and further embedding political accountability, as giving Timor-Leste the best chance for the future. There remain, however, some challenges to human security in Timor-Leste, even in these areas of relative success.

Ongoing political and security challenges

According to Bu Wilson (2012, p. 83), a convergence of perverse incentives in the security field, not only principally related to the legacy of the UN's work in the country but also with an eye to future relevance and employment opportunities, has led to a continuing over-rosy rewriting of achievements in Timor-Leste. Timor-Leste has a working and competitive party system with free elections with the capacity to produce a change of government. Dennis Shoesmith (2012, pp. 34, 50) is concerned however, that multiparty politics and the proliferation of small parties, encouraged by a proportional electoral system, undermine the coherence of national governance and risk encouraging 'the habituation of patrimonial and clientelist politics, and the deployment of state resources to pursue personal benefit as well as to satisfy political ambition'. That being said, only four of the 21 parties and party coalitions competing in the 2012 parliamentary election crossed the 3 per cent threshold to win seats in Parliament: National Congress for Timorese Reconstruction (CNRT), FRETILIN, Partido Democratico (PD) and Frenti-Mudansa (F-M). The CNRT increased its share from 18 to 30 seats, and went into coalition its former coalition partner PD (eight seats) and F-M (two seats), with FRETILIN (25 seats) continuing as the only party in opposition.

Other commentators are, however, worried about potential transition toward exclusionary and/or authoritarian politics in Timor-Leste (Simonsen, 2006, p. 595; Siapno, 2006, pp. 325–6). Linked to this is the perceived heavy-handedness of indigenous security forces. Blunt warnings that those who caused trouble in the lead-up to the election would be shot were backed up with high-profile joint patrols and those contemplating violence seem to have got the message (Della-Giacoma, 2012b). Indeed, it is possible that strong actions, or at least strong words, are necessary to deter outbreaks of violence, particularly during election periods. A broad range of people informed ICG in 2012 that 'the single-biggest contributor to deterring violence during the elections was the threat from both the police and the army commanders that troublemakers would be shot, paired with a significant police and army presence' (Nolan, 2012). But international observers may be concerned by the political legitimacy of an administration whose president, Xanana Gusmão blithely announced:

> Once the UN are gone ... if you continue to hurl [stones] at one another, I will arrest you and not give you any food; if you continue to fight one another, I will arrest you and not give you any food. If I need to go to the International Human Rights Court, then I'll go. It's in order to protect you. In order to protect your name is one reason, to protect your younger

> siblings, to protect ... us all. Because we are now a reference point for the world. [...] Dialogue. Talk to one another. You can't throw stones or hurt one another. If I find that one of you has killed another? Then you'll be locked up for a week without even water. (Nolan, 2012)

There are very real concerns that Timor-Leste could head down the path taken by Myanmar, and described in Chapter 7, whereby the human security of the individual is sacrificed in the interests of something called 'national security'. On the other hand, while it is easy to question the motivations of those who govern committing violence in the name of the state, it is also important to address why there are groups of individuals who want to throw stones and disrupt elections. National and international agencies in Timor-Leste have been relatively successful addressing the threat posed by malcontented veterans of the liberation struggle, petitioners, and IDPs. Measures like the US$72 million (6 per cent of the state budget) set aside for veterans' benefits in 2011 have eased discontent among dissident former Forças Armadas de LibertaçãoNacional de Timor-Leste (FALINTIL) fighters, and all but a few IDPs have taken the compensation listed above, despite ongoing chronic land disputes (Della-Giacoma, 2011). Nevertheless, the problems posed by disaffected youth groups are only likely to increase in the short to medium term.

The nation-building process of Timor-Leste faces significant demographic challenges due to a population growth which is the fastest in Asia and among the fastest in the world, spurred by extremely high total fertility rate (2.41) which is also among the highest in the world. If the current fertility rate and its implied population growth continue as predicted, the population of Timor-Leste will double in 17 years (Saikia and Hosgelen, 2010, p. 133). Timor-Leste also has a distorted demographic curve with an early peak and a long tailing-off due to a large younger generation while many of the older generation perished during the struggle against Indonesia. The average age is only 17.3 years (Asahi, 2012, p. 14). The East Timorese youth have become heavily involved with so-called 'martial arts groups', some of which have taken on the characteristics of violent armed gangs. These groups have exacerbated and inflamed each crisis since independence, and disrupted elections with internecine violence, attacks against the instruments of the state, and intimidation and victimization of civil society.

Yet it seems that the stimulus for Timorese youths to join these groups and engage in the destabilizing activities listed above is primarily economic, related to a failure of those who govern to provide havens free from want for the most vulnerable sections of society. Timor-Leste has a 'shockingly high' unemployment rate, particularly among the youth (Guterres, 2008, p. 368). Indeed, in a 2012 report for the US Congress, unemployment and underemployment combined in Timor-Leste were listed as high as 70 per cent, with 20 per cent unemployment in urban areas and a 40 per cent rate among youth (Dolven *et al.*, 2012, p. 5). A total of 10,000–15,000 unemployed youths are added to these figures each year (Akara, 2011). Therefore, we must return to the notion of spillover between underdevelopment and insecurity and between human and national security considerations. The next section addresses the ongoing development challenges faced by Timor-Leste and the implications for human security of both the narrow and broad definition.

Development, distribution, and human security

The World Development Report 2011 found that on average post-conflict countries take between 15 and 30 years – a full generation – to transition out of fragility and to build resilience, thus according to the World Bank, social and economic development in Timor-Leste can be seen as nothing short of remarkable (World Bank, 2011). Indeed, Timor-Leste now ranks as a lower middle income country, and is predicted to have the sixth highest rate of economic growth in the world in 2013 (The Economist, 2013). There are, however, a number of caveats to go along with this remarkable success. First, remarkable rates of growth have occurred as a result of starting from such a low base, and also on the back of a tremendous influx of aid, international investment, and petrodollars from its oil fund. Second, as shown by the very high unemployment and underemployment rates, among other indicators addressed below, this wealth has not been evenly distributed. Third, as a result of the first two caveats, there remain a great number of challenges to the human security of the most vulnerable sections of East Timorese society, and therefore sources of potential future instability.

Limits to development

The Petroleum Fund finances around 90 per cent of government spending, making Timor-Leste one of the most energy-dependent economies in the world. Rises in revenue from this fund account for much of Timor-Leste's perceived economic success. Based on June 2008 prices, East Timor's oil revenue doubled over the previous year, to US$200 million a month, and boasted the Petroleum Fund from US$2 billion in 2007 to US$5 billion in 2008. This is what pushed Timor-Leste's per capita GDP to a nominal US$4500, meaning that it was quickly approaching the status of a 'middle income' country with per capita GDP US$6,000 (Kingsbury, 2009, p. 365). The Petroleum Fund Law sets the upper limit of money extracted from the Fund for the national budget at the level of 3 per cent of estimated total oil assets (or, Estimated Sustainable Income: ESI). The Fund had a balance of around US$10 billion as of the end of 2011 (Asahi, 2012, p. 10). Over the past two years, Timor-Leste has announced substantial increases in government spending, with the FY2012 budget rising 30 per cent from FY2011. 'In addition to directing funds towards traditional areas such as infrastructure, rural development and public services, it has also created new funding vehicles for large-scale infrastructure and human capital' (Dolven *et al.*, 2012, p. 3).

Kingsbury (2009, p. 365) has, however, noted that most East Timorese remain unaware, or at least are not recipients, of their country's increasing economic status, and that there is concern that having access to large amounts of direct income, rather than using earned interest, could lead to fiscal irresponsibility, with money being thrown at programs that produce little if any concrete outcomes. The political opposition certainly has alleged that the government is spending unsustainably, that its investments are reaching a small minority of the population, and that the expansionary budget has brought inflation that stands around 18 per cent (Dolven *et al.*, 2012, p. 3). The main opposition party, the FRETILIN, further argues that increased government expenditure primarily benefited the 'Dili-based political elite and their families' and fears over corruption have intensified with allegations in recent years spiraling all the way to the prime minister's family (Arnold, 2011, p. 219).

Further than this, there is widespread recognition of the significant danger that Timor-Leste may become, or indeed has already become trapped by a 'resource curse', with increased potential for rent-seeking and corruption, resource related conflict, and natural resource waste (Doraisami, 2009, p. 168). In 2010, Transparency International ranked Timor-Leste 127 out of 180 countries in terms of corruption, representing a significant improvement from the 2008 low of 145 (and reflecting the impact of anti-corruption drives by the government), but showing the persistence of significant problems and still short of the 123 place in the listings achieved in 2007. 'In contrast to allocating 30 per cent of the budget to a stabilization fund, the budget allocates approximately 3.98 per cent to the agricultural sector where over 80 per cent of the population is employed. The same proportion is also devoted to the health sector while education received 6.64 per cent' (*ibid.*, pp. 169–70). Readily available funds from resources have led to poor planning and management, and currently high levels of expenditure have done little to significantly improve infrastructure, are not in line with the economy's absorption capacity, and are unlikely to increase private sector activity or employment (*ibid.*, p. 72).

At US$800, Timor-Leste has one of the lowest per capita GDPs (when adjusted for Purchasing Power Parity) in the world (Easttimorgovernment). The dominance of oil production in the economic figures for Timor-Leste is also reflected in the fact that per capita non-oil GDP is only US$348 (Doraisami, 2009, p. 164). Likewise, Timor-Leste's HDI score is 0.495, ranking the country only 147 out of 187 countries with comparable data. Thus, despite some improvements, Timor-Leste remains well below the contemporary regional average for East Asia and the Pacific of 0.671, while 37.19 per cent of civilians live below the international poverty line of 1.25 dollars a day, and 23 per cent of the population is malnourished (UNDP, 2012). By some measurements, Timor-Leste in fact remains the poorest country in Asia (Asahi, 2012, p. 2). Telecommunications and power infrastructures were severely damaged during the Indonesian withdraw, and have yet to be satisfactorily repaired. Timor-Leste is ranked 133 out of 134 countries in the world in terms of overall network readiness index, has low teledensities with 6.8 mobile lines per 100 persons and 0.21 main telephone lines per 100 persons, and only 32 per cent of households have access to electricity. Telecommunications and energy costs are extremely high, with nearly all of its electricity generated by imported diesel, and there is a culture of non-payment for services, erratic electricity supply, low human capacity, and lack of institutional structure (Doraisami, 2009, p. 172).

Within the country, however, there are further concerns that it is not just the absolute level of development that is lacking, but in particular, the development and human security of the most vulnerable sections of society – the poorest, the most remote, the unemployed, the young, and women.

Limits to distribution

Severe inequalities in the distribution of newfound economic benefits are evident. Indeed, Timor-Leste's inequality adjusted HDI is significantly lower at 0.332 than figures for its regular HDI (UNDP, 2012). Average mean income, in fact remains low, at around US$500–600 per person, while those outside the main towns continue to survive in an often largely cash-less economy (Kingsbury, 2009, p. 367). Both national and international governance agencies have encountered severe difficulties in spreading the benefits of economic development much beyond the boundaries of the capital, Dili. Despite expending US$32 million in 2010 on the Decentralized Development Package, aimed at infrastructure development in rural communities, critics contended that overall spending was still too concentrated in Dili and failed to benefit the 90-plus per cent of the population living in rural districts (Arnold, 2011, pp. 218–19).

Challenges to the human security of the most vulnerable sections of East Timorese society are reflected in high figures for maternal and infant mortality in the HDI and MDG indicators. Despite drastic improvements (when compared with 928.6 in 2008 and 1016.3 in 1990), there is still a maternal mortality ratio of 370 per 100,000 live births, an under-five mortality rate of 60 per 1,000 births, and a neonatal mortality as a percentage of under-five mortality of 48 (UNFPA, 2011, pp. 138–9). These figures are now better than comparable ones for all the other case studies represented in this volume, but still lag significantly behind those of more developed regional countries (Maternal Mortality Portal). Indeed, the maternal mortality rate remains one of the highest in the world, with 42 per cent of all deaths of women aged 15 to 49 related to pregnancy (Timor-Leste, 2011, p. 49). Thus, to a certain extent the much of the improvement is due to starting from a truly awful base.

East Timorese women have, in fact, always borne, and continue to endure a disproportionate share of the human security challenges faced by the population. During the Indonesian occupation, the military raped and forcibly sterilized thousands of women and girls. Indeed, local women have claimed that 'there was never a day without rape' (Farsetta, 2004, p. 51). Following independence, while, as described above, the physical security of men has improved significantly, the distribution of human security advancement has left women behind. Sexual slavery continued in the refugee camps immediately after independence (Smith, 2002, p. 71). During the transitional period, governance was through a complex and unusual hybrid of the colonial legal system as mandated by Indonesian law, the United Nations Transitional Administration in East Timor (UNTAET) regulations, and the local judicial systems, all of which failed adequately to address gender-based violence (Groves *et al.*, 2009, p. 187).

Domestic violence, which continues to be an issue in independent Timor-Leste, is the most common form of gender-based violence reported to the police, and according to a baseline study in two Timorese districts, published in 2009, is a 'normal' occurrence for many Timorese women and is often viewed as a private or family matter (Timor-Leste, 2011, p. 50). To address this problem, in 2009, domestic violence was entered in the penal code, making it a punishable crime for the first time, and also a public crime, which means people other than the victim have the power to report incidents of domestic violence to the police. 'The recognition of domestic violence as a crime made it possible for the National Parliament to pass a long awaited Law Against Domestic Violence in May 2010' (*ibid.*). Since the passing of the law, however, continued obstacles such as 'lack of rule of law, a feeble judicial system, economic dependence, and a culture of silence' mean that it remains the country's number one crime, accounting for around 50 per cent of all crimes, and nearly one-third of all women have experienced some form of violence or assault since the age of 15, rising to one in two in the capital Dili (Hodal, 2012).

Women continue to be marginalized in socioeconomic terms in Timor-Leste, and while girls are now represented in all levels of state schooling at over 90 per cent of the rate of boys, the enrollment of women in higher education continues to lag far behind that of men. Furthermore, while some progress has been made, adult female illiteracy still stands at 32 per cent compared to 21 per cent for men (Timor-Leste, 2011, pp. 20–4, 49). Indeed, Rita Reddy (2011), Senior Gender Advisor to UNMIT, has noted that not only has conflict delayed women's advancement in Timor-Leste and that the androcentric, patriarchal, overwhelmingly Catholic and conservative traditional society continues to place obstacles in front of them but also that poverty, unemployment, gangs, and martial arts clubs are further endangering women. Furthermore, disappearances of women for internal and cross-border trafficking are on the rise (*ibid.*).

A focus on security governance, a lack of development, and unequal distribution of resources mean, therefore, that Timor-Leste continues to face significant challenges to human security, despite (uneven) progress in some areas. Rural communities, where the majority of East Timorese live, are particularly vulnerable due to the concentration of development spending in the capital and on 'stabilization' projects.

Human security challenges – lack of freedom from want

Perhaps the most serious and immediate human security threat to the most vulnerable sections of East Timorese society is that posed by food insecurity. Food security is a measure of ensured access to essential nutrition. The World Health Organization defines three facets of food security: food availability, food access, and food use. Food availability is having available sufficient quantities of food on a consistent basis. Food access is having sufficient resources, both economic and physical, to obtain appropriate foods for a nutritious diet. Food use is the appropriate use based on knowledge of basic nutrition and care, as well as adequate water and sanitation (WHO, 2006). To this can be added a fourth facet: the stability of the first three dimensions of food security over time (FAO, 2006).

All of these face impediments in Timor-Leste, with sporadic outbreaks of famine, significant sections of the population malnourished or lacking access to adequate water and sanitation, increasing food prices, shortages of dietary staples, scarcity of arable land, and the impact of natural disasters (Dolven *et al.*, 2012, p. 9). Indeed, almost half of all children under the age of five are malnourished, while about half of the country's population lives with extreme hunger (World Vision, 2012). Chronic malnutrition among children in Timor-Leste thus remains very high, although the situation is improving, and one-third of children under the age of five and one-third of all women suffer from anemia (Timor-Leste, 2011, p. 35).

Despite the overwhelming majority of East Timorese living and working in rural communities, the harvests are not sufficient in terms of quantity or quality to sustain the population, and the country is still a net importer of foodstuffs. The people of Timor-Leste have a long history of malnutrition and chronic food shortages, and this problem has continued unabated and, indeed, has been worsened by the continuing drought that affected the region, despite government attempts in 2008 to alleviate the problem by purchasing more foodstuffs on the international market (Kingsbury, 2009, p. 365). Oxfam (2008, p. 4) found that food insecurity in Timor-Leste is likely to continue to pose a serious problem with 70 per cent of households moderately to severely food insecure.

Access to water is also problematic, with shortages severely impacting on crop abundance as well as sanitation and drinking water supply. Water has always been a critical resource in Timor-Leste, where much of the country is covered in shallow rocky soils that are alkaline, are not particularly fertile, do not store water well, and easily erode (Barnett *et al.*, 2007, p. 373). Climate change could, however, result in a drier dry season; rain may fall as fewer but more intense events; El Niño events, which result in delayed rain and less rain, may become more severe; all of which may exacerbate Timor-Leste's existing problems with drought, floods, and water quality (*ibid.*, p. 374).

There are problems with the types of crops grown in Timor-Leste. Maize is the most abundant and the most important source of food supply. It is grown in shallow soils on steep slopes using shifting cultivation practices involving burning existing vegetation (up to 20 per cent of landmass of the entire country at any one time) and planting seeds in the ashes. 'In mountainous areas, population densities are sufficiently high, and the amount of land available restricted because of coffee plantations, that there is not enough land to allow for sufficient periods of fallow for this to be an ecologically sustainable form of production' (*ibid.*, p. 376). This means a vicious cycle of changing rainfall regimes, declining yields, soil erosion, and nutrient depletion. In recent years, declining maize yields have seriously imperiled the food security of several regions in Timor-Leste (Oxfam, 2008, p. 5). Meanwhile rice production, the second most important food crop in Timor-Leste in terms of volume produced, yields far less per hectare than comparable fields in the rest of Southeast Asia, again as a result of soil quality and climate limiting most to a single crop per year, and where a second crop is produced, to a very low second harvest. Coffee, the major cash crop, is also vulnerable to water shortages and climate change, but faces becoming increasingly unviable due to decline in real terms of global coffee prices. Many of the causes of problems surrounding poor crop selection and food insecurity can, however, be laid at the feet of colonial and neo-colonial administrations of Timor-Leste.

Historically, rather than maize and rice, many rural communities in Timor-Leste have cultivated cassava, an extremely drought-tolerant and good source of carbohydrates, as well as a wide range of perennial food crops such as orange, pawpaw, mango, jackfruit, banana, and coconut. Cassava is cultivated for household consumption and as a livestock feed is stored in the ground and harvested on demand and, along with the other traditional crops, constitutes an important source of household food security and diet diversity (Oxfam, 2008, p. 5). Unfortunately, these crops do not generate much in the way of income, thus cultivation prioritization shifted under the Portuguese to coffee, and under the Indonesian administration, to rice (which also reflected a shift in diet), as well as a continuous shift toward maize under both, which has resulted in its current place of dominance. Increased demand for rice, in part due to the massive influx of international agencies, has been reflected in the market, where a 50 kg bag sufficient to feed a family now costs over US$20 while many try to survive on 50 cents per day (Akara, 2011). This is exacerbated among poorer sections of society where extended families of five to six people are routinely dependent on a single source of income, or the income from several under- or irregularly employed members of the family. The final analytical section looks at additional consequences of external governance for human security in Timor-Leste.

Imperial and neo-imperial legacies

As might be expected, Portuguese and Indonesian administrations had serious direct consequences for the human security of the people of Timor-Leste. Long after these colonial powers had abdicated their respective periods of governance, however, the enduring legacies of their rule continue to impact negatively on the chances of securing freedom from want and freedom from fear. Furthermore, although, on the whole, the presence of the UN, Australia, and other members of the international community in post-colonial Timor-Leste has contributed substantively to securing freedom from fear; in some areas relating to freedom from want, the impact of these actors and their representatives has been less positive, and potentially even counter-productive. Given the *de facto* governance of Timor-Leste by international actors, even post-independence, these negative impacts will be referred to as neo-imperial legacies.

The first imperial legacy is that of linguistic division. For instance, the predominant use of Portuguese for legislation, legal decisions, and state-operated accreditation has divided the ruling elite from the population as a whole, with less than 10 per cent of the population speaking the language well (Marriott, 2012, p. 59). This was further complicated by the proliferation of Indonesian as the language of governance during the period of occupation, and then English during the Australian-led UN administration. Linguistic barriers not only exclude the least empowered sections of society but they also undermine nation-building as opposed to state-building, as demonstrated by the violence of pro-Indonesian militia after the vote for independence. Ethnic groups that existed prior to the colonial interlude were further reflected in the broad linguistic divide that characterized much of the conflict of 2006 and the 2007 elections in which 'FRETILIN won most strongly in areas identified with the east in the 2006 conflict, and in which parties that came to form the coalition AMP government identified with the west during the conflict' (Kingsbury, 2012b, p. 21).

The second legacy is a geographic one to which this chapter has already alluded, whereby development and resources are concentrated in Dili. As a result, human security challenges in rural and remote communities are perpetuated. This concentration can also, however, have negative impacts within Dili itself. In the capital, wage inflation as a result of high demand among international agencies and NGOs for local personnel has driven wages up to an unsustainable level above that of relatively wealthy Malaysia, and well above that of neighboring Indonesia (Akara, 2011). During the artificial boom created by the international presence in Timor-Leste, growth was primarily generated by consumption (Doraisami, 2009, pp. 166–7). With the drawdown of the international presence, there is a danger of an economic slump. In addition, high levels of capital flight and repatriation of funds to Indonesia have resulted in as much as 70 per cent of each dollar leaving the country (de Vasconcelos,

2011). Linked to the divide between the metropolis and the rest of the country is the evolving relationship between traditional and modern forms of political authority in local government and a 'clash of paradigms' between traditional and liberal democratic ideas of legitimacy (Cummins and Leach, 2012, p. 89). Ongoing land disputes between groups, each claiming legitimacy based on different traditions, further complicate geographic colonial legacies.

The third set of divisive imperial legacies concerns the residue of anti-imperial resistance experiences. Some groups ended up being perceived as collaborators. Others left Timor-Leste to pursue the struggle through international support and networking. Still others stayed to fight. Each group has continued legitimacy problems when claiming to act on behalf of the whole of the East Timorese people when elected or elevated to positions of governance authority. Each has perpetuated divisions in politics, the military, the police, and civil society groups. These linguistic, geographic, and historical legacies of imperialism are mutually reinforcing. To a certain extent they have also been stimulated by the experience of decolonization and independence, competition for the new state's resources, and removal of the common imperial enemy. The midwifery of the UN administration and the roles of other international actors have also however left negative legacies.

Gusmão himself claimed that the UN intervention must bear some of the blame for the events of 2006 as it did not do an adequate job in preparing East Timor for independence, lacked respect for local culture, and the conspicuous consumption of the UN bureaucracy was an affront to the mass poverty surrounding them (Paul, 2010, p. 112). Mericio Akara (2011), founder of Luta Hamatuk, concurs, asking where the money went, while noting that if the US$9 billion emergency aid from 2000 to 2002 had been spent in accordance with good governance and planning, the ongoing problems would be nowhere near as severe. The main problem he argues is that it was spent on consumption rather than investment. While West Timor's budget of US$400 million stretches to cover 4 million citizens, in Timor-Leste, US$1.3 billion is spent on 1.1 million citizens. Francisco M. de Vasconcelos (2011) blames the discrepancy on too many international advisors. Exclusionary practices and the lack of capacity-building increased reliance on outsiders and led to local wariness about imposed and unreliable systems while 'new institutions have not tended to provide human security or protection' (Stanley, 2007, p. 131).

Meanwhile, Erik Paul (2010, p. 113) notes that, 'while Australia spent more than A$2 billion on its military intervention, what was needed was an equivalent Marshall plan to put the country on its feet'. Ines Martins (2011) of La'o Hamatuk likewise criticizes international organizations for paying attention to physical security when the biggest problems faced in Timor-Leste were the other societal sectors such as colonial legacies, the need for justice, accountability of perpetrators, rural poverty, and land rights. And for Elizabeth Stanley (2007, p. 125), 'overall, international state-building has contributed to an insecure Timor-Leste, has intensified divisions and conflict, deepened poverty, and encouraged a culture of dependency on external actors, shaping conditions under which further harms and crimes, including transnational crimes, have occurred and will occur'.

Conclusion

While Stanley's view may be a little overly pessimistic, and there have been some very real progress made in Timor-Leste by both national and international governance authorities. These legacies demonstrate that the job is at best only half done, and that it is time to refocus efforts on the broader aspects of human security and the distribution of development benefits to the most vulnerable sections of society.

This has been recognized by the government in its *Strategic Development Plan 2011–2030* which aims at working toward Timor-Leste becoming a nation with a 'well-educated and skilled population, quality universal health care, good infrastructure, a strong private sector operating in a diversified economy and a prosperous society with adequate income, food and shelter for all our people' (Timor-Leste, 2011, p. 18). In the summary of strategies, actions, and targets, the main goal categories in the short-, medium- and long-term identified as social capital include education and training, health, social inclusion, environment, culture, and heritage (*ibid.*, pp. 220–2).

References

Akara, Mericio (2011) Interview with Author, Dili, Timor-Leste, 5 August 2011.

Arnold, M. B. (2009) 'Challenges Too Strong for the Nascent State of Timor-Leste: Petitioners and Mutineers', *Asian Survey,* 49(3), 429–49.

Arnold, M. B. (2011) 'Timor-Leste in 2010: The Window for a "Normal" Future?', *Asian Survey,* 51(1), 215–20.

Asahi, H. (2012) 'An Uneasy Future for East Timor', http://www2.jiia.or.jp/en/pdf/research/20120628e-An_Uneasy_Future_of_East_Timor.pdf.

BBC (2012) 'East Timor: UN Ends Peacekeeping Mission', BBC, 31 December 2012, http://www.bbc.co.uk/news/world-asia-20873267.

Barnett, J., Suraje, D. and Roger, N. J. (2007) 'Vulnerability to Climate Variability and Change in East Timor', *Ambio,* 36(5), 372–8.

Benzing, M. (2005) 'Midwifing a New State: The United Nations in East Timor' in A. von Bogdandy and R. Wolfrum (eds), *Max Planck Yearbook of United Nations Law,* vol. 9, pp. 295–372 (Leiden: Brill).

4th High Level Forum on Aid Effectiveness (Busan) (2012) *The New Deal for Engagement in Fragile States,* http://www.aideffectiveness.org/busanhlf4/images/stories/hlf4/english.pdf.

Cummins, D. and Leach, M. (2012) 'Democracy Old and New: The Interaction of Modern and Traditional Authority in East Timorese Local Government', *Asian Politics & Policy,* 4(1), 89–104.

Della-Giacoma, J. (2011) 'Timor-Leste's Veterans: An Unfinished Struggle?' International Crisis Group, http://www.crisisgroup.org/en/regions/asia/south-east-asia/timor-leste/B129-timor-lestes-veterans-an-unfinished-struggle.aspx.

Della-Giacoma, J. (2012a) 'Timor-Leste: Everybody Needs Good Neighbours', International Crisis Group, http://www.crisisgroup.org/en/regions/asia/south-east-asia/op-eds/della-giacoma-timor-leste-everybody-needs-good-neighbours.aspx.

Della-Giacoma, J. (2012b) 'Has Timor-Leste Left Behind Its Violent Past?', International Crisis Group, http://www.crisisgroupblogs.org/resolvingconflict/2012/07/09/has-timor-leste-left-behind-its-violent-past/?utm_source=wu9july&utm_medium=timorlesteblog&utm_campaign=wuemail.

de Vasconcelos, F. M. (2011) Program Manager for Luta Hamatuk and Member of the Petro Fund Council, Interview with Author, Dili, Timor-Leste, 4 August 2011.

Dolven, B., Rhoda, M. and Vaughn, B. (2012) 'Timor-Leste: Political Dynamics, Development, and International Involvement', *Congressional Research Service,* July 3.

Doraisami, A. (2009) 'Fiscal Policy Challenges in Timor Leste: Is the Resources Curse on the Horizon?', *ASEAN Economic Bulletin,* 26(2), 164–73.

Easttimorgovernment, http://www.easttimorgovernment.com/, 14 March 2013.

The Economist (2013) 'The Fastest-Growing Economies of 2013: Speed is Not Everything', 2 January 2013, http://www.economist.com/blogs/theworldin2013/2013/01/fastest-growing-economies-2013.

Farsetta, D. (2004) 'Women Call for Justice', *Off Our Backs,* 34(3/4), 51–2.

Food and Agriculture Organization of the UN (FAO) (2006) 'Food Security', *Policy Brief,* June 2006, Issue 2, 1.

Groves, Gabrielle Eva Carol, Bernadette P. Resurreccion and Philippe Doneys (2009) 'Keeping the Peace is Not Enough: Human Security and Gender-based Violence during the Transitional Period of Timor-Leste', *Sojourn: Journal of Social Issues in Southeast Asia,* 24(2), 186–210.

Guterres, J. C. (2008) 'Timor Leste: A Year of Democratic Elections', *Southeast Asian Affairs,* (Singapore: Institute of Southeast Asian Studies) 359–72.

Hodal, K. (2012) 'Timor-Leste Strives to Overcome Culture of Domestic Violence', *The Guardian,* 24 August 2012, http://www.guardian.co.uk/global-development/2012/aug/24/timor-leste-strives-overcome-domestic-violence.

Kingsbury, D. (2009) 'East Timor in 2008: Year of Reconstruction', *Southeast Asian Affairs,* (Singapore: Institute of Southeast Asian Studies) 357–69.

Kingsbury, D. (2012a) 'East Timor 10 Years On and the Two Saving Graces', *Crikey,* 18 May 2012, http://www.crikey.com.au/2012/05/18/east-timor-10-years-on-and-the-two-saving-graces/?wpmp_switcher=mobile.

Kingsbury, D. (2012b) 'Challenges of Constructing Postcolonial Unity: Timor-Leste as a Case Study', *Asian Politics & Policy,* 4(1), 15–32.

Macaulay, J. (2003) 'Timor Leste: Newest and Poorest of Asian Nations', *Geography,* 88(1), 40–6.

Marriott, A. (2012) 'Justice Sector Dynamics in Timor-Leste: Institutions and Individuals', *Asian Politics & Policy,* 4(1), 53–71.

Martins, I. (2011) Board Member of La'oHamatuk, Interview with author, Dili, Timor-Leste, 4 August 2011.

Maternal Mortality Portal 'South-East Asia', http://maternalmortalityportal.org/taxonomy/term/13.

Nolan, C. (2012) '"Trickery" and the Rule of Law in Timor-Leste', International Crisis Group, http://www.crisisgroupblogs.org/resolvingconflict/2012/12/11/trickery-and-the-rule-of-law-in-timor-leste/.

Organisation for Economic Co-operation and Development (OECD) (2007) *Principles for Good International Engagement in Fragile States and Institutions,* http://www.oecd.org/development/incaf/38368714.pdf.

Oxfam (2008) *Timor Leste Food Security Baseline Survey Report,* http://www.oxfam.org.nz/resources/Timor-Leste%20Food-Security-Baseline-Survey.pdf.

Paul, E. (2010) *Obstacles to Democratization in Southeast Asia: A Study of the Nation State, Regional and Global Order* (Basingstoke: Macmillan).

Ramos-Horta, J. (2012) 'We Are Learning How to Reconcile Plural Interests in Timorese Society', Praxis: A Review of Policy Practice, *Asian Politics & Policy*, 4(1), 105–18.

Reddy, R. (2011) Senior Gender Advisor to UNMIT, Interview with author, Dili, Timor-Leste, 4 August 2011.

Sahin, S. B. (2007) 'Building the State in Timor-Leste', *Asian Survey*, 47(2), 250–67.

Saikia, U. and Hosgelen, M. (2010) 'Timor-Leste's Demographic Destiny and Its Implications for the Health Sector by 2020', *Journal of Population Research,* 27(2), 133–46.

Shoesmith, D. (2012) 'Is Small Beautiful? Multiparty Politics and Democratic Consolidation in Timor-Leste', *Asian Politics & Policy,* 4(1), 33–51.

Siapno, J. (2006) 'Timor Lest: On a Path to Authoritarianism?', *Southeast Asian Affairs,* 1, 325–42.

Silva, R. and Ball, P. (2006) *The Profile of Human Rights Violations in Timor-Leste, 1974–1999*. A Report by the Benetech Human Rights Data Analysis Group to the Commission on Reception, Truth and Reconciliation of Timor-Leste.

Simonsen, S. G. (2006) 'The Authoritarian Temptation in East Timor: Nationbuilding and the Need for Inclusive Governance', *Asian Survey*, 46(4), 575–96.

Smith, A. L. (2002) 'Timor Leste, Timor Timur, East Timor, Timor Lorosa'e: What's in a Name?', *Southeast Asian Affairs*, 54–77.

Stanley, E. (2007) 'Transnational Crime and State-Building: The Case of Timor-Leste', *Social Justice*, 34(2), 124–37.

Government of the Republic of Timor-Leste (Timor-Leste) (2011) *Strategic Development Plan 2011–2030,* Dili.

United Nations Development Programme (UNDP) (2012) 'Timor-Leste Country Profile: Human Development Indicators 2011', http://hdrstats.undp.org/en/countries/profiles/TLS.html.

United Nations Foundation (UN Foundation) (2002) 'United Nations Peacekeeping Success Story: East Timor Celebrates First Independence Day', http://www.unfoundation.org/news-and-media/press-releases/2005-1997/2002/un-peacekeeping-sucess-story-east-timor.html.

United Nations Population Fund (UNFPA) (2011) *State of the World's Midwifery,* http://www.unfpa.org/sowmy/resources/docs/country_info/profile/en_TimorLeste_SoWMy_Profile.pdf.

Wilson, Bu V. E. (2012) 'To 2012 and Beyond: International Assistance to Police and Security Sector Development in Timor-Leste', *Asian Politics & Policy,* 4(1), 73–88.

World Bank (2011) 'Timor-Leste Overview', http://www.worldbank.org/en/country/timor-leste/overview.

World Health Organization (WHO) 'Food Security', http://www.who.int/trade/glossary/story028/en/.

World Vision (2012) 'Supporting Our Neighbours in Timor-Leste with 40 Hour Famine Funds', http://www.famine.org.nz/documents/EastTimor.aspx.

Part III
East Asian Actors

9
Human Security and Japanese Strategic Aid

Introduction

Of the three East Asian economic power houses, Japan may be seen as first among equals in terms of providing for human security and development in the region. Japan was the first East Asian country to graduate to membership of the OECD and also to join the OECD DAC, leading to unprecedented contributions to international development assistance and regional human security. Not surprisingly, following Japan's remarkable post-war boom and evolution into an economic powerhouse, other regional economies looked to follow Tokyo's lead with policies such as Malaysia's 'Look East', and the 'Learn from Japan', campaigns of both Laos and Singapore contributing to a perception both within and outside the region of a 'flying geese' mode of East Asian capitalism with Japan as the lead goose.

Thus, the first way in which Japan has contributed to human security and development in the region is as a benchmark or paradigmatic example of good development governance. Japan has also, however, provided a model of action and leadership in independent non-military foreign policy carried out in the shadow of a close, even stifling relationship with the global leader, the United States. Japan's role in the development of regional human security action is a model of what can be achieved by a medium-ranked power in terms of making an international issue its own and serving as a normative 'shining city on the hill' in much the same way that the United States is reputed to do in terms of the global promotion of Western liberal political and economic values.

This chapter, however, also addresses several related criticisms of Japan's role in the promotion and protection of human security in both theory and practice in the East Asian region. First, that successive administrations in

This chapter benefited from significant research assistance from Suyoun Jang and also contributions from Tsukasa Takamine.

Japan have prioritized Japanese interests in their international aid and assistance policies. Second, that Japan does not really have a coherent foreign and security policy, and that the human security paradigm is no substitute as it has left the military behind in favor of bureaucratic administration and development implementation by the Ministry of Foreign Affairs (MOFA) and Japan International Cooperation Agency (JICA) (Ho, 2008, p. 101; Hynek, 2012b, p. 62). Third, that Japan's embrace of the human security paradigm was likewise motivated by self-interest and has waned whenever Tokyo has failed to get its way, as well as contributing to the schism between narrow and broad human security policy communities (Edström, 2008, pp. 109–10). This chapter considers each of these concerns in turn.

In terms of the foreign aid literature which has long been critical of Japan's prioritization of its own national interest in determining aid policy (Ensign, 1992; Schrader *et al.*, 1998), this chapter concedes that Japan has historically had a significantly higher ratio of tied to untied aid than many other donors, and also has often used soft loans instead of aid; nevertheless, regardless of motives and forms, Japan's contributions to Asian countries have been substantial, have been on the whole well-received, and have the potential to contribute a substantial positive effect on regional development. Furthermore, in recent years, Japan's ODA program has shifted its focus from physical capital development, which was a feature of Japan's aid programs for several decades, to human capital development, prioritizing those areas of well-being related to human security within recipient countries (Furuoka *et al.*, 2010).

This chapter also admits a lack of Japanese security policy and a failure to bring on board the military or responsibility to protect dimension of human security. In traditional security terms, Japan has been and continues to be 'reactive' with regards to the United States, and resistant to peacekeeping, peace-building, and humanitarian intervention initiatives under the R2P. Nevertheless, ODA and other forms of international assistance can be viewed not only as an area of autonomous Japanese foreign policy formation that defies the reactivist hypothesis, but even as an alternative form of security policy formation. Non-military assistance continues to be the means by which the Japanese government promotes the comprehensive human security agenda internationally simultaneously with its national interest. Through economic and development assistance, Japan can improve not only the human security of neighboring countries, but also its own comprehensive security, leading to a greater strategic commitment. In terms of leaving behind the narrower security dimensions of human security promoted by Canada, this can also yield benefits in terms of the acceptability of Japanese intervention and engagement in regional challenging case studies in contrast to that of the West, as highlighted in Chapter 7 on Burma/Myanmar.

Finally, this chapter agrees with critics that Japanese multilateral initiatives in the field of human security do appear to have slowed somewhat following the unsuccessful parallel strategic drive to gain a permanent seat in the UNSC in the late 1990s, and the uncertainty of party politics culminating in the defeat of the Liberal Democratic Party (LDP) in 2009 by the Democratic Party of Japan (DPJ) (Edström, 2011, p. 44). It also concedes that perhaps the achievements in terms of bottom-line results have been less than satisfactory. Nevertheless, the inspirational and aspirational contributions Japan has made to the region endure, with other actors taking up the baton. Furthermore, within Japan, the non-military approach to the pursuit of strategic interests remains the only game in town, given the absence of sufficient support from internal and external constituencies for a more assertive military option (Furuoka *et al.*, 2010). It remains the official doctrinal focus point of the key agencies, and given the bureaucratic inertia of Japanese governmental decision-making is unlikely to be replaced any time soon. The major political parties have failed to produce clear policy choices to the voters; thus, human security remains the default foreign policy preference. Hence the Japanese government will continue to promote a broad human security agenda but distinct from the R2P mission.

All-in-all, therefore, this chapter contends that Japanese policy initiatives have impacted significantly in a positive manner on human security and development in East Asia while simultaneously fulfilling Japanese strategic agendas. Due to incremental drift in Tokyo's policy-making and the lack of constituencies supporting radical alternatives, this set of circumstances is likely to persist for the foreseeable future. This in turn potentially ensures greater commitment by Tokyo toward regional challenging case studies than may be the case from strategically less interested Western actors, and also a greater receptivity among recipients of Japanese assistance due to its non-military and non-interventionary focus. This chapter therefore addresses the positive impact of Japanese commitment to human security and development agendas in East Asia.

Japanese aid

Despite a long history and continuous efforts to improve socioeconomic conditions in recipient countries, Japan's aid-giving activities have rarely received positive evaluations on the international level, and Japan has received little respect as an aid-giving country (Furuoka *et al.*, 2010). Margee Ensign (1992) noted that in the 1990s, despite assertions by Japanese officials that aid had been 'untied', Japanese aid remains substantially tied to Japanese business interests. Indeed, according to the neo-mercantile commercial self-interest thesis, Japanese aid is purely or substantially a commercially motivated policy, largely premised on commercial benefit to private Japanese companies, or increased access to markets and raw materials (Long, 1999, pp. 328–9). Yet recipients of Japanese assistance, even if, due to the degree to which it fulfills Japanese interests, it cannot be considered largesse, nevertheless have received significant development boosts, and, it will be argued here, the most vulnerable peoples of the region have received significant collateral benefit in human security terms.

As can be seen in Figure 9.1, Japan is by far the largest contributor of ODA to Asia with around 30 per cent of total ODA disbursements to the region. Figure 9.2 shows that Asia, and particularly East Asia, historically has received the largest proportion of Japanese ODA.

Much of this aid has been targeted toward Japan's greatest regional rival, China. Since the start of its official China aid program in 1979, successive

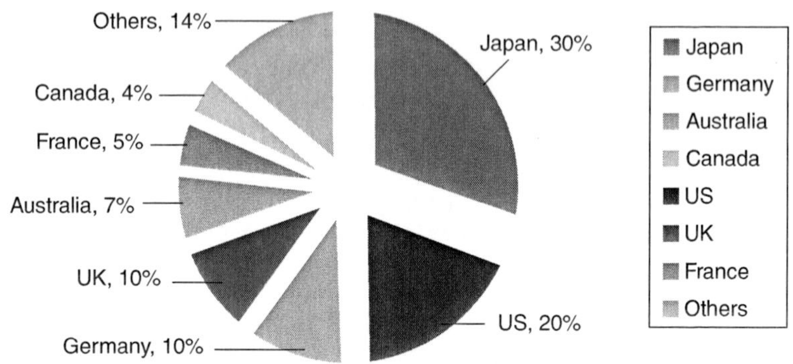

Figure 9.1 OECD/DAC's ODA disbursements to Asia, 2007–08 average
Source: 'DRC 2010 Statistical Annex' in Development Co-operation Report 2010, OECD.

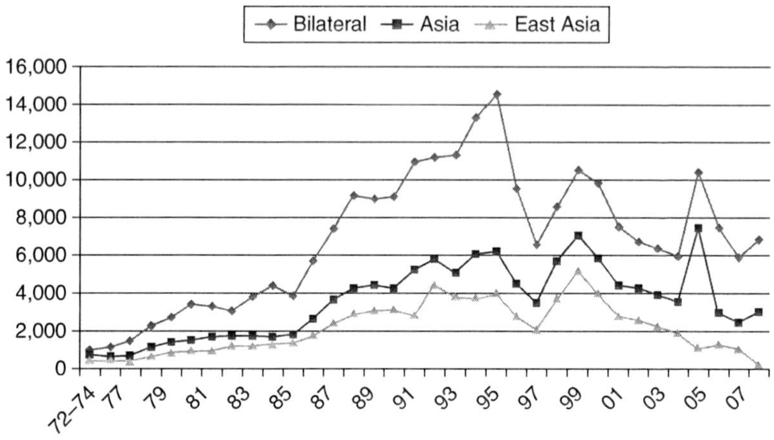

Figure 9.2 Japanese ODA disbursements to Asia, US$ million
Source: OECD, Query Wizard for International Development Statistics.

Japanese governments consistently have provided China with ODA in the form of government loans, grant aid, and technical cooperation. In terms of net-disbursement, the cumulative total of Japanese ODA to China from 1979 to 2008 approaches US$21 billion. Among China's aid donors, Japan is easily the largest. As revealed in Figure 9.3, Japan provided more than 50 per cent of China's total bilateral ODA between 1979 and 1998, while Germany and France, the next most important ODA donors for China, provided 15 per cent and 5 per cent respectively on average.

For political, economic, and ethical reasons, Japanese governments have actively directed aid to China with the aim of steering China in an economically sustainable, socially stable, and politically liberal direction. The fact that they have done so because it suits Japan's national economic and security interests to have a large, more positively disposed, less threatening trading neighbor does not necessarily lessen the importance of Japan's aid policy to China from the recipient's perspective.

Japan's development assistance whether in terms of ODA or soft loans can be seen as having contributed to China's phenomenal economic growth and increasing openness, by supporting the development of infrastructure, foreign direct investment (FDI), and trade. Although it is statistically impossible conclusively to prove the causality of Japanese assistance upon Chinese development, a positive, albeit indirect, link between Japanese ODA and/or soft loans and the growth and globalization of the Chinese economy works as follows: (1) Japanese assistance contributed to the development of China's industrial infrastructure, (2) the strengthening of Chinese infrastructure

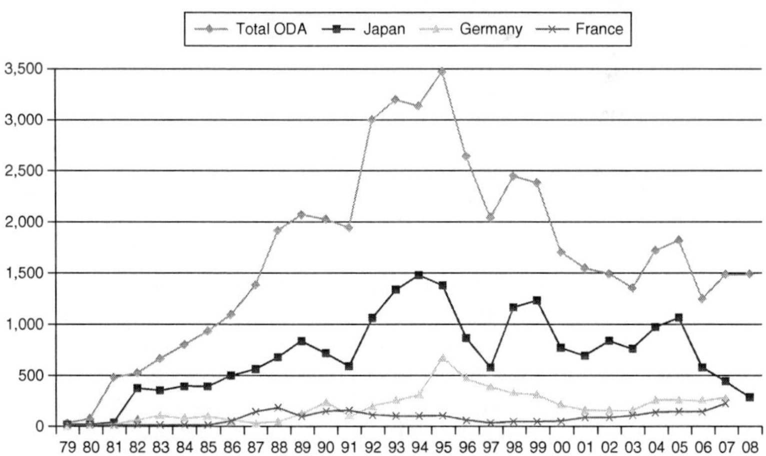

Figure 9.3 ODA disbursements to China (USD million)

Source: OECD Query Wizard (2012) for International Development Statistics.

attracted and facilitated the inflow of FDI from MNCs around the world into China, (3) these FDI encouraged the expansion and diversification of China's foreign trade, and (4) the expanded and diversified Chinese foreign trade promoted economic development and the incorporation of the Chinese economy into the market-based global economic system.

FDI inflows from MNCs around the world have been the major driving force behind the rapid development and globalization of the Chinese economy (Hilpert and Nakagani, 2002; Fu, 2004). By helping fund the development of industrial infrastructure in China during the 1980s and 1990s, however, Japanese assistance conceivably also contributed to facilitate the inflow of FDI. For example, during the period from 1979 to 1998, yen loans contributed to the construction of 38 per cent (or 3842 kilometers) of China's total electric rail network, 25 per cent of its total chemical fertilizer production, 13 per cent of its total port facilities, and 3 per cent of its total power-generating capability. During this period, yen loans also contributed to the building of 35 per cent of China's sewage control facilities, which can deal with 4 million tons of sewage per day.

The financial contribution of Japanese assistance to the development of industrial infrastructure in China was especially significant during the 1980s when the nation suffered a severe foreign currency shortage (Inada, 2001). China's economic development and the rapid expansion of a market-based economy, which Japan assisted through ODA, have also generated a profound social transformation in China at both the institutional and structural levels. Institutional transformation in China refers to the change from a highly centralized planned economic system to a more market-oriented economic system, or what the Chinese government calls a socialist market economy. On the other hand, structural transformation means the change from a traditional China, characterized by agriculture, village and closed society, to a modern society, characterized by industry, urbanization, and openness (Hishida, 2000).

Japan has also given a high priority to Southeast Asia and has been the region's largest aid donor since the late the 1970s (Yanagihara and Emig, 1991, p. 37; Paul, 1996, p. 394). It is stipulated in the Japanese ODA charter that Asia, in particular member countries of the ASEAN, 'will continue to be a priority region for Japan's ODA' for historical, geographical, political and economic reasons (MOFA, 2003). Again, there are sound strategic reasons for perceived Japanese largesse in the sub-region. Japan craves the markets and raw materials which could be opened up through development, but Japan have to overcome not only the historical legacy of mistrust following the region's experience of the Greater East Asia Co-Prosperity Sphere but also the current and future challenge of China's influence.

Beijing's 'charm offensive' toward its neighbors contrasts with recent unilateral, illiberal, and 'charmless' US policy, and the policies historically pursued by Japan itself (Kurlantzick, 2006). Nevertheless, once again, as Japan attempts to gain political capital, there are substantial collateral benefits for the region. Indonesia, Thailand, the Philippines, Malaysia, Myanmar, and Vietnam consistently feature in the top ten recipients of Japan's ODA and Japan's share of total ODA flows to those countries have been in the order of 50 per cent to 80 per cent (see Table 9.1 below).

As in China, Japanese assistance (both ODA and loans) has supported the industrial development of Southeast Asia by investing in the building of infrastructure. Japan's policies toward Southeast Asia have, however, experienced dramatic changes with, in essence, three phases of contributions to the sub-region: war reparation payments (1950s–60s); ODA, FDI, and trade expansion (1970s–80s); and the evolution of Japanese assistance as human security-based ODA (1990s–present) (Hirono, 2001).

Japan's aid policy toward Southeast Asia began with war reparations to Burma in 1954. Japan established a Fund for the Economic Development of Southeast Asia in the Eximbank of Japan to assist Southeast Asian countries to promote their economic development and had provided US$1,152 million in damages and US$737 million in loans by the end of the 1960s. In addition, as Japan achieved rapid economic growth with an average annual rate of 10 per cent, its aid grew exponentially (Sueo, 2002). In the following period from the 1970s to 1980s, Japan provided huge amounts of assistance, in particular soft yen loans to Southeast Asia. In 1977, when Japan's reparation payments came to an end, Tokyo designed an 'aid-doubling plan' which was successfully implemented as Japan's ODA (US$1.4 billion) in 1977, and more than doubled by the end of 1980 to US$3.3 billion and reached US$10 billion in 1988 (*ibid.*).

Table 9.1 The top five DAC Countries ODA disbursements to Southeast Asian countries, 1967–2007 average (per cent)

	1	2	3	4	5
Cambodia	Japan (17.5)	United States	France	Australia	Germany
Indonesia	Japan (45.9)	United States	Australia	Germany	Netherlands
Laos	Japan (22.7)	United States	Sweden	France	Germany
Malaysia	Japan (61.9)	Australia	United Kingdom	Germany	Denmark
Myanmar	Japan (46)	Germany	Australia	United Kingdom	United States
Philippines	Japan (50.4)	United States	Germany	Australia	Netherlands
Thailand	Japan (54.3)	United States	Germany	Australia	France
Viet Nam	Japan (23.9)	United States	Sweden	France	Germany

Source: OECD, DAC Development Database on Aid.

Around 60 per cent of assistance was allocated to expansion and improvement of road, transport, telecommunications, and power infrastructures, as well as agriculture and industry (OECD DAC, 1999). This helped improve the environment for investment by foreign capital and utilize the vitality of the private sectors. In Indonesia, this included the construction and renovation of 12 per cent (or 799 kilometers) of its railway systems, the construction of 15 per cent (or 56 kilometers) of its toll roads, the construction of 60 per cent of the intra-city communication transmission cable conduit system of Jakarta, and the construction of 54 per cent of the city's water filtration facilities (9,600 tone/second) (MOFA, 1994). In the case of the Philippines, the second largest recipient, more than 60 per cent of aid was spent on infrastructure projects such as transport, education, and public work. At the same time, Japan began to open up its market and promoted the expansion of FDI (Soesastro, 2004).

More than half of Japanese FDI has been implemented in Southeast Asia and focused on manufacturing sectors such as food and textile industries, electrical machinery, telecommunication equipment, and domestic electric goods. This has helped develop the domestic private sector, promoted exports, and thus helped modernization and industrialization of Southeast Asian countries (Blaise, 2009). Japan has also been particularly supportive in political and economic terms of the process of ASEAN integration, facilitating the construction of a zone of peace within which freedom from fear has been considerably enhanced, and as a result of which a peace dividend has been generated and win-win economic cooperation encouraged (Yoshimatsu and Trinidad, 2010). Essentially Japanese aid has been politicized, and even securitized, but has nevertheless contributed in a number of positive ways to development and human security first in China and then throughout Southeast Asia. The next section considers the extent to which strategic aid and human security have gravitated toward the programmatic core of Japanese foreign and security policy, thereby forming part of Japanese national interest and ensuring continued commitment.

Strategic aid and human security in Japanese policy-making

Bert Edström (2003, p. 220) has argued that Japanese human security is concerned almost exclusively with economic development and humanitarianism rather than national security policy. Likewise, Nik Hynek (2012b, p. 62) attests that 'in the Japanese case more than in any other the profound separation of the military from the rest of the state apparatus has been responsible for the country's inability to bridge peacekeeping and peace-enforcement practices with human security'. On the other hand, Hynek (2012a, p. 120) also points out the errors of the 'general belief that the Japanese approach has always rested on humanitarian and non-military solutions and has not been primarily shaped by political motives'. He emphasizes that 'once the international and domestic sides of Japanese human security are put under the microscope together, Japanese human security can no longer be understood as resting on either liberal values or a combination of liberal values and "Asian' values" but rather through a "domopolitical" diagram concerned with national security' (*ibid.,* p. 121). The combination of international and domestic constraints is what gives Japanese strategic policy-making in general, and its human security prioritization in particular, its distinctive characteristics. Japanese policy is fundamentally non-military as a result of internal constraints, but it is certainly still concerned with security, both national and human.

Constrained by its pacifist constitution and lingering animosity in the region over Japan's historic role, planners have looked to non-traditional security policies to further Japanese interests. These conditions have provided added impetus for successive Japanese governments to develop non-military concepts of security and to practice them in order to play a leadership role in the global politico-strategic sphere. In particular, the emergence of the human security concept within security discourse allowed the country to combine its traditional regional aid operations with an initiative with global reach.

Kent Calder (1988), the originator of the 'reactive state' hypothesis sees Japan as occupying the unique position of having the power potential of a mid-range European state, yet the political leverage of much smaller and weaker reactive states. Perhaps most importantly, Calder claims that the fragmented character of state authority in Japan makes decisive action more difficult than in countries with strong chief executives, such as the United States thereby explaining Japanese passivity in international affairs when activism would have been both possible and beneficial for Japan (*ibid.,* pp. 518–28). Such has been the impact of Calder's hypothesis that the dominant view of Japan's international behavior is one where Japan is portrayed as passive, risk-avoiding, and ineffective in conducting foreign policy (Hirata, 1998, p. 1).

Calder (2006) more recently claimed that his major contentions have weathered the test of time, noting that Japan has not, despite a huge economy, emerged as an effective 'rule-maker' in international affairs. Koji Taira (1991, pp. 161–2) concurs, noting that 'Japan has a psychological disadvantage in dealing with the United States, which relegates it to the status of junior partner or pupil'. This deference toward the United States finds its way into official Japanese government publications in which the United States is viewed as the 'most important country for Japan', and the Japan-US security system is viewed as 'central to the relationship' (Task Force, 2002). Deference to and security dependence on the United States has even led Japan to be described as a 'semi-sovereign state' (Mearsheimer, 2001, p. 382). Japan is essentially seen as a power that inevitably bandwagons on the policy initiatives of the global hegemonic leader.

Other commentators have been even more dismissive of Japanese security policy – or rather its absence (Van Wolferen, 1990, pp. 5–26; Green, 2003, p. 1). Bad enough that Japan is a reactive state, but such interpretations imply that Japan does not even react. Indeed, even many Japanese do not believe Japan has a coherent security policy, but rather is left 'groping' (*mosaku*) for strategy (Samuels, 2007, p. 1). Indeed some seem uncertain whether Japan has any independent agenda, with Michael Green (2003, p. 11) challenging: '*Japanese* foreign policy? Let me know if you find any!!'.

ODA and other forms of international assistance can, however been seen not only as an area of autonomous Japanese foreign policy formation that defies the reactivist hypothesis, but even as an alternative form of security policy formation. William Long (1999) notes that although Japanese economic assistance can be a response to foreign (primarily United States) pressure (the so-called *gaiatsu* thesis), or can be motivated by Japan's desire to expand export and investment markets for Japanese firms (the neo-mercantile thesis), it can also be viewed as a form of 'comprehensive security'. Given internal and external structural constraints on the use of force, Japan has consistently tried to pursue its foreign policy through economic means such as ODA, FDI, and loans rather than by military means (Von Feigenblatt, 2007, p. 57).

Japan was at the forefront of moves to establish APEC, the ADB, East Asian Community, ASEAN+3, the East Asia Summit (EAS), the Six-Party Talks, and Economic Partnership Agreements with ASEAN countries and the Republic of Korea. Japan is the largest supporter of the ADB and has always held the presidency, and Japan continues to be the biggest trading partner, investing country, and ODA donor for ASEAN. Japan has followed a mixture of proactive and reactive policies to allay the misgivings of other Asian states.

This is particularly apparent when we consider Japanese policy toward Southeast Asia. Following violent anti-Japanese demonstrations in Southeast Asian capitals in 1974 during visits by then Premier Kakuei Tanaka, Prime Minister Takeo Fukuda announced in 1977 what was to become known as the 'Fukuda doctrine', which stated that Japan would reject a military role in the region in favor of 'heart-to-heart dialogues' (Singh, 2002, p. 284). This was a rational, clearly thought out, and ultimately effective non-traditional response to a threat to Japanese interests. Japan has continued with such overtures under successive administrations.

In the early 1980s, Japan adopted a 'comprehensive security' (*sogo anzen hosho*) policy under the direction of Prime Minister Zenko Suzuki (following the recommendations of a group commissioned by his predecessor Masayoshi Ohira from the National Institute for the Advancement of Research commissioned to study change in the international environment and Japan's response). Comprehensive security not only looked beyond the traditional security elements of individual self-defense by focusing on regional and global security arrangements but also stressed the need to take into account other aspects vital to national stability such as food, energy, environment, communication, and social security (Akaha, 1991; Radtke and Feddema, 2000). It was an explicitly inclusive approach that emphasized multilateralism, and the concept as such can be traced to Japanese thinking on security as far back as the fifties (Long, 1999).

In the 1990s, Japan more sharply defined the security-related goals related to offers of economic assistance, developing guidelines for distributing official foreign assistance, and an ODA Charter, that included a clear non-proliferation objective. 'In making aid decisions, policy makers were to consider the following policies in recipient states: (1) trends in military expenditures; (2) development and production of weapons of mass destruction and missiles; (3) exports or imports of arms; and (4) democratization efforts, development of market-oriented economies, and status of human rights and freedom' (*ibid.*, p. 329).

While human security was introduced to the mainstream of Japanese foreign policy by Prime Minister Keizo Obuchi in 1998, a similar concept was first outlined as a key foreign policy perspective and main objective of Japanese ODA disbursement in 1995 (Fukushima, 2003, p. 132). According to a speech by Prime Minister Tomiichi Murayama at the UN World Summit for Social Development held in Copenhagen in 1995, Japan was trying to create a 'human-centered society' and emphasized 'human-centered social development' as a focus of Japanese ODA (Murayama, 1995), thereby further embedding the notion of a strategic link between development, human security, and Japanese foreign and state security policy.

The recognition of the concept of human security in Japan is related to both the Asian financial crisis and the desire to play a bigger role in international society under the concept of proactive pacifism (Acharya and Acharya, 2000, p. 12; Soeya, 2005). The crisis had a devastating impact on Asia's economy, increasing poverty and political instability, and underscoring the crucial need for social safety nets for the poor and for a new understanding of security, focusing on Asian peoples rather than states. (Acharya and Acharya, 2000) In the context of the crisis, Prime Minister Keizo Obuchi delivered the following opening remarks at the 'Intellectual Dialogue on Building Asia's Tomorrow' on 2 December 1998:

> The current economic crisis has aggravated those strains, threatening the daily lives of many people. Taking this fact fully into consideration, I believe that we must deal with these difficulties with due consideration for the socially vulnerable segments of population, in the light of "Human Security", and that we must seek new strategies for economic development which attach importance to human security with a view to enhancing the long term development of our region ... "human security" is ... the key which comprehensively covers all the menaces that threaten

> the survival, daily life, and dignity of human beings and strengthens the efforts to confront those threats. (Obuchi, 1998a)

Obuchi committed to help Asian countries overcome crises and assist socially vulnerable people. He emphasized his perception of human security as being people- rather than state-centric, and that his understanding of human security was analogous to that of the UNDP. At 'the ASEAN+3 Summit' in Hanoi on December 16, he advanced a vision of human security as 'a comprehensive view of all threats to human survival, life and dignity' and as one of the three areas on which Asia should focus for a 'century of peace and prosperity', stressing the need to 'implement measures for the socially vulnerable who are affected by the Asian economic crisis'. The other two areas were Asia's recovery from economic crisis and the further promotion of intellectual dialogue to tackle numerous other challenges after overcoming the Asian economic crisis (Obuchi, 1998b).

Obuchi also contributed 500 million yen (US$4.2 million) for the establishment of the human security fund under the UN, (later renamed the United Nations Trust Fund for Human Security, UNTFHS), as an expression of Japan's commitment to promoting the paradigm and supporting related projects by UN agencies. Together, these speeches laid the foundation for the rise to prominence of human security as the main pillar of Japan's foreign policy agenda. With the fusion of human security and ODA, Japanese aid policy has been transformed into a vehicle for transporting the human security idea (Konrad, 2006, p. 22).

As previously mentioned, by focusing on the economic and development aspects of human security, and supporting wholeheartedly the broad approach outlined by the UNDP, Japan has been accused of contributing to a schism within the paradigm and community, placing the Japanese approach at odds with that of Western countries such as Canada and the Nordic states (Edström, 2008, pp. 109–10). Knowing the apprehension of developing countries toward the interventionary turn taken by other approaches, however, it is perhaps understandable that the Japanese government has focused on the developmental and economic aspect of human security (Edström, 2011, p. 21). Japan's ability to work in politically problematic and/or (post-) conflict territories has been facilitated by its approach to human security and development, with its discursive emphasis on human security welcomed as a 'particularly suitable replacement for Western liberal discourses on human rights, which are deeply unpopular in Asia and Africa' (Hynek, 2012a, p. 70).

This is still not to suggest, however, that Japanese human security promotion is somehow apolitical or entirely altruistic. Rather, policy-makers have identified a niche area where Japan can punch up to its weight in the international arena, if not above it, the pursuance of which will promote national interest at the same time as improving the image of Japan as a benevolent international actor. At the same time, collateral benefit accrues to the human security of the most vulnerable sections of Asian societies, and the concept is elevated on the global stage through Japanese support. As pointed out by Edström, 'it seems that countries pursuing policies on human security have devised them to fit policies where they have seen themselves having a comparative advantage' (2011, p. 25).

The concept of human security first appeared in *Japan's Diplomatic Bluebook* in 1999. It defined human security as all aspects 'that threaten human survival, daily life and dignity – for example, environmental degradation, violations of human rights, transnational organized crime, illicit drugs, refugees, poverty, anti-personnel landmines, and other infectious diseases such as AIDS – and strengthens efforts to confront these threats' (MOFA, 1999a). In addition, *Japan's ODA Annual Report 1999*, which was renamed in 2001 as *Japan's ODA White Paper*, contained a section on 'Human Security and ODA' which referred to human security as 'a policy idea, which Japan is conveying to the international community as one of the essential principles for the conduct of Japanese foreign policy in twenty-first century' (MOFA, 1999b). Although the concept of human security was mentioned as a policy agenda in the subsequent White Papers, it was only from 2003 that the concept was prioritized in Japan's ODA policy through the revision of the ODA charter.

The revised ODA charter begins by stating that the 'objectives of Japan's ODA are to contribute to the peace and development of the international community and thereby to help ensure Japan's own security and prosperity' (MOFA, 2003). The document then proceeds to explain that human security is one of the 'basic policies' of ODA and the first 'priority issue'. In other words, ODA policies reflect the concept of human security. The document clearly states that Japan will implement ODA to protect and empower people (*ibid.*). In addition, in policy papers to implement ODA in accordance with the ODA charter, ODA should be made up of 'assistance that puts people at the center of concerns and that effectively reaches the people' (MOFA, 2005). Thus, the concept of human security is used throughout Japanese public papers on ODA as a way to link the concept and ODA policy and to give ODA a sense of purpose.

This represents a 'sea change' of Japanese ODA policies aimed at replicating some version of Japan's miracle economy and good governance in developing countries (Leheny, 2005, p. 18). Since the ODA Charter was revised in 2003, Japan has increased the share of assistance allocated to BHN such as social infrastructure and services, and emergency aid, largely through the extension of grants and technical cooperation. A government report issued by the Advisory Council on International Cooperation[1] reveals some of the objectives behind Japan's ODA activity in general and its use of ODA to promote human security in particular (MOFA, 2008, p. 1). The Report states:

> It is true that ODA serves as Japan's "national interests" as it is an important source of Japanese diplomatic power. However, Japanese ODA also

> serves as "global interests" as it is necessary to solve humanitarian and other problems that developing countries face in order to turn ODA activity into actual diplomatic power. ODA could be sustainable if we could incorporate "global interests" into "national interests" and paradoxically integrate "national interests" with "global interests". (MOFA, 2008)

The reasons for Japan's leadership in human security promotion are in fact threefold: To advance its diplomatic interests by using ODA effectively as a diplomatic tool; to benefit vulnerable sections of the global community; and to secure bureaucratic interests by gaining public support for ODA through active commitment to human security. From MOFA's point of view, human security is a very useful public relations tool to secure the ODA budget it controls and also to regain pubic supports in an era of economic recession and the resultant budget deficit. In addition, Japan's human security initiative can partly be understood as an inevitable consequence of ODA budget cuts. ODA for human security which mainly supports grassroots projects by NGOs requires relatively small amounts of funding compared to ODA for industrial infrastructure development carried out as yen loan projects. Not surprisingly, therefore, the Japanese government has shifted the focus of its ODA activity from infrastructure development to human security promotion in response to a shrinking development budget.

Edström (2011, p. 50), in one of his detailed critiques of Japanese human security contributions, notes that there is a paradoxical aspect of Japan's pursuit of human security, in which 'in Japan's foreign policy rhetoric, human security has continued to be portrayed as a key element of foreign policy also after it had been made a part of Japan's ODA policy, that is, by definition, no longer a part of Japan's foreign policy'. While it is true that in a strict, technical sense ODA does not, or perhaps should not, fall under the purview of foreign ministries, in a practical sense it has always been political, and therefore, on the international stage, part of foreign policy and national interest promotion.

In Edström's 'Life Story of "Human Security", 1999 –' he documents the stages of the rise and fall of human security in Japanese foreign policy: Phase 1: 1999–2000 A pillar-to-be of Japan's long-term foreign policy; Phase 2: 2001–2003 A priority of Japan's foreign policy; Phase 3: 2004–2006 A pillar of Japan's ODA policy; Phase 4: 2007 – One of five key concepts of Japan's ODA policy (2011, p. 48). The next section of this chapter acknowledges a shift from the security and foreign policy platform to that of development assistance for the concept, and even achievements that fall far short of desires and thus a lessening of interest among policy elites. But, nevertheless, it points to a continued commitment within Japan (even if only as a result of a dearth of alternatives), and a continued inspiration to other actors in the region.

Human security and Japanese policy implementation

Human security lies at the heart of JICA's policy on ODA implementation. Indeed, Japan has already played a very active human security role in East Asia, especially in crisis and disaster response scenarios. This includes providing massive financial assistance and currency swap arrangements in the aftermath of the Asian financial crisis to stabilize the regional economies and strengthen social and political stability; engaging in peacemaking in Cambodia and Aceh, and peace-building in East Timor, Aceh, and Mindanao; offering financial and medical assistance when East Asia was hit by the SARS epidemic; and deploying the largest contingent of Japanese troops since the end of World War II for humanitarian assistance to tsunami-stricken Aceh in early 2005 (Lam, 2006, p. 143).

In the case of Cambodia, where human capital had decreased and the legal system had been undermined by a long period of armed conflict, Japan provided technical assistance to improve institutional capacity and enhance public awareness on human rights and legal procedures (JICA, 2008). After peace was restored with the help of Japanese personnel under the framework of a UN peacekeeping operation, Japanese and Cambodian experts worked together to establish legal and judicial frameworks by revising and drafting the Cambodian Civil Code and Code of procedure and training legal professionals. In addition, JICA continues to work jointly with local NGOs to improve people's access to justice and heighten human rights awareness. In this case, unlike previous huge infrastructure projects, ODA was used for the purpose of improving intangible assets such as public awareness on human rights and the establishment of a legal basis for the capacity of government (Von Feigenblatt, 2007).

Likewise, in Timor-Leste, Japan dispatched an International Peace Cooperation team to engage in activities such as road and bridge maintenance and repair work. In addition, JICA has implemented governance, capacity-building, and civil infrastructure measures to meet human security objectives of protecting and empowering individuals and communities (Hsien-Li, 2010). Japanese expertise trained the more than 300 Timorese civil servants who formed a new generation of public officials. Meanwhile in Mindanao, Southern Philippines, where the national government and Islamic and communist rebels have been fighting for several decades, JICA also provided social and economic infrastructure as an important peace-builder.

In addition, when the life-endangering SARS epidemic spread rapidly throughout the world, and when a powerful tsunami hit the coasts of Southeast Asian countries, Japan provided financial assistance to affected Southeast Asian countries and dispatched experts to protect the people. Japan has, in fact, contributed the greatest amount of financial support (US$500 million) to countries suffering from natural disasters (Lam, 2006). Such efforts are guided by the human security concept of providing for the safety of individuals rather than protecting sovereign states. But JICA's peacemaking and peace-building in post-conflict and conflict areas also serve as paths for Japan to play an active role in international high political arenas through soft power such as economic and technical assistance rather than military might.

At the more local and practical level, Grant Assistance for Grass-roots Human Security Projects (GGS) has provided non-refundable assistance to local governments, NGOs, and other non-profit associations for quick response to local needs. It was first established in 1989 and renamed in 2003 by the Japanese government from its original name of Grant Assistance for Grass-roots Projects, in recognition of the additional dimension of human security and in order to address the emerging needs of post-conflict countries that require peace-building processes (The External Advisory Meeting on ODA Evaluation, 2006). The basic principles of GGS are in line with the principles and the priority areas of assistance specified in the new ODA Charter: (1) direct support to the people at the grassroots level, (2) flexible response to various needs of the grassroots level, and (3) prompt response to the needs. Therefore, these grant assistance schemes strongly reflect the principles of 'human security' and have proven effective in delivering directly benefits to the target community, as they assist the projects at the grassroots level. This instrument provides support to relatively small projects in BHN sectors at the grassroots level with a maximum grant amount of US$1 million (MOFA, 2007).

In addition to its domestic and bilateral regional efforts, since human security is also a means to strengthen Japan's reputation in the international arena, Tokyo looks to strengthen the paradigm in international forums. Indeed, for Gilson and Purvis (2003, p. 198), the UNDP reports on human security have been central to Japan's interpretation of the term, 'and its participation in forums like the WTO (World Trade Organization), IMF (International Monetary Fund) and World Bank similarly affects Japan's normative preferences'. But as Japan pushes human security, it also takes advantage of the existing structures. In this way, Japan does strengthen the human security system not only internationally but it also relies on a strong network of skilled and well-trained personnel.

In the international field, human security provides a safe umbrella for constructive contributions. Tokyo funnels much of its bilateral through multilateral mechanisms, adding the legitimacy of international collective action to its policies. Japan has also begun to behave proactively in dealing with development problems through the UN, 'believing it to be the only global organization capable of tackling the issues as part of broader definition of security' (Hook *et al.*, 2005, p. 380). Thus, the concepts and institutions of human security have allowed Japan to step out of the reactive shadow, and in this field, Japan has emerged as a truly capable international actor.

The CHS has been Japan's main international theoretical policy vehicle. An independent commission under the chairmanship of Sadako Ogata and

Amartya Sen, the CHS was established in 2000 through an initiative of the Government of Japan and in response to the UN Secretary-General's call at the 2000 Millennium Summit for a world free from want and free from fear (UNTFHS, 2009). In its final report, *Human Security Now,* the CHS aimed to mobilize support and provide a concrete framework for the institutionalization of the concept of human security. As mentioned in Chapter 2, the CHS adopted an even broader definition of human security than did the 1994 UNDP report, arguing that 'it should entail a vision of security which would protect the vital core of all human lives in ways that enhance human freedoms and human fulfillment' (CHS, 2003, p. 4). The final report referred to 'political, environmental, economic, military, and cultural systems that together give people the building blocks of survival, livelihood and dignity', and suggested a list of ten 'starting points' to address human security, in contrast to the seven components of human security listed by the UNDP (*ibid.*, p. 133).

The CHS's notion of security has expanded the concept to include human dignity, means for financing human security in post-conflict situations, and linking the issues of human security to fair trade, minimum living standards, access to education, and respect for diversity. Although the CHS was established as an independent commission, the influence of the Japan's funding can be seen in the fact that the report was preliminarily presented to Prime Minister Junichiro Koizumi in February 2003 (Konrad, 2006, p. 31). Likewise, the broad human security approach of the government of Japan is very close to that of CHS. Thus, from a theoretical perspective, Japan initiated the creation of the CHS which has strongly influenced the international community in conceptualizing human security.

Japan has also been at the forefront of the practical implementation of these concepts. The most significant action taken by the Japanese Government was the incorporation of the UNTFHS (*ibid.*, p. 33). Japan established the Trust Fund with the UN Secretariat to finance UN human security projects and in order to increase the operational impact of human security projects (UNTFHS, 2009, p. 55). The UNTFHS funds projects related to key thematic areas in human security, including 'post-conflict peace-building, persistence and chronic poverty, disaster risk reduction, human trafficking and food security' (*ibid.*, p. 57). In addition, it follows guidelines provided by the Human Security Unit which was established to manage the works of UNTFHS and distribute its funding. The guidelines determine that the UNTFHS 'finances projects carried out by organizations in the UN system, and when appropriate in partnership with non-UN entities, to advance the operational impact' and names parameters, targets, geographical areas, and the budgets (*ibid.*, p. 1).

Japan strongly influences these projects through its donations to the fund. Japan did not only initiate the fund, but also, until now, it remains the only major donor, although since 2007 Thailand and Slovenia have joined the UNTFHS as additional donors (*ibid.*, p. 56). When the Fund was established in 1999, Japan initially contributed approximately 500 million yen or US$4.63 million. Japan additionally contributed an estimated 6.6 million yen or US$55.05 million for Kosovo's reconstruction and the repatriation of refugees and for East Timor's reconstruction (MOFA, 2009). By 2009, total contributions, amounted to some US$347 million and exceeded the total approved budget of US$303.4 million.

Furthermore, the UNTFHS is managed in accordance with guidelines agreed between the government of Japan and the UN Secretariat. Thus, the objectives of the fund are the same as those of Japan's ODA policy: namely, realizing the human security concept and applying the principles of 'protection' and 'empowerment' (UNTFHS, 2009, pp. 9–10). The UNTFHS has allocated approximately 36 per cent of its budget to the Asian region, and 71 projects out of 194 were implemented in Asia. The prioritization of Southeast Asian recipient countries in the UNTFHS mirrors that of Japan's aid policy.

Since the late 1980s, Japan's top six recipient countries in Southeast Asia have included Indonesia, the Philippines, Thailand, Malaysia, Myanmar, and Viet Nam (OECD, 2010). Likewise, more than 50 per cent of UNTFHS' Asian budget has been distributed to Southeast Asian countries including Thailand, East Timor, Philippines, Cambodia, Indonesia, Viet Nam, Myanmar, and Lao PDR (MOFA, 2009; The External Advisory Meeting on ODA Evaluation, 2010). In addition, much of UNTFHS' budget (US$97 million or 34 per cent) has been allocated to dealing with conflict situations and transition from war to peace, further reflecting Japan's comprehensive and integrative approach to security and development.

Edström (2011, p. 22) has been deeply critical of Japan's human security role in the UN. He notes that the CHS wound up its activities in 2003 and 'exists now only in historical annals and Japanese foreign policy rhetoric' and that the UNTFHS has 'largely become a Japanese pursuit, with its activities even reported on the homepage of the Japanese foreign ministry, as if the TFHS were a Japanese governmental agency'. Japan did not join the Canadian-influenced HSN either as a result of doctrinal and policy divergence, or because Japan was unwilling to play second fiddle, and the Japanese-initiated Friends of Human Security (FHS) which seeks to bridge HSN and non-HSN countries can be seen as an attempt by Tokyo to regain the initiative.

These criticism do not necessarily, however, impact on the key points raised by this chapter, that Japan is committed to human security initiatives precisely because they are in Japan's national interest. Furthermore, while Edström is dismissive of the FHS (*ibid.*, p. 24), the fact remains that a growing number of states have joined up, and such informal collaboration may be more acceptable to potential recipients or hosts of human security initiatives, and also seen as the way of the future in terms of holistic collaboration on simultaneously on the freedom from fear and freedom from want frontiers, as perhaps is shown by the challenging case studies in this book. More serious is Edström's contention that human security is no longer a priority for Japan itself as evinced by the downgrading of human security in the Diplomatic Bluebook for 2009 and 2010 and in the ODA White Paper in 2009 after significant rises in 2005, 2007, and 2008 (2011, pp. 44–5). Again, however, these criticisms are not as compelling as they would seem at first sight.

While Japanese statesmen and institutions may be backing away from the express use of human security terminology, they are still following policies guided by related principles. In part, this is because there is no alternative. The Japanese public is deeply wedded to the idea of non-militarism in their nation's foreign policy. There is no political constituency for transforming the Japanese Self Defense Forces into a force capable of force projection, and the country's aging population and the existence of a resilient, mature democracy works against a revival of militarism. Opinion polls in 2007 and 2008 found that only 39 per cent supported the renewal of the law (which initially expired on 1 November 2007) permitting the dispatch of the Maritime Self Defense Forces to the Indian Ocean in support of anti-terrorism measures in Afghanistan, and only 35 per cent were in favor of allowing the Self Defense Forces to be dispatched overseas.[2] There is, however, continued support for the Japanese government to play a more active role in non-traditional areas of foreign and security policy. Ninety-two per cent thought that Japan should be more forceful in its diplomatic efforts to persuade other countries to reduce their emissions of carbon dioxide and other gases.[3]

Thus, although the DPJ came to power in August 2009 after half century of almost uninterrupted LDP dominance with a stronger mandate and apparently a more stable coalition (at least until they lost control of the Upper House of parliament in the elections of July 2010) than the previous brief ousting of the LDP from 1993 to 1994, there has been little change in Japan's geopolitical code. Furthermore, Japanese policy-making faces tremendous bureaucratic inertia when compared to that of other nations. As a result, policy is only created through a process of 'disjointed incrementalism' (for example, small undirected steps), and rather than grand strategic policy-making, for the vast majority of the time, 'incremental drift' or slight modifications of existing policy is the norm (Baybrooke and Lindblom, 1969, p. 233).

The prioritization of human security by successive administrations may be seen to already have fulfilled its strategic objectives, thereby helping to explain why Tokyo is less prone to restate the central tenets. Like its human security policy rival Canada, Japan will always be associated with the normatively positive human security agenda and the pursuance of an 'ethical' foreign policy, even after both countries have backed away from active support of the paradigm. This has contributed greatly to Japan's prestige in international affairs. It has also softened attitudes toward Japan in East Asia, thereby supplementing Japanese strategic interests.

Finally, even if Japan is no longer promoting its brand of human security as actively as it has in the past, other regional actors are 'learning from Japan' in terms of pursuing normative policy agendas as well as in terms of economic development and governance. In particular, South Korea, the subject of Chapter 10, has tried strategically to position itself as an honest broker of G20 good governance agendas, and as the chief proponent of 'Green Growth' in the UN. Indeed, green growth has become the national strategic model for the Republic of Korea in much the same way that human security became the fundamental strategic theme for Japan, and the incoming President of Korea, Park Geun-hye, has already committed to follow in the footsteps of her predecessor, Lee Myung-bak, when it comes to normative strategic and foreign policy.

Conclusion

The Government of Japan has played a leading role in financing East Asian development and, despite some crisis-inspired budget constraints, remains committed to such a path due in part to its own strategic self-interest. Tokyo also remains committed to promoting human security in a number of ways: promotion of the concept of human security (although this is receding), the practice of human security by bilateral ODA through JICA and GGS, and multilateral ODA through the UNTFHS. Through these multiple channels, Japan has contributed to enhancing the human security of many of the most vulnerable inhabitants of East Asia (Lam, 2006, p. 149).

The concepts of human security and development, as well as those of ODA and Japan's foreign policy and non-traditional security agenda, have become increasingly entwined. Such a conflation of motives and objectives is not without its critics. Indeed, Japanese policy may be seen as a classic example of 'securitization' where an issue is first politicized (requiring state action *within* the standard framework of the political system), and then securitized (requiring emergency action *outside* of the boundaries of the established norms), which in turn frames the issue as one of existential threat to a referent object (Emmers, 2007, pp. 110–13). For Beall *et al.* (2006), 'all too often the development-security nexus exists to manipulate development for "them" with the ultimate purpose of enhancing security for "us", and security concerns may eventually undermine the legitimacy of the development assistance'.

Likewise, Ben Saul (2006, p. 29) is concerned that a broadly defined concept of human security 'collapses and conflates the whole spectrum of human problems' causing great harm to the fragile architecture of human rights law, blurring the particularity of diverse problems, and obscuring concrete solutions. He also notes that one of the aims of treating developmental issues as security threats is to invoke a sense of crisis and urgency about those issues, and that is may be rhetorically or strategically advantageous to do so in the political arena (*ibid.*, p. 10, 29).

The thrust of this chapter, however, is that despite the conflation of human security, development, and national interest, nevertheless Japanese assistance has contributed to the furtherance of both East Asian development and human security precisely because these tenets have come to form the bedrock of Tokyo's foreign and security policy toward the region. And precisely because Japanese assistance and human security promotion are tied up with Tokyo's own national interest and strategic priorities, a higher degree of commitment is likely to be forthcoming, particularly with regard to East Asian needs, than is found among Western donors and actors in the region.

Notes

1. This is an advisory council established by the Japanese Ministry of Foreign Affairs in 2007 and includes 14 prominent academics, business leaders and NGO leaders as its core members. The tasks of the council are to discuss ODA-related issues and make policy recommendations to Foreign Minister to improve Japan's ODA performance.
2. Nikkei Shimbun Opinion Polls, December 2007 and January 2008.
3. Yomiuri Shimbun Opinion Polls, 19 and 20 May 2007.

References

Acharya, A. and Acharya, A. (2000) 'Human Security in Asia Pacific: Puzzle, Panacea or Peril?' *Canadian Consortium on Asia Pacific Security Bulletin,* 27.

Akaha, T. (1991) 'Japan's Comprehensive Security Policy: A New East Asian Environment', *Asian Survey,* 31(4), 324–40.

Baybrooke, D. and Lindblom, C. (1969) 'Types of Decision Making' in J. Rosenau (ed.), *International Politics and Foreign Policy: A Reader in Research and Theory* (New York: The Free Press).

Beall, J., Goodfellow, T., and Putzel, J. (2006) 'Introductory Article: On the Discourse of Terrorism, Security and Development', *Journal of International Development,* 18(1), 51–67.

Blaise, S. (2009) 'Japanese Aid as a Prerequisite for FDI: The Case of Southeast Asian Countries', *Asia Pacific Economic Papers,* 385, 1–38.

Calder, K. (1988) 'Japanese Foreign Economic Policy Formation: Explaining the Reactive State', *World Politics,* 40(4), 517–41.

Calder, K. (2006) 'Halfway to Hegemony: Japan's Tortured Trajectory', *Harvard International Review,* 27(3), 46–9.

CHS (Commission on Human Security) (2003) *Human Security Now: Final Report* (New York: CHS).

Emmers, R. (2007) 'Securitization' in A. Collins (ed.), *Contemporary Security Studies* (Oxford: Oxford University Press).

Ensign, M. M. (1992) *Doing Good or Doing Well? Japan's Foreign Aid Program* (New York: Columbia University Press).

Edström, B. (2003) 'Japan's Foreign Policy and Human Security', *Japan Forum,* 15(2), 209–25.

Edström, B. (2008) *Japan and the Challenge of Human Security: The Founding of a New Policy 1995–2003* (Stockholm: Institute for Security and Development Policy).

Edström, B. (2011) *Japan and Human Security: The Derailing of a Foreign Policy Vision* (Stockholm: Institute for Security and Development Policy).

Fu, X. (2004) *Exports, Foreign Direct Investment and Economic Development in China* (New York: Palgrave Macmillan).

Fukushima, A. (2003)'Human Security and Japanese Foreign Policy', Paper presented at UNESCO/Korea Conference on Human Security, Seoul, Korea, 16–17 June 2003, http://unesdoc.unesco.org/images/0013/001365/136506e.pdf.

Furuoka, F., Oishi, M., and Kato, I. (2010) 'From Aid Recipient to Aid Donor: Tracing the Historical Transformation of Japan's Foreign Aid Policy', *Electronic Journal of Contemporary Japanese Studies,* Volume 10, Issue 3, Article Number 3, http://www.japanesestudies.org.uk/articles/2010/FuruokaOishiKato.html.

Gilson, J. and Purvis, P. (2003) 'Japan's Pursuit of Human Security: Humanitarian Agenda or Political Pragmatism?', *Japan Forum,* 15(2), 193–207.

Green, M. (2003) Japan's Reluctant Realism: Foreign Policy Challenges in an Era of Uncertain Power (New York: Palgrave).

Hilpert, H. G. and Nakagani, K. (2002) 'Economic Relations: What Can We Learn from Trade and FDI?' in M. Soederberg (ed.), *Chinese-Japanese Relations in the Twenty-first Century: Complementarity and Conflict* (London and New York: European Institute of Japanese Studies).

Hirata, K. (1998) 'Japan as a Reactive State? Analyzing Japan's Relations with the Socialist Republic of Vietnam', *Japanese Studies,* 18(2), 1–31.

Hirono, R. (2001) 'Economic Cooperation as a Step toward an East Asian Community' in Hirono, R. (ed.), *ASEAN-Japan Cooperation: A Foundation for East Asian Community* (Tokyo: Japan Center for International Exchange), http://www.jcie.org/researchpdfs/ASEAN/asean_hirono.pdf.

Hishida, M. (2000) *Gendai chugoku ni okeru kokka to shakai [State and Society in Contemporary China]* (Tokyo: Tokyo University Press).

Ho, S. (2008) 'Japan's Human Security Policy: A Critical Review of its Limits and Failures', *Japanese Studies,* 28(1), 101–12, 2008 Special Issue: New Directions in Japanese Foreign Policy.

Hook, G. D., Gilson, J., Hughes, C.W., and Dobson, H. (2005) *Japan's International Relations, Politics, Economics and Security* (London and New York: Routledge).

Hsien-Li, T. (2010) 'Not Just Global Rhetoric: Japan's Substantive Actualization of its Human Security Foreign Policy', *International Relations of the Asia-Pacific,* 10, 159–87.

Hynek, N. (2012a) 'The Domopolitics of Japanese Human Security', *Security Dialogue,* 43(2), 119–37.

Hynek, N. (2012b) 'Japan's Return to the Chequebook? From Military Peace Support to Human Security Appropriation', *International Peacekeeping,* 19(1), 62–76.

Inada, J. (2001) Political Economist at Senshu University and a Senior Research Fellow at the Japan Institute of International Affairs, Interviewed by Tsukasa Takamine in Tokyo, Japan, 28 March 2001.

JICA (2008) *Terminal Evaluation: Legal and Judicial Cooperation Project (Phase II),* http://www.jica.go.jp/english/our_work/evaluation/tech_and_grant/project/term/asia/c8h0vm000001rr8t-att/cam_01_1.pdf.

Konrad, C. (2006) 'The Japanese Approach: Tracks of Human Security Implementation', *Human Security Perspectives,* 1(3), 22–38.

Kurlantzick, J. (2006) 'China's Charm Offensive in Southeast Asia', *Current History,* September 2006, 270–6.

Lam, P. E. (2006) 'Japan's Human Security Role in Southeast Asia', *Contemporary Southeast Asia,* 28(1), 141–59.

Leheny, D. (2005) 'Terrorism, Law Enforcement, and Foreign Policy: Evaluating Japan's Counter Terrorism Assistance Initiatives', *Asia Program Special Report,* 128, 17–21.

Long, W. (1999) 'Nonproliferation as a Goal of Japanese Foreign Assistance', *Asian Survey,* 39(2), 328–9.

Mearsheimer, J. (2001) *The Tragedy of Great Power Politics* (New York: W.W. Norton & Company).

MOFA (Ministry of Foreign Affairs) (1994) 'Japan's Official Development Assistance Annual Report 1994', http://www.mofa.go.jp/policy/oda/summary/1994/index.html.

MOFA (1999a) *Japan's Diplomatic Bluebook (*Tokyo: MOFA).

MOFA (1999b) 'Japan's Official Development Assistance Annual Report 1999', http://www.mofa.go.jp/policy/oda/summary/1999/index.html.

MOFA (2003) 'Japan's Official Development Assistance Charter', http://www.mofa.go.jp/region/n-america/us/q&a/oda/3.html.

MOFA (2005) *Japan's Medium-Term Policy on Official Development Assistance* (Tokyo: Government of Japan).

MOFA (2007) *Japan's Official Development Assistance White Paper 2007* (Tokyo: MOFA).

MOFA (2008) *Kokusai kyoryoku ni kansuru yushikisha kaigi hokoku* [Report by the Advisory Council on International Cooperation] (Tokyo: MOFA).

MOFA (2009) *The Trust Fund for Human Security: For the 'Human-centered' 21st Century* (Tokyo: MOFA, Global Issues Cooperation Division).

Murayama, T. (1995) Statement at World Summit for Social Development, Copenhagen, 11 March 1995, http://www.un.org/documents/ga/conf166/gov/950311074922.htm.

Obuchi, K. (1998a) Opening Remarks by Prime Minister Obuchi at an Intellectual Dialogue on Building Asia's Tomorrow, http://www.mofa.go.jp/announce/pm/obuchi/index.html.

Obuchi, K. (1998b) Policy Speech, Toward the Creation of a Bright Future for Asia, 16 December 1998, http://www.mofa.go.jp/region/asia-paci/asean/pmv9812/policyspeech.html.

Organisation for Economic Co-operation and Development (OECD) (2010) *Development Co-operation Report 2010* (Paris: OECD).

OECD/DAC (Development Assistance Committee) (1999) *Development Cooperation Review Series: Japan, no. 34* (Paris: OECD).

OECD Query Wizard (2010) *International Development Statistics,* http://stats.oecd.org/qwids/.

Paul, E. (1996) 'Japan in Southeast Asia: A Geopolitical Perspective', *Journal of the Asia Pacific Economy,* 1(3), 391–410.

Radtke, K. W. and Feddema, R. (2000) *Comprehensive Security in Asia: Views from Asia and the West on a Changing Security Environment* (Boston: Brill Academic Publishers).

Samuels, R. J. (2007) *Securing Japan: Tokyo's Grand Strategy and the Future of East Asia* (Ithaca: Cornell University Press).

Saul, B. (2006) 'The Dangers of the United Nations' "New Security Agenda": "Human Security" in the Asia-Pacific Region', *Asian Journal of Comparative Law,* 1(1), 1–35.

Schrader, P. J., Hook, S. W., and Taylor, B. (1998) 'Clarifying the Foreign Aid Puzzle: A Comparison of American, Japanese, French, and Swedish Aid Flows', *World Politics,* 50(2), 294–323.

Singh, B. (2002) 'ASEAN's perceptions of Japan: Change and Continuity', *Asian Survey,* 42(2), 276–96.

Soesastro, H. (2004) 'Sustaining East Asia's Economic Dynamism: The Role of Aid', *PRI-OECD Research Project,* May 2004, 1–31.

Soeya, Y. (2005) 'Japanese Security Policy in Transition: The Rise of International and Human Security', *Asia-Pacific Review,* 12(1), 103–16.

Sueo, S. (2002) *The International Relations of Japan and South East Asia: Forging a New Regionalism* (London and New York: Routledge).

Taira, K. (1991) 'Japan an Imminent Hegemon?'*Annals of the American Academy of Political and Social Science,* 513, 161–2.

Task Force on Foreign Relations for the Prime Minister (2002) *Basic Strategies for Japan's Foreign Policy in the 21st Century New Era, New Vision, New Diplomacy,* http://www.kantei.go.jp/foreign/policy/2002/1128tf_e.html.

The External Advisory Meeting on ODA Evaluation (2006) *Evaluation of Japan's Grant Assistance for Grassroots Human Security Projects (GGP Scheme)* (Tokyo: MOFA).

The External Advisory Meeting on ODA Evaluation (2010) *Evaluation on Multilateral ODA: The United Nations Trust Fund for Human Security* (Tokyo: MOFA).

UN Trust Fund for Human Security (UNTFHS) (2008) *Guidelines for the United Nations Trust Fund for Human Security* (New York: Human Security Unit).

UNTFHS (2009) *Human Security in Theory and Practice: Application of the Human Security Concept and the United Nations Trust Fund for Human Security* (New York: Human Security Unit).

Van Wolferen, K. (1990) *The Enigma of Japanese Power: People and Politics in a Stateless Nation* (New York: Vintage Press).

Von Feigenblatt, O. F. (2007) *Japan and Human Security: 21st Century Official Development Policy Apologetics and Discursive Co-optation,* http://papers.ssrn.com/sol3/papers.cfm?abstract_id=1395012.

Yanagihara, T. and Emig, A. (1991) 'An Overview of Japan's Foreign Aid' in S. Islam (ed.), *Yen for Development: Japanese Foreign Aid and the Politics of Burden-Sharing* (New York: Council on Foreign Relations Press).

Yoshimatsu, H. and Trinidad, F. (2010)'Development Assistance, Strategic Interests, and the China Factor in Japan's Role in ASEAN Integration', *Japanese Journal of Political Science,* 11(2), 199–219.

10
South Korea's Contribution to the Promotion of Human Security

Introduction

South Korea has grown from being one of the poorest countries in the world, and heavily dependent on ODA for 50 years (1945–95), to become the newest member of the OECD DAC. The last two decades have also seen dramatic progress in political governance in the Republic of Korea (ROK), as a successful transition to democracy was followed by democratic consolidation. Korea firmly established its place in what has become known as the 'Third Wave of Democratization' (Huntington, 1991) and is now, according to the CIA World Factbook (2013) 'a fully functioning modern democracy'. South Korea is also a dynamic new player in regional and global governance, and its new assertiveness has seen the country host both the G20 and the High Level Forum (HLF) on Aid Effectiveness. In accordance with its new responsibilities under DAC guidelines, South Korea is looking to dramatically expand its ODA budget. It further hosts many governance and development fact-finding missions, and sponsors the studies, through the Korean Overseas International Co-operation Agency (KOICA), of large numbers of graduate students from small- and medium-sized regional economies, who perhaps see in the ROK a role model closely analogous to their own conditions and experiences.

South Korea has been criticized not only for its relatively low level of ODA as a proportion of GDP but also for its high levels of tied aid. Nevertheless, as a new emerging donor of ODA, South Korea embodies three things: (1) a rapid rise from one of the poorest countries in the world to the 13th largest economy sending a message of hope to other developing countries, (2) rapid economic development accompanied by democratization, and (3) the achievement of these milestones in the context of insecurity. South Korea

Research for this chapter was carried out jointly by the author and Suyoun Jang. Additional contributions were made by Dong Jin Kim.

is also unique among donors in not suffering from any neo-imperial baggage. Finally, successive administrations in Seoul have actively looked to promote the country's interests and influence through non-traditional power projection including not only ODA and related economic assistance as previously initiated by Japan but also through leadership in international organizations in niche policy areas such as 'green growth', through 'public diplomacy', and through active support of the cultural soft power projection known as 'Hallyu' or the Korean wave, which has seen all things Korean imitated, supported, and absorbed across the region.

It was not until the late 1980s and early 1990s that South Korea looked to build economic, policy, and scholarly interests in the development of Asia in general, and Southeast Asia in particular. This late start in Korean involvement is not surprising considering that it was still overshadowed by its major East Asian neighbors, China and Japan, in its relationships with Southeast Asia. South Korea was also, for a long time, caught up with its own development challenges and the subordinate role it played to the United States, and was therefore unable to pursue its independent foreign policy (Steinberg, 2010). As Korea has achieved dramatic economic, political, social, and cultural progress since the 1980s however, its influence in the region, bought through investment and development aid, and the example set by the country's achievements, has experienced a corresponding upsurge. Likewise, Seoul's interest and political and strategic involvement in the region have increased exponentially. Southeast Asia is now Korea's fifth most important trading partner, the second destination for its development assistance, and the third most important direct investment target (Kim, 2010).

While South Korea has neither officially nor explicitly used the term human security in its policy documentation, like Japan, many of its new policy initiatives and policy prioritizations seem nevertheless to reflect concern for the most vulnerable. South Korea also seems to follow Japan in terms of a broad approach to human security through development assistance and efforts at nation-building and reconstruction through humanitarian assistance. But the ROK offers something more and different in the fields of human security and development than just aping Japanese precedents. Indeed, although Japan has been regarded as the foremost contributor to regional development and human security, South Korea's unique experiences of a rapid rise from being a war-devastated, poor country to a new emerging donor seem to be more immediately relevant, appealing, and worthy of emulation by developing countries in the region.

In addition to South Korea's commitment to East Asian economic development, it has contributed to the promotion of peace in the region. As mentioned in Chapter 3, Asian perspectives on human security do not mean that they allow national governments to violate entitlement rights of their citizens or the safe havens of the most vulnerable people and communities. Rather, East Asian actors contribute to human security in the region in different ways from the West. Although South Korea strategically has had to prioritize national security in the face of the lingering challenge of the DPRK, it has demonstrated a capacity and willingness to contribute to regional peace-building through still meager but increasing amounts of humanitarian assistance. Furthermore, it supports the R2P principle and the strengthening of human rights and civilian protection, and is actively involved in discussions on reshaping regional security architecture in response to NTS threats.

South Korea's new president, Park Geun-hye, has stipulated in her campaign promises in the 2012 presidential election and in her inaugural address on 25 February 2013, that human security considerations would be further brought to the fore in both domestic and international policy-making. She has pledged to usher in an era of hope focused on 'economic democratization' and the 'happiness' of South Korean citizens, while actively promoting the spread and flourishing of Korean culture. With regard to North Korea, she has emphasized 'strategic patience' focused on 'trustpolitik' and humanitarian assistance, despite recent inflammatory speeches issued from Pyongyang in the wake of international sanctions following the DPRK's successful missile (or satellite) launch and third nuclear test (Cha and Kim, 2013).

Indeed, as a result of a combination of national security concerns, genuine humanitarian motivation, and an awareness of the close relationship between development and security, South Korea has been a large donor of humanitarian assistance to North Korea. Due to the lack of mutual diplomatic recognition of the *de facto* and *de jure* existence of the two Korean states, this assistance is not considered ODA. Furthermore, as might be expected, 'feeding the enemy' is a controversial policy and has faced obstacles from opponents who see little strategic value being offered in return by Pyongyang. Nevertheless, humanitarian imperatives and empathy among South Korea's population, combined with its consolidated democracy and the information revolution, mean that no administration in Seoul can simply leave the most vulnerable in North Korea to suffer and die. As has been addressed previously in this volume, from a strategic perspective, it would also not be in the strategic rational self-interest of ROK decision-makers to ignore insecurity in the North.

This chapter therefore addresses four ways in which the ROK contributes to the protection and promotion of human security in East Asia. First, it considers the example South Korea sets as a post-conflict ODA recipient development and governance success story. Second, it examines South Korea's expanding influence on, and relations with, countries in East Asia in terms of South Korea's ODA practice and strategy with an emphasis on regional economic development (broad considerations of human security). Third, it explores South Korea's cautious but growing involvement in regional security affairs and its contribution to the promotion of narrow visions of human security in the region. Fourth, it evaluates the ROK's humanitarian engagement with the DPRK.

South Korea's development experience

Ranging from emergency relief to structural adjustment programs, ODA significantly contributed to Korea's economic and social development. In particular, ODA was the only available source of capital following the devastation of the ROK economy by the Korean War. From 1945 to the early 1990s, South Korea received ODA from other countries amounting to a total of US$12 billion (ODA Korea, 2013). During the period of rapid economic growth from 1961 to 1975, more concessional loans and other forms of financial investment came to Korea, allowing it to build social and economic infrastructure and promote industrial development. The 'Miracle on the Han River' saw South Korea grow from one of the world's poorest countries with a GDP per capita of US$67 in 1953 to the world's 15th largest economy. Its subsequent development to its current status as one of the world's leading economies is one of the few aid success stories, and South Korea sees its own experience as an asset it can provide to other recipients of aid. Thus, South Korea has become increasingly actively involved in the international development community and has endorsed a 'Knowledge Sharing Program' (KSP) in its development cooperation efforts. This section examines the extent to which South Korea can represent a positive example of externally stimulated and internally generated development and governance success.

South Korea's aid experience can be categorized in five distinct stages: (1) the 1945–48 period of early, post-World War II foreign assistance, primarily from the United States, (2) the 1949–60 period of foreign assistance aimed at state-building and reconstruction, (3) the 1961–75 period representing not only the middle stage of foreign assistance but also the support by Japanese reparations following the normalization of relations in 1965, focused on boosting economic and social development, (4) the 1976–90 period characterized as a late stage of foreign assistance designed for a modern industrialized economy, and (5) the 1991–99 period of transformation from a recipient to a donor (Lee, 2004, pp. 29–34). In each stage, Korea has pursued different economic development strategies, and the roles and types of ODA have varied.

South Korea's history as a recipient of ODA began in 1945 after Japan's defeat in World War II. Korea was divided at the 38th parallel north in accordance with UN directives, with the South administered by the United States, and the North by the Soviet Union. The Soviets and the Americans were unable to agree on the implementation of joint trusteeship over the whole of the Korean Peninsula; thus, the division became formalized in

1948 with the establishment of two governments at Pyongyang in the North and Seoul in the South – capitals of the DPRK and the ROK respectively. During the period of US tutelage or trusteeship, Washington provided aid for the South from the Government Appropriations for Relief in Occupied Area (GARIOA) and Economic Rehabilitation in Occupied Area (EROA) (Lee, 2004). GARIOA constituted emergency relief aid to assist with US-occupied areas in need of basic subsistence including food, medicine, and fuel, while EROA was for the development of infrastructure in US-occupied areas. In addition to grant aid, the United States also provided concessional loans from the Office of the Foreign Liquidation Commissioner (OFLC) totaling US$24.9 million. The total ODA provided by the United States amounted to US$434.3 million (*ibid.*, pp. 35–7).

After the ROK was officially established in August 1948, it continued to receive aid. The newly established government in Seoul, however, lacked the capability and clear national economic plans necessary to use foreign assistance for national economic development, and thus most foreign assistance was provided as a form of emergency relief (Kim, 2011). Following the Korean War, which resulted in the devastation of over 80 per cent of the Korean Peninsula, foreign aid played an even more important part in rapid national reconstruction. During the first two development periods covering the timeframe 1945–60, foreign aid was almost the only source of investment for post-conflict rehabilitation and construction, economic stability, and growth. In particular, between 1953 and 1958, foreign aid amounted to 9.3 per cent of South Korea's GDP (Chung, 2007).

During the third stage of foreign aid in 1961–75, the types of foreign aid shifted from grants to concessional loans. While over 98 per cent of foreign aid to South Korea was grant aid in the period of first stage, beginning in the 1960s, loans increased substantially and peaked around the early 1980s. ODA to South Korea totaled US$3,941.4 million during the period 1961–75, of which 50.7 per cent was provided in grant aid and 49.3 per cent in concessional loans (Lee, 2004, p. 59). Likewise, the nature of foreign aid changed from relief aid to development assistance. South Korea experienced rapid economic growth during this period, and foreign assistance, mostly loans, was used to support the ROK's economic development plans. In particular, the largest proportion of loans was used to finance the building of economic infrastructure, including electric power, transportation, communication, water systems, and construction (Kim, 2011, p. 278). For example, around 57 per cent of the funds from the United States Agency for International Development (USAID) program was invested in building basic social infrastructure (Chung, 2007, p. 331).

Foreign loans were also used to finance large industrial projects such as the construction of heavy chemical industries (HCIs) production facilities. Of the US$960 million devoted to HCIs between 1972 and 1981, US$580 million or 60 per cent of the total came from foreign loans (*ibid.*). During the third stage of foreign assistance, therefore, foreign loans were mainly used to support the government's economic development and industrialization plans. By 1975, South Korea's GNP per capita reached US$574 and thus it was no longer eligible for a low-income economy classification by the International Development Association.

In the last two stages of foreign assistance, ODA to South Korea decreased to US$3,510.8 million in 1976–90 and to US$2,226.2 million in 1991–99, as its economy continued to grow (Lee, 2004, p. 74). The government focused on specific industries including chemical industry within the HCIs, oil refineries, and fertilizer plants. In addition, it aimed to promote promising industries such as automobiles, machinery, electronics, and semiconductors, while reducing the country's dependence on labor-intensive industries such as textiles and footwear (Chung, 2007, p. 145). During these periods, Korea registered an average growth rate of 8.2 per cent from 1976 to 1990 and 7.3 in the 1990s before the Asian Financial Crisis (World Bank, 2013). Finally, in 1995, South Korea graduated from being a recipient when it paid off its final structural adjustment loan to the World Bank. It was removed from the OECD's list of recipient nations in 2000.

South Korea's economic growth can be seen, therefore, as having been fueled by foreign aid and, especially from the 1960s, ODA provided to South Korea acted like domestic capital, allowing the South Korean government to utilize these funds to support its industrial policies (Kim, 1997). In this sense, it is critical to examine the role of ODA in understanding South Korea's remarkable economic development. Furthermore, however, it is important to recognize that in the Korean case, economic development has been accompanied by human development. Indeed, it would seem that much of the remarkable economic recovery and growth in the ROK was precisely because of the prioritization of human development, particularly in the realm of education and capacity building. Economic growth and human development have interacted with each other in the Korean economy, and the government-led economic development plans have been directly reflected in education policy and planning (Lee, 1997). As will be discussed below, these prioritizations were then transferred to South Korea's role as a donor.

Until the 1960s, the role of the South Korean government in providing education was limited by financial shortcoming, with foreign aid largely contributing to the expansion of educational opportunities. During the period from 1945 to 1948, two-thirds of the operating costs of running the primary schools were financed by the US Military Government (USMG) in South Korea. Foreign aid, mostly from the United States, and amounting to US$100 million in 1952–66, provided the resources for classroom construction and thereby facilitated the quantitative expansion of student enrollment and the number of schools (McGinn, 1980). Despite financial limitations, however, the Korean government initiated a 'national campaign for literacy' contributing to the increase in the adult literacy rate from 22 per cent in 1945 to approximately 80 per cent in 1960 (Pillay, 2010, p. 10).

Since the 1960s, the government has been successful in providing and expanding the education system based on the industrial needs for human resources (*ibid.*, p. 73). The focus of the government's educational plan has moved from primary to secondary education and finally to the tertiary level, according to its economic advancement. For example, during the early stage of industrialization in the 1960s and 1970s, during which workers with a lower level of technical skill were required, the government implemented an effort to expand vocational training and the supply of secondary school technical graduates. Later in the 1980s, in order to absorb more advanced technology, more support was given to two-year junior technical colleges, colleges, and universities for a supply of skilled workers and technicians (Lee, 1997). Consequently, South Korea has achieved the largest increase in human capital stock. The average years of schooling of the population aged 15 and above more than doubled from 4.2 years in 1960 to 9.9 years in 1990, which exceeds the average of the OECD countries as a whole (*ibid.*).

Education has also, however, laid the foundations upon which democratic principles and institutions are based (Pillay, 2010, p. 74). It has promoted political knowledge, changed political behavior patterns, and shaped political attitudes and values. At the same time, education has imbued the people with commitment to modernization and citizenship. Increased educational opportunities have made upward social mobility possible, and the middle class has expanded as a result. South Korea has a history, therefore, of prioritizing human capacity building and education, while at the same time promoting rapid economic development – an ambition to which many challenging case studies in the region could aspire. Education and human resource investment, as well as, through these initiatives, the development of an educated and skilled workforce, have led to rapid and sustained economic growth. But they have also contributed to political governance gains, democratic transition, and consolidation. In this regard, South Korea has also achieved significant progress in the human security related aspects of development from which others could learn.

Indeed many developing countries in the East Asian region and from further afield have been looking to learn the lessons of the Korean development experience. South Korea represents a rare case of an ODA recipient success story, a country which has overcome the dual challenges of post-conflict under-development and insecurity, a 'miracle' of economic and political governance development, and a country which embraces both macro- and human-centered development in its policy prioritization. Since becoming a donor, however, South Korea has also looked actively to export these lessons rather than being content to serve merely as a developmental shining city on the hill. This is considered further in the next section.

South Korea's ODA strategies and human security

South Korea became a donor of ODA in 1963 when it was asked by USAID to participate in a joint training project. It was not, however, until the late 1980s and early 1990s when South Korea became an independent donor of ODA. In 1987, after South Korea had enjoyed nearly three decades of rapid industrialization, it established the economic development cooperation fund (EDCF) under the Export-Import Bank of Korea (Eximbank) in order to handle concessional loans. KOICA was established in 1991 to deal with the grant aid. The aid system was quite similar to the Japanese aid agencies which were also divided into JICA and Japan Bank for International Cooperation (JBIC) which dealt with grant aid and concessional loans respectively.

Since South Korea joined the OECD in 1996 and the DAC in 2010, it has worked hard to boost its aid and to contribute to global development efforts. South Korea strengthened its legal framework for a more effective ODA system by enacting the *Framework Act on International Development Cooperation (Framework Act)* and *Presidential Decree*, and devised the *Strategic Plan for International Development cooperation (Strategic Plan)* to provide a greater clarification for managing its development budget (National Assembly of the Republic of Korea, 2010; PMO, 2010a; GOK, 2010). In addition to strengthening its own development assistance, South Korea has been active in international debates and global process (OECD, 2012). South Korea hosted the G20 Summit in 2010 and played a leading role in expanding G20's agenda to include development issues. In addition, during the Fourth High Level Forum on Aid Effectiveness (HLF-4) at Busan in 2011, South Korea, paved the way to enhancing global partnership between DAC members and recipients.

Despite recent efforts and a willingness to take a leading role in the international development community, South Korea faces challenges in terms of its ODA volume. South Korean aid only topped US$500 million in the mid-2000s, and while it reached US$1,325 million in 2011, this was only equivalent to 0.12 per cent of its GNI (OECD, 2012). While Korea's ODA volume in 2011 was 6 per cent greater than 2010, when Korea's aid surpassed US$1 billion for the first time, its ODA/GNI ratio was unchanged from 2010 and below DAC members' average of 0.32 per cent as well as its target of 0.13 per cent for the year. South Korea committed to increase the total volume of ODA to about US$3 billion and ODA/GNI to 0.25 per cent by 2015. South Korea's total volume of ODA and its ODA/GNI ratio remain, however, relatively small when compared to other traditional donor countries in North America, Western Europe, and in particular, the Nordic countries. In achieving its commitment, Korea should more than double its ODA/GNI ration over the next three years and must manage the steep aid increase effectively (*ibid.*).

As has been mentioned in previous chapters, it is common for East Asian actors to take a broad and economically focused perspective on human security, and South Korea is certainly no exception in this regard. In particular, the ROK draws upon the UNDP's holistic approach in formulating its human security related policies. As outlined in Chapter 2, the UNDP's Human Development Report in 1994 introduced the concept of human security to the governance community, listing seven components of human security including economic security. According to the report, economic insecurity results in increasing poverty and homelessness, and thus security income through economic development, especially in developing countries, is important (1994, pp. 25–6). The report approaches economic development and poverty from the perspective of human rights, emphasizing the importance of protecting individuals from fear and want. Therefore, economic development is one of the goals as well as tools to achieve human security, and South Korea's contribution to human security in East Asian region can be examined from this perspective.

A large share of Korea's aid has been directed to Asia to strengthen development cooperation as a top priority. As can be seen in Figure 10.1, Asia, particularly East Asia, received the largest portion of bilateral ODA with approximately 50 per cent during 2006–10, and Figure 10.2 shows that the

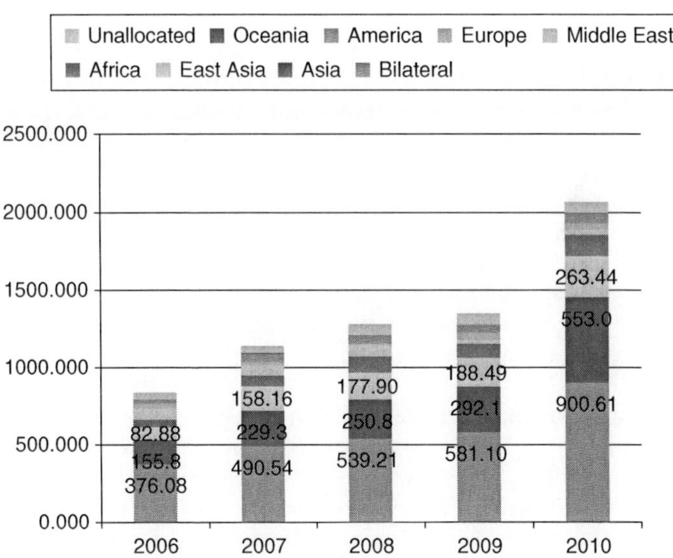

Figure 10.1 Korea's bilateral ODA by region, 2006–10 average (net disbursements, in per cent)

Source: OECD, International Development Statistics (2013).

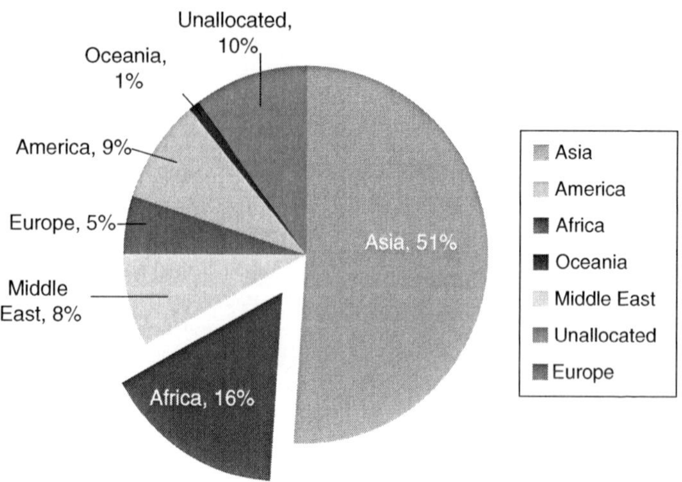

Figure 10.2 Korea's bilateral ODA by region, 2006–10 (net disbursements, US$ million)

Source: OECD, International Development Statistics (2013).

volume itself has gradually increased. According to the *Strategic Plan* and the *Mid-term ODA Policy for 2011–2015,* which describe strategic orientations and allocation principles for each region, strategic priority is given to the Asian region (GOK, 2010; PMO, 2010b). Furthermore, in early March 2009, the then President Lee Myung-bak announced the 'New Asia Initiative', intended to enhance Korea's cooperation with neighboring Asian countries, including a plan for increasing ODA contributions to developing countries in Asia (MOFAT, 2009). Although Korea recognizes the importance of Africa in its commitment to join the global efforts to fight poverty through the MDGs, Korea has closer ties with Asian countries due to geographical proximity and cultural familiarity. Of 26 priority partner countries, 11 are located in Asia, and Korea pledges to increase its amount of aid to these Asian partner countries to 55 per cent by 2015 (PMO, 2010b).

Specifically, since the start of Korea's official aid program in 1987, the largest volume of aid has been given to Vietnam, followed by Indonesia, Sri Lanka, Bangladesh, and Cambodia (OECD, 2013). All of its five largest recipients are classified as low or lower-middle income countries by the World Bank, and its top 15 recipients include all of the poorest East Asian countries, with only one, Angola, from a continent other than Asia.[1] This shows somewhat different geographical patterns of ODA allocation from Japan, which puts priority on East Asian upper-middle income countries including China and Indonesia.

As discussed in Chapter 9, the Japanese government sees its ODA partially as a strategic or diplomatic tool to pursue its foreign policy under the given external structural constraints on the use of force. In addition, Japanese aid contributed greatly to Japan's economic interests by facilitating the inflow of Japanese FDI. Some argue that beyond the institutional resemblances, Korea is also following Japan with regard to the primary direction of its aid policy being based on the national and economic interests of the donor (Kang *et al.*, 2011, Kim and Oh, 2012). First, as also noted in Chapter 9, this need not be a catastrophic failure, as such would imply a greater commitment to giving aid to the region and can result in collateral benefit to the most vulnerable. In addition, however, South Korea does appear to be following a pattern more in line with DAC recommendations in terms of aid to LDCs and low-income countries. Indeed, in 2010, Korea allocated 61 per cent of its gross bilateral ODA to these two groups of countries, which is above the DAC average of 53 per cent whereas Japan distributed 23 per cent (OECD, 2012).

In terms of sectors, more than half of South Korea's assistance has been directed toward areas such as economic infrastructure and production sectors. In the last decade, however, the economic infrastructure sector has accounted for 37 per cent whereas the share of Korea's ODA for the social infrastructure sector is 46 per cent, which is 15 per cent higher than the overall average of DAC members (Figure 10.3). During the five years after 2002, in particular, two-thirds of South Korean aid has been targeted toward the social sector, the field most closely associated with the provision of human-centered security and development. This large increase in the proportion of aid allocated to social infrastructure since the early 2000s is mainly due to an increase in water supply, health, and government and civil society initiatives in response to the international community's commitment to the MDGs (EDCF, 2003).

Indeed South Korea has changed its development goals and priority sectors. According to the EDCF's *Annual Report 2003*, development goals included 'economic development and industrialization of developing countries' by 'sharing Korea's development experience and transferring technological expertise accumulated during its economic development' (2003, p. 9). By 2004, however, the emphasis had shifted to the sustainable development of partner countries and Korea's participation in development efforts of the international community such as the MDGs (EDCF, 2004, p. 11). In addition, South Korea began to place a higher priority on improving the quality of lives of people by providing more assistance to enhance water supply, public health, and education (*Ibid.*; EDCF, 2005, p. 11). Considering that one of the traditional features of Japanese aid which distinguishes it from that of other DAC members' is its emphasis on economic infrastructure, Korea seems to show different priorities, much closer to DAC norms, than those of Japan.

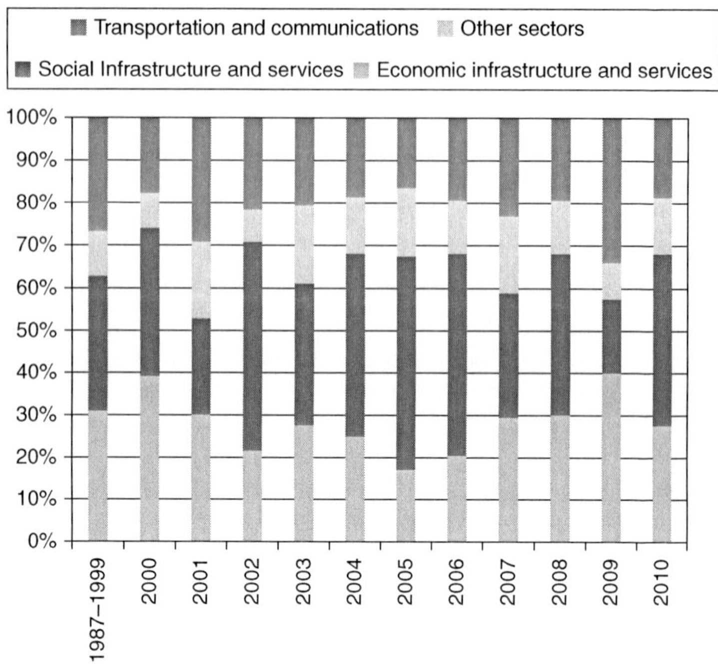

Figure 10.3 Korea's bilateral ODA by sector (net disbursements, in per cent)
Source: OECD, International Development Statistics (2013).

That being said, Korea's ODA within the social sector varies significantly across time, with an ongoing sub-sector emphasis on economic infrastructure development. A significant portion of financial resources has been allocated to economic infrastructure projects in the areas of transportation and telecommunication, with 30 per cent on average in the 2000s (Figure 10.3). In addition, across sectors, Korea has shown a strong preference for financing the building of basic hard infrastructure over that of social services, budget support, and humanitarian aid. For example, in 2002, when social infrastructure sector accounted for 63 per cent of bilateral ODA, assistance toward the education sector took up 43 per cent of social sector allocation. Such a significant increase was due to the construction of large vocational training centers and the establishment of a computer network in an elementary school (EDCF, 2003, p. 32). This type of aid aimed at increase in physical capital is classified as project-type interventions by OECD, and Korea has provided over 60 per cent of bilateral aid as project-type interventions since 1987 (Eximbank, 2012).

In this sense, South Korea has attempted to balance between social and economic infrastructure, not to change radically its ODA prioritization.

This is reflective of South Korea's own development experience whereby the foundations for growth are laid by concentrating ODA to social and economic infrastructure projects (EDCF, 2004, p. 14). The East Asian approach to ODA as a whole draws heavily upon the very successful economic case histories of the region, and South Korea's KSP is perhaps the embodiment of this approach. The KSP, initiated by the Ministry of Strategy and Finance and implemented by the Korean Development Institute, is a comprehensive consultation program designed to assist development partner countries in key policy areas by sharing Korea's development experience (Kim and Tcha, 2012). Such policy areas include economic development strategy, industrialization and export promotion, economic crisis management, knowledge-based economy, and human resource development (KSP, 2013). South Korea has successfully completed policy consultation for 107 countries on more than 440 topics up to 2012, and most of the countries asking to consult are located in Asia. The KSP budget has increased 17-fold between 2004 and 2012 (Kim and Tcha, pp. 3–4).

In addition, South Korea has helped developing countries in the region promote other dimensions of human security within their own borders. First of all, it has supported the human resources development of developing countries through the KOICA training program. The training program aims to share important technical skills and knowledge as well as to build capacities for sustainable development (KOICA, 2013). Since 1991, KOICA has offered more than 2,000 courses on sectors such as education, governance, rural development, and information and communication technology, and trained 44,321 people from 173 developing countries. In particular, fully funded Master's degree programs at Korean universities provide long-term, continuous, and sustainable training environments. Every year, approximately 290 participants from developing countries, at 15 different universities in Korea, are funded to participate in long-term research programs leading to professional Master's degrees.

South Korea also keeps pace with international efforts to mainstream environment and climate change issues into ODA. As part of its efforts, KOICA produced the *Environment Guideline* to make its grants environment-conscious and upgraded it to the *Environmental Mainstreaming Guideline* in 2012 to mainstream cross-cutting issues in ODA strategy (KOICA, 2012). In addition, in 2008, Korea established the *East Asian Climate Partnership (EACP)*, a development cooperation initiative aimed to help developing countries address climate change and achieve green growth, funded to the tune of US$200 million for five years from 2008 to 2012 (EACP, 2013).

South Korea's humanitarian assistance and human security

In addition to economic development, South Korea actively supports and participates in collective international efforts to promote human security and protect the entitlement rights of those in crises caused by hunger, diseases, or natural and man-made disasters. The ROK supports all internationally agreed humanitarian principles such as humanity, impartiality, neutrality, and independence and applies them to foreign, security, and assistance policies. As part of its efforts, South Korea has made good progress toward ensuring better humanitarian donorship through a legislative framework for its humanitarian action and a commitment to increase its humanitarian aid.

In March 2007, Korea enacted the *Overseas Emergency Relief Act* designed to allow the Korean government to provide more effective and prompt overseas emergency relief in order to play a greater role in the concerted efforts of the global community toward disaster management. In addition, the *Framework Act* of 2010 recognizes that humanitarian assistance is an integral part of South Korean development cooperation (National Assembly of the Republic of Korea, 2010). Furthermore, humanitarian assistance is outlined as one of the six objectives of the ROK's *Strategic Plan* (GOK, 2010). Thus, South Korea has a strong legislative mandate for its humanitarian activities, although it still lacks a cross-government policy to focus and guide its humanitarian program (OECD, 2012).

South Korea's humanitarian aid amounted to US$241 million or 2.1 per cent of ODA between 1991 and 2011 and South Korea allocated around US$22.7 million to humanitarian assistance, which is 1.25 per cent of total ODA, in 2012 (OECD, 2013). This budget share is much lower than the average of all donors reporting to the OECD/DAC in this period of 6.2 per cent. If, however, South Korea meets its commitment to increase the share of the ODA budget allocated to humanitarian assistance to 6 per cent by 2015, this will bring South Korea more or less in line with other DAC donors. Recipients of Korea's humanitarian aid are also concentrated in Asia, although the geographical allocation of humanitarian aid is less concentrated than that of development assistance. As can be seen in Table 10.1, East and Southeast Asian countries appear in the top three of recipients of South Korean humanitarian aid 13 times.

In addition to humanitarian aid, South Korea has participated in building the region's peace and security. Over the last decade, the regional security environment in Southeast Asia has changed dramatically. Along with the emergence of the concept of human security, there is growing recognition among Asian countries that newly emerging NTS threats are proving to be more severe and more likely to inflict harm to a greater number of people than the traditional threats of interstate and civil wars. According to the definition by the Consortium of Non-Traditional Security Studies in Asia (NTS-Asia), NTS refers to challenges to the survival and well-being of peoples and states that arise primarily out of non-military sources, such as climate change, infectious diseases, natural disasters, irregular migration, food shortages, smuggling of persons, drug trafficking, and other forms of transnational crime (Caballero-Anthony, 2010, p. 1).

Table 10.1 Korea's top three humanitarian aid recipients (US$ million)

	1	2	3		1	2	3
2000	Serbia	Pakistan	Ethiopia	**2005**	Sri Lanka	Iraq	Indonesia
	0.2	0.1	0.1		7.2	5.7	4
2001	Serbia	Guinea	Tanzania	**2006**	Indonesia	Iraq	Philippines
	0.3	0.2	0.2		9.8	7	1
2002	Afghanistan	Timor-Leste	Ethiopia	**2007**	Iraq	Lebanon	Bangladesh
	2.3	0.4	0.1		5.4	1.7	1.1
2003	China	Iran	Algeria	**2008**	China	Iraq	Myanmar
	0.3	0.2	0.1		5.9	3	2.6
2004	Afghanistan	Thailand	Indonesia	**2009**	Palestine	Sri Lanka	Indonesia
	11.8	0.2	0.2		3.1	2.1	1.6

Source: OECD, International Development Statistics (2013).

Against this new security environment, regional institutions like ASEAN, ASEAN+3 (APT), ASEAN Regional Forum (ARF), and Asia-Pacific Economic Cooperation (APEC) have responded to new security challenges, and South Korea has participated actively within these regional dialogues. The APT, in particular, has beenan arena wherein the ROK and its partners have moved beyond the promotion of regional financial cooperation, to address international cooperation against terrorism and HIV/AIDS, and the importance of energy security (Caballero-Anthony, 2010, p. 1). Although the ASEAN-South Korea relationships remain the weakest vis-à-vis those of ASEAN and East Asian neighboring countries China and Japan, it was the ROK which suggested establishing the East Asia Vision Group (EAVG) and the East Asia Study Group (EASG) in the early 2000s in order to accelerate not only economic cooperation but also cross-sectoral, socio-cultural, and political and security cooperation (Hernandez, 2007, p. 41, 43). Furthermore, South Korea, as a founding member of the Council for Security Cooperation in the Asia Pacific (CSCAP), has participated in promoting dialogue and research on regional peace and security (CSCAP, 2013).

Finally, South Korea has also made good progress in strengthening its humanitarian partnerships with international organizations including UN agencies. For example, it increased its humanitarian budget allocation to UN agencies from 7 per cent of total humanitarian budget in 2006 to 63 per cent in 2010 (OECD, 2012). South Korea also takes part in the UN humanitarian mechanisms such as the Office for the Coordination of Humanitarian Affairs (OCHA), which is the main UN body designed to strengthen the UN's response to both complex emergencies and natural disasters. As part of its effort to strengthen its partnership with OCHA, Korea joined the OCHA Donors Support Group (ODSG) in 2006, and has been part of the UN Disaster Assessment and Coordination (UNDAC) teams since 2003, and the International Search and Rescue Advisory Group (INSARAG) since 1999. Since Korea specializes in search and rescue efforts, it has participated in the OCHA-administered Asia-Pacific Humanitarian Partnership (APHP) since its establishment in 2004. In 2009, Korea signed up to the Good Humanitarian Donorship (GHD) initiative and became the 36th member.

More recently, Korea officially expressed its support for the R2P principles but, as mentioned in Chapter 3, in a cautious way (Park, 2009). Prior to and during the 2005 World Summit's deliberation on the R2P, Korea was a consistent supporter of the Principle. It has, however, emphasized the R2P's prevention component and the international community's role in assisting states to build the capacity needed to deliver on their responsibility to protect their own population (APC, 2008). In this sense, South Korea still stressed the narrow scope in activating R2P and distinguished it from humanitarian intervention in terms of collective actions authorized by the UN Security Council (Park, 2009). Again, however, this stance makes the ROK a less threatening humanitarian partner than other states with more imperial and/or interventionary baggage. Despite a heavy US military presence within the country, South Korea is closely attuned to East Asian perspectives on security and intervention. Hence, the ROK did not support the rather interventionary US North Korean Human Rights Act of 2004, with Seoul expressing concern that the Act would 'negatively affect cooperation between the two Koreas and six-way talks' (Goodenough, 2004).[2] In fact, as detailed in the next and final section, the ROK has consistently promoted humanitarian issues in the DPRK, despite, or because of national security concerns between the two Koreas.

Assistance to North Korea

Nowhere is South Korean international assistance more substantial, more important, and yet more controversial than that which has been offered and delivered to the fraternal enemy state of North Korea. Indeed, there are problems in even terming this international assistance, and it is never referred to as official development assistance or ODA, for both political entities on the Korean Peninsula consider themselves as the sole legitimate state responsible for the governance of all Koreans living there, regardless of which side of the DMZ they live. Yet both states have been admitted to the UN and have been recognized by the international community as possessing both *de facto* and *de jure* sovereignty. Regardless of how the politicians on both sides may protest the nuances, aid passing from one to the other at the very least constitutes international assistance, even if it is not classified as ODA.

Seoul has multiple, overlapping reasons for wanting and needing to give assistance to North Korea. From a development perspective, there is hope that economic growth will lead to gradual and peaceful regime transformation in the North, or at the very least a modification of the erratic, self-destructive, and dangerous policies pursued by Pyongyang. From a security perspective (as detailed in Chapter 4), addressing some of the internal insecurity issues of North Korea may help steer Pyongyang away from the *songun* philosophy which has proved so damaging to internal human security and so threatening to international peace. From a human rights perspective, Seoul is obligated to help Koreans in the North, first as a state claiming to govern in the interests of all Koreans on the peninsula, and second, due to the obligations placed on all members of the international community when a state (in this case the DPRK) fails in its responsibility to protect its citizens and to provide for their human security. So great is the commitment in Seoul that successive administrations in the ROK have continued to give humanitarian assistance to the DPRK even while Pyongyang has been threatening or carrying out hostile acts.

In 1995, in the face of a humanitarian catastrophe in North Korea, and with Pyongyang making an international appeal for assistance to meet its population's dire need, an agreement was reached between Japan and the ROK to jointly supply food aid to the DPRK. Seoul announced that it would provide the DPRK with 150,000 tons of rice, after an abrupt semi-official talk in Beijing on June 17 (Noland *et al.*, 1999, p. 9). To explain this sudden policy reversal, the South Korean public was told that the aid would help to build trust with North Korea. Kim Yong-sam even sent his prime minister, Lee Hong Koo, to the port of Donghae to celebrate the first shipment of South Korean rice to the North (Oberdorfer, 2001, p. 372). The ROK government eventually decided to pledge US$3 million worth of aid, in the form of mixed grains and dried milk, to the DPRK through the WFP and UNICEF. Public sentiment in favor of assisting the North grew, and by the summer of 1997, the Kim Young-sam administration had provided another US$24.13 million worth of food aid, which included mixed grains, maize, corn-soya blend, and dried milk, through the WFP and the UNICEF (Moon, 2011, p. 19).

In 1998, the newly elected South Korean President Kim Dae-jung initiated a positive engagement policy toward North Korea called the 'Sunshine Policy', which emphasized reconciliation and cooperation between the two sides (Kim, 1999, pp. 12, 64–5). In pursuit of these goals, the ROK government provided the DPRK with 30,000 tons of maize and 10,000 tons of flour through the WFP in 1998. Immediately after sending aid through the WFP, Seoul attempted bilateral assistance. In March 1999, the ROK government decided to provide 115,000 tons of chemical fertilizer to the DPRK with no pre-conditions. To procure the fertilizer, the government spent 33.9 million won from the Inter-Korea Cooperation Fund, while another 12.3 million won was raised from the civilian sector through the South Korean Red Cross (Chae, 2001, p. 7). Afterwards, the North adopted a more positive attitude toward the Sunshine Policy (Lee, 2009, pp. 119–20). Learning from past experiences, the Kim Dae-jung administration's new engagement policy took on practical operating principles such as 'Easy tasks first, difficult tasks later', 'Economy first, politics later', 'Non-governmental organizations first, government later', and 'Give first, take later' (Moon, 2012, p. 26).

The Kim Dae-jung administration continued to promote this policy even during tense moments in the inter-Korean relationship, including during the shooting incidents between the two sides' warships off the west coast of the Korean peninsula, North Korea's launching of a ballistic missile, and the financial crisis (Kim, 2001, pp. 248–9). The continuation of the policy led to the first inter-Korean summit in June 2000 and the June 15 North-South Joint Declaration, which dramatically stimulated economic cooperation and exchange between the North and South (Moon, 2012, p. 49). The ROK government pledged to provide 200,000 tons of fertilizer in June and an additional 100,000 tons in August. In September, for the first time since the famine started, the DPRK officially requested food aid from the ROK, to which the ROK responded with a long-term loan of 300,000 tons of rice and 200,000 tons of maize. In addition to the food loan, the Kim Dae-jung administration also provided multilateral assistance in 2001. The ROK government pledged 100,000 tons of maize through the WFP and contributed US$460,000 to preventing the spread of malaria through the WHO. The ROK also provided 200,000 tons of fertilizer in 2001 (Chae, 2001, p. 8). Even with the souring of relations between the DPRK and ROK's patron, the United States, the Kim Dae-jung administration never stopped providing assistance to the North.

The Roh Moo-hyun administration's North Korea policy, the 'Peace and Prosperity Policy', largely inherited the main tenets of the Sunshine Policy. But the mounting tension between the United States and the DPRK over the nuclear issue, and criticisms from conservative sectors of the South Korean public over sending aid without pre-conditions caused the new ROK government to put greater emphasis on the principle of reciprocity than the previous administration had done (Koh, 2005, pp. 203–4). The Roh Moo-hyun Administration nevertheless tried to avoid damaging the improved South Korean relationship with the North, which had been established during the Kim Dae-jung presidency, by pledging to supply 500,000 tons of food and 300,000 tons of fertilizer per annum. Following this, the ROK government granted 400,000 tons of rice on loan terms, sent 300,000 tons of fertilizer directly, and provided 100,000 tons of maize through the WFP in 2003 and 2004 (Kim, 2005, p. 16). In 2003, the ROK government also managed to persuade the United States to reach out to North Korea through a multilateral initiative to resolve the nuclear crisis: the so-called 'Six-Party Talks'.

During this period, the ROK government used aid as a bargaining chip to attract the DPRK back to the table. Responding to an appeal from the North Koreans to provide fertilizer in 2005, the South Korean government asked them to hold the inter-Korean vice-ministerial meetings in return, ultimately leading to the vice-ministerial meeting in May 2005. The ROK sent 350,000 tons of fertilizer and provided 500,000 tons of rice on loan terms in exchange in 2005 (MOU, 2005, p. 174). This progress was, however, set back almost immediately by the Banco Delta Asia scandal resulting in the United States freezing North Korean funds, after accusing the DPRK of counterfeiting and laundering US dollars. In July, North Korea conducted ballistic missile tests, followed by a nuclear test in October 2006 (Hamid-ur-Rehman, 2010, p. 10). After the missile tests, the ROK government suspended a food loan and the delivery of 100,000 tons of rice which had been pledged to North Korean flood victims in 2006 (Moon, 2011, pp. 21, 155).

In late 2006, relations between the United States and the DPRK began to improve, with some of the North Korean funds released. Furthermore, on 14 February 2007, the Six-Party Talks progressed toward an agreement to implement a first phase of the September 19 joint statement, which caused the South Korean government to resume aid to the North. In 2007, the ROK government provided 400,000 tons of rice in the form of a loan, as well as 300,000 tons of fertilizer and 44,000 tons of food aid through the WFP (Moon, 2011, p. 18; Gyeonggi, 2012, p. 340). As the inter-Korean relationship improved, the Second Inter-Korean Summit was held in October 2007 between Kim Jong-il and Roh Moo-hyun. In the October 4 South-North Joint Declaration, on the final day of the summit, North Korea and South Korea reaffirmed the spirit of the June 15 Declaration, and showed their willingness to build peace on the Korean peninsula through international relations and their economic cooperation with one other (Korea Times, 2007).

As inter-Korean relations failed to improve, and indeed worsened, with growing exasperation in the South at the intransigence of Pyongyang and the discrediting of unconditional assistance, the new Lee Myung-bak administration in Seoul reverted to a more coercive engagement with the North, linking assistance with verifiable progress on certain key issues. After his inauguration in 2008, President Lee introduced his 'Vision 3000' policy, which stated that if North Korea would implement a complete and verifiable dismantlement of its nuclear weapons program and introduce a market-oriented open economic system, then South Korea would assist the DPRK in improving its economy and education, and finance and welfare systems (Kim, 2008, p. 8).

The DPRK reacted sharply against the new South Korean policy. Shortly after the announcement of the new policy, North Korea disconnected the direct hotline between the North and South, which had been set up in 2000 during the Kim Dae-jung administration (Korea Times, 2008). The North Korean state news agency 'Korean Central News Agency' (KCNA) denounced South Korean policy as 'nothing but sheer sophism', and criticized Lee Myung-bak, saying that he 'does not want the improvement of the inter-Korean relations but goes reckless, unable to judge the situation, hell-bent on escalating confrontation with fellow countrymen' (KCNA, 2009).

In 2010, the relationship between the two Korean governments worsened even more, especially after the 26 March 2010 sinking of the South Korean warship, the *Cheonan*, which claimed all 46 lives aboard (Korea Times, 2010). The ROK government formally accused the DPRK of attacking and sinking the ship and announced the May 24 Measures, which suspended all inter-Korean cooperation with the exception of the Kaesong Industrial Park and certain limited humanitarian assistance for the most vulnerable groups in the DPRK (KBS World, 2012). Although in 2010 Seoul provided 5000 tons of rice to North Korean flood victims, and in 2011, it contributed 6.5 billion won through UNICEF to support infants and children, the overall humanitarian assistance to the DPRK in 2011 decreased by almost 70 per cent compared to the previous year (Gyeonggi, 2012, pp. 336–8).

It seems, however, that despite recent escalations, hostile posturing, and saber rattling by both sides, the idea that North Korea must somehow be engaged from both humanitarian and national security perspectives has become received wisdom in the South. In the 2012 Presidential elections, both front-running candidates, the eventual victor, Park Geun-hye, and her defeated rival, Moon Jae-in, campaigned on the need for more constructive dialogue and engagement with the DPRK. As mentioned in the introduction to this chapter, since becoming president, Park Geun-hye has made this her policy platform through an emphasis on trustpolitik and humanitarian assistance, even while acknowledging through the Presidential Transition Team that the new government would increase national defense budget 'above the rate of increase in national spending to show its firm determination regarding national security' (Park, 2013).

Conclusion

The ROK remains one of the few ODA development success stories, overcoming the legacies of conflict, extreme poverty, insecurity, and authoritarian regimes to become a dual (economic and political governance) miracle on the Han. It has emerged from the ashes of war, to a situation where it is able to provide havens safe from fear and want for the majority of its people, and even become a regional economic powerhouse and global political player in the course of a mere half century. As such, it serves as a tremendous example to other regional challenging case studies of what can be achieved.

Based on its own development experience, South Korea has prioritized its assistance to others on building socioeconomic infrastructure as a ground for growth. Based on a combination of national interest and local knowledge/identity, the ROK has geographically concentrated its assistance toward the East Asian region. When economic development is considered as a tool for enhancing human security, as well as a goal in and of itself, such policies can be seen to contribute extensively toward providing freedom from fear and want. In addition, however, South Korea acts more directly to promote human security through humanitarian assistance and regional and global peace and security dialogues.

Although South Korea has been criticized not only for its relatively low level of ODA as a proportion of GDP, but also for high levels of loans, more important than just the volume of aid itself is what South Korea brings to the development cooperation community. First of all, South Korea was never a colonizer of other nations, but rather was a victim of colonization, and is seen as less of a threat than regional great powers to national sovereignty. That is, unlike Western donors and its East Asian neighbors China and Japan, South Korea can operate with a greater reservoir of trust among developing countries. Second, as the newest member of OECD/DAC, South Korea cannot be criticized (as China has been) for providing development assistance with little regard to international development norms and guidelines. Likewise, in some respects, South Korea is also different from Japan, which, as described in Chapter 9, has been criticized for the over-prioritization of its own national security interest in determining aid policy. Rather, South Korea has made an effort to make its mark on the global stage and meet its growing role as an emerging donor of development through hosting the fifth G20 Summit and the HLF-4, as well as through supporting various environmental, NTS, and humanitarian initiatives.

Finally, ROK humanitarian assistance to the DPRK has become a cornerstone of its security and humanitarian policy-making, and has become embedded in the large body politic. Thus South Korea stands not only as an example of the protection and promotion of human security in its own right, to be emulated by other East Asian states, but also as the first of a new breed of actors and donors from the region. The potential contributions of other new regional actors and donors form the backdrop of Chapter 11 of this volume.

Notes

1. Korea's top 15 recipients include Vietnam, Iraq, Indonesia, Sri Lanka, Bangladesh, Cambodia, China, Afghanistan, Philippines, Mongolia, Laos, Uzbekistan, Angola, Myanmar, and Nepal.
2. For a detailed discussion of the perceived shortcomings of this act see Brendan Howe (2006), 'Strategic Implications of the 2004 US North Korean Human Rights Act', *Asian Perspective* 30(1) 191–219 (Portland State University, Spring 2006).

References

APC (Asia-Pacific Center for the Responsibility to Protect) (2009) 'Japan and Korea on Responsibility to Protect', http://www.responsibilitytoprotect.org/files/Japan%20and%20Korea%20on%20R2P.pdf.

Caballero-Anthony, M. (2010) 'Non-Traditional Security Challenges, Regional Governance, and the ASEAN Political-Security Community (APSC)', Asia Security Initiative Policy Series: Working Paper, 7, 1–17.

Cha, V. and Kim, E. (2013) 'Inauguration of South Korea's New President Park Guen-hye', Center for Strategic & International Studies (CSIS), 6 February 2013, csis.org/publication/inauguration-south-koreas-new-president-park-geun-hye.

Chae, K. (2001) 'The Future of the Sunshine Policy: Strategies for Survival', *East Asian Review*, 13(4), 3–17.

Chung, Y. I. (2007) *South Korea in the Fast Lane: Economic Development and Capital Formation* (New York: Oxford University Press).

CIA (2013) 'The World Factbook', https://www.cia.gov/library/publications/the-world-factbook/geos/ks.html.

CSCAP (Council for Security Cooperation in the Asia Pacific) (2013) 'The Kuala Lumpur Statement', http://www.cscap.org/index.php?page=about-us.

EACP (East Asia Climate Partnership) (2013) 'EACP Initiatives, Introduction', http://eacp.koica.go.kr.

EDCF (Economic Development Cooperation Fund) (2003) *EDCF Annual Report 2003* (Seoul: EDCF).

EDCF (2004) *EDCF Annual Report 2004* (Seoul: EDCF).

EDCF (2005) *EDCF Annual Report 2005* (Seoul: EDCF).

Eximbank (Export-Import Bank of Korea) (2012) 'Sutjaro boneun ODA 2012: Urinara ODA tongyejaryojip [Facts and Figures on Korean ODA 2012]', http://www.edcfkorea.go.kr/edcf/bbs/puba/list.jsp?bbs_code_id=1311914922967&bbs_code_tp=BBS_4.

Goodenough, P. (2004) 'S Korea Wary of US Law Targeting North Korea Human Rights', CNS News, 21 October 2004, http://cnsnews.com/news/article/s-korea-wary-us-law-targeting-north-korean-human-rights.

GOK (Government of Korea) (2010) *Strategic Plan for International Development Co-operation* (Seoul: GOK).

Gyeonggi Province (2012) 'The White Paper on Gyeonggi Province's Inter-Korean Exchanges & Cooperation 2001–2011', Gyeonggi Province.

Hamid-ur-Rehman (2010) 'The Korean Peninsula: Peaceful Engagement for Humanitarian Concerns', NTS-Asia Research Paper No. 3 (Singapore: RSIS Centre for Non-Traditional Security (NTS) Studies).

Hernandez, C. G. (2007) 'Strengthening ASEAN-Korea Co-operation in Non-Traditional Security Issues' in: K. L. Ho (ed.) *ASEAN-Korea Relations: Security Trade and Community Building* (Singapore: ISEAS Publishing).

Huntington, S. (1991) *The Third Wave: Democratization in the Late 20th Century* (Norman: University of Oklahoma Press).

Kang, S. J., Lee, H. S. and Park, B. (2011) 'Does Korea Follow Japan in Foreign Aid? Relationships between Aid and Foreign Investment', *Japan and the World Economy*, 23, 19–27.

KBS WORLD (2012) 'May 24th Measures: First Two Years', http://world.kbs.co.kr/english/event/nkorea_nuclear/now_02_detail.htm?No=1329.

Korea Central News Agency (KCNA) (2009) 'Traitor Lee Myung Bak's Anti-Reunification Remarks Rebuffed', http://www.kcna.co.jp/item/2009/200901/news04.20090104-06ee.html.

Kim, C. N. (2005) 'The Roh Moo Hyun Government's Policy Toward North Korea', East-West Center Working Papers, 11.

Kim, D. J. (1999) *Government of the People – Collected Speeches of President* (Seoul: Office of the President, the Republic of Korea).

Kim, E. M. (1997) *Big Business, Strong State: Collusion and Conflict in South Korean Development, 1960–1990* (New York: State University of New York Press).

Kim, E. M. and Oh, J. H. (2012) 'Determinants of Foreign Aid: The Case of South Korea', *Journal of East Asian Studies*, 12, 251–73.

Kim, H. J. (2001) 'Recent Transformation in Inter-Korean Relations: The North-South Summit Conference, the North-South Joint Declaration, Subsequent Event, and Their Meaning' in C. I. Moon, O. A. Westad and G.H. Kahng (eds), *Ending the Cold War in Korea: Theoretical and Historical Perspectives* (Seoul: Yonsei University Press).

Kim, J. K. (2010) 'Korea's Economic Relations with Southeast Asia' in D. I. Steinberg (ed.), *Korea's Changing Roles in Southeast Asia: Expanding Influence and Relations* (Seoul: ASEAM-Korea Centre).

Kim, J. Y. (2011) 'Foreign Aid and Economic Development: The Success Story of South Korea', *Pacific Focus*, 26 (2), 260–86.

Kim, K. S. (2008) 'Lee Myung-bak Government's Paradigm for Foreign and Security Policy', *Korea and World Affairs*, 32(1) (Seoul: Research Center for Peace and Unification of Korea).

Kim, Y. L. and Tcha, M. (2012) 'Introduction to the Knowledge Sharing Porgram (KSP) of Korea', http://keia.org/publication/introduction-knowledge-sharing-program-ksp-korea.

Koh, Y. H. (2005) 'Two Years of the Roh Moo-hyun Administration's North Korea Policy', *Sejong Policy Studies*, 1(2), 1–20 (Seoul: The Sejong Institute).

KOICA (Korea International Cooperation Agency) (2012) 'Environmental Mainstreaming Guideline', http://210.90.109.15/search/media/img/CAT000000034617?metsno=000000011082&fileid=M000000011082_FILE000002.

KOICA (2013) 'Schemes, Training Program', http://www.koica.go.kr/.

Korea Times (2007) 'Full Text of Joint Declaration', http://www.koreatimes.co.kr/www/news/nation/2007/10/116_11347.html.

Korea Times (2008) 'Inter-Korean Hotline No Longer Functioning', 13 July, 2008, http://www.koreatimes.co.kr/www/news/nation/2008/07/116_27500/html.

Korea Times (2010) 'Lee to Reveal Stern Countermeasures to Cheonan Today', 23 May, 2010, http://www.koreatimes.co.kr/www/news/nation/2010/06/116_66352.html.

KSP (Knowledge Sharing Program) (2013) 'Bilateral Consultation', http://www.ksp.go.kr/.

Lee, J. M. (2009) 'The History of South Korean Aid to DPRK and its Transition to Development Assistance: Aid to DPRK in the Context of the Inter-Korean Relationship', in International Conference on Humanitarian and Development Assistance to DPRK, Seoul, 24–26 November, 2009.

Lee, J. W. (1997) 'Economic Growth and Human Development in the Republic of Korea, 1945–1992', Occasional Paper, No. 24 (New York: UNDP), http://hdr.undp.org/en/reports/global/hdr1997/papers/jong-wha_lee.pdf.

Lee, K. K. (2004) *Hangugedaehan kaebalwŏnjowa hyŏmnyŏk* [Development Assistance and Cooperation to South Korea: A Review of ODA for South Korea as a Recipient and Case Studies] in Korean (Seoul: KOICA).

McGinn, N. F., Sondgrass, D. R., Kim, Y. B., Kim, S. B. and Kim, Q. Y. (1980) *Education and Development in Korea* (Cambridge: Harvard University Press).
MOFAT (Ministry of Foreign Affairs and Trade) (2009) 'Introduction to New Asian Initiative', www.mofat.go.kr/mofat/pcrm/eng5.doc.
Moon, C. I. (2012) *Sunshine Policy: In Defense of Engagement as a Path to Peace in Korea* (Seoul: Yonsei University Press).
Moon, K. Y. (2011) 'The Role of Humanitarian NGOs: Impact on South Korean Food Aid Policy towards North Korea from 1995–2007', PhD Thesis, Cranfield University.
Ministry of Unification (MOU) (2005) *Unification White Paper* (Seoul: Ministry of Unification).
National Assembly of the Republic of Korea (2010) *Framework Act on International Development Co-operation* (Seoul: National Assembly).
Noland, M., Robinson, S. and Wang, T. (1999)' Famine in North Korea: Causes and Cures', Working Paper Series WP99-2, Peterson Institute for International Economics.
Oberdorfer, D. (2001) *The Two Koreas: A Contemporary History* (Indianapolis: Basic Books).
ODA Korea (2013) 'History of Korea's ODA', http://www.odakorea.go.kr/index.jsp.
OECD (Organisation for Economic Co-operation and Development) (2012) *DAC Peer Review of Korea* (Paris: OECD), http://www.oecd.org/dac/peerreviewsofdacmembers/Korea%20CRC%20-%20FINAL%2021%20JAN.pdf.
OECD (2013) 'International Development Statistics', http://stats.oecd.org/qwids/.
Park, B. S. (2013) 'Incoming Park Administration Plans to Increase Defense Spending', The Hankyoreh, 22 February 2013, http://english.hani.co.kr/arti/english_edition/e_national/575126.html.
Park, I. K. (2009) 'Plenary Meeting of the General Assembly on Responsibility to Protect, Statement', 23 July 2009, http://www.responsibilitytoprotect.org/Korea_ENG.pdf.
Pillay, P. N. (2010) *Linking Higher Education and Economic Development: Implications for Africa from Three Successful Systems* (Wynberg: Center for Higher Education Transformation (CHET)).
PMO (Prime Minister's Office) (2010a) *Presidential Decree of the Framework Act on International Development Co-operation* (Seoul: PMO).
PMO (2010b) *The Mid-term ODA Policy for 2011–2015* (Seoul: PMO).
Steinberg, D. I. (2010) 'Tenuous Beginnings, Vigorous Developments' in D. I. Steinberg (ed.), *Korea's Changing Roles in Southeast Asia: Expanding Influence and Relations* (Seoul: ASEAN-Korea Centre).
UNDP (United Nations Development Programme) (1994) *Human Development Report: New Dimensions of Human Security* (New York: Oxford University Press).
World Bank (2013) 'World Development Indicators', http://databank.worldbank.org/ddp/home.do?Step=3&id=4.

11
Future Contributions to East Asian Human Security

Introduction

As outlined in Chapter 1, there is no doubt that, from a state-centric perspective, East Asia represents an extremely successful region of development in terms of both economic growth and stable and secure governance. The challenging case studies in this volume demonstrate, however, that some states in the region and some regions within states have yet to share in this success. Moreover, this book identifies serious shortcomings, from both normative and pragmatic perspectives, in adhering solely to state-centric measurements of security, development, and governance. Although East Asia has been identified as a region particularly wedded to Westphalian notions of statehood, the region is gradually becoming suffused with human-centric governance norms as a result of influence and pressure from internal and external normative constituencies. This has led to something of an overlapping consensus, where, from different historical and normative backgrounds, nevertheless, those who govern have become aware of an imperative to consider the protection and promotion of human security through the provision of havens free from fear and want.

Chapters 9 and 10 have identified how some states in the region have, in fact, even become champions of alternative approaches to human security and that in certain circumstances these approaches may hold a comparative advantage over those pursued by extra-regional actors when dealing with regional challenging case studies. Thus, in the future, not only is the East Asian region likely to continue to be influenced by the international normative and pragmatic consensus on human-centric good governance but it is also likely to be the source of valuable new approaches to achieving good governance objectives. This final chapter, therefore, considers possible contributions from the two most important emerging actors in the region, the PRC and ASEAN. Both might be considered unlikely candidates for inclusion, given that China's normative impact is generally considered in negative terms, and the ASEAN Way champions non-interference and state sovereignty. Nevertheless, while both could be considered further obstacles to protecting and providing for human security in East Asia, this chapter briefly explores ways in which these two major regional players could have a positive impact.

China's emerging impact

Due to its size, China can have a tremendous impact on human security in East Asia for the better or for the worse through two mechanisms: First, domestic policy implementation, development and governance can drastically alter measurements of human well-being in the region due to the sheer number of Chinese and peoples from neighboring countries who are impacted. Second, through an increasingly confident and assertive role on the international stage, China has great potential to change the parameters of national governance in challenging cases and regional governance as a whole.

A recent volume edited by Guoguang Wu focuses on the challenges posed by China to human security through both its foreign relations and the global implications of its domestic policies (2013). In particular, a chapter by Qing *et al.* (2013, pp. 164–92) assesses the environmental costs of China's participation in global capitalism, while Gaye Christofferson looks at the human security implications of China's foreign energy relations (2013, pp. 193–214). Gabriel Botel (2013, pp. 215–44) further develops these concerns by looking at how China's increasing demands for energy are fuelling human insecurity in Myanmar. Aung San Suu Kyi (2011) has also expressed her concerns about the negative impact of the operations of Chinese energy companies upon human security, as well as those of South Korea, within the borders of Myanmar. Finally, Australian Federal Police (AFP) Commissioner Mick Keelty, in his 2007 dire warnings about the regional security impact of environmental degradations described in Chapter 2, singled out China's need to increase its food production by about 50 per cent above today's levels to feed its predicted 2030 population. He asked, 'How does it achieve this if its available land is dramatically shrinking and millions of people are on the move because of land and water?' (Lauder, 2007).

Yet China does seem to at least have made some progress toward addressing human security challenges at home through governance initiatives. In February 2001, China's National People's Congress (NPC) and the Chinese legislature ratified the International Covenant on Economic, Social, and Cultural Rights, which had been signed by the Chinese government in 1997. Li Peng, chairman of the NPC Standing Committee, declared that 'China will take legislative, judicial, and administrative measures to carry out the rights and obligations in the covenant' (Chu, 2002, p. 12). And certainly there seems to be some evidence to back up this claim. Between 1980 and 2012, China's HDI rose by 2.0 per cent annually from 0.407 to 0.699 today, which gives the country a rank of 101 out of 187 countries with comparable data. 'The HDI of East Asia and the Pacific as a region increased from 0.432 in 1980 to 0.683 today, placing China above the regional average' (UNDP, 2013).

In addressing the MDG of halving the global poverty rate from its 1990 level by 2015, World Bank measurements would seem to indicate that this is well within reach, but as pointed out by The Economist, this 'victory' is mainly due to a drop in China's poverty rate from 60 per cent in 1990 to 16 per cent in 2005. 'Because China and India accounted for over 62 per cent of the planet's poor in 1990, changes to the world's poverty rate depend heavily on their performance' (The Economist, 2010). Dramatic progress toward achieving the MDGs has, in fact, been made in the country, despite the challenges posed by the pursuit of macro-economic development projects such as the Three Gorges Dam and environmental degradation. In 2008, the Chinese Ministry of Foreign Affairs and the UN System in China found that China is likely to achieve all the MDGs by 2015, although the country should focus more attention on promoting gender equality and empowering women, containing and reversing the spread of HIV/AIDS by 2015, and reversing environmental and resource degradation by 2015 (CHDR, 2010, p. 9). The PRC has pulled some 500 million out of poverty, and at the same time committed to tackle their carbon footprint. In December 2009, China made its commitment to reduce carbon dioxide emissions per unit of GDP in 2020 by 40 per cent to 45 per cent compared with 2005 levels' (CHDR, 2010, pp. i and 1). Overall, therefore, China has experienced considerable progress on human and environmental security. In part, this is a by-product of not only development success, but also in part due to a shift in policy prioritization.

This policy shift itself is, as outlined in Chapter 3, part of a realignment of understandings of national security along more comprehensive lines throughout the region, but in particular in China where those who govern face increasingly vociferous demands from their citizens for more open and egalitarian governance. Growth has not benefited all, and the geographic and socioeconomic distribution of both the good and the bad (horizontal and vertical axis) is cause for concern. It is in the national interest to keep the people happy and also to sustain their environment. Shulong Chu is thus correct to point out how Chinese security doctrine and approaches have been repositions in the post-Cold War era, with the scope of security being enlarged and new levels of understanding being developed. 'Internal stability, which includes political stability and social stability, has become a major concern for the party and the government' (Chu, 2002, p. 2). Chinese concepts of security now encompass 'economic security, food security, energy security, financial security, environmental security, cooperative security/security cooperation, common security, and multilateral security', and all these terms have entered the national discourse through official language, academic writing, the news media, and expressions of public opinion (*ibid.*). Ordinary Chinese are notably more concerned about domestic security challenges such as the energy shortage, pollution, and spread of pandemics than by their surrounding powers' economic and military challenges (Jung, 2012, p. 9).

Although, like South Korea, the leadership of PRC has shied away from actually using the term 'human security' primarily due to its close approximation in Chinese to the human rights terminology identified in Chapter 2 as problematic, nevertheless, the idea of 'constructing a harmonious world' advocated by Chinese leaders is, in practice, closely correlated. The guiding principle of building a harmonious world involve 'people-centered scientific development', by which is meant the fundamental interests of the broadest possible segment of the masses, and the realization of the overall development of the people is taken as the starting and end point for economic and social development (Hu, 2011). A recent emphasis on 'people's safety' would seem to reflect some of the freedom from fear concerns of the human security paradigm, while the efforts made by the government to control the prices of vegetables and housing can be seen to reflect a desire to provide freedom from want. Thus, it might be that in the future East Asian countries may look to the PRC not only as an exemplar of macro-economic development but also even as a regional example of sound governance, although it must be admitted that at the moment there are at least as many negatives as positives for the human security of the most vulnerable when ruled from Beijing.

At the international level, China has also started to make an impact on human security, in both negative and positive ways. There are concerns that China's policies aimed at improving the human security of its own citizens negatively impacts on the human security of those under other jurisdictions (Bron, 2010). The PRC has been extensively criticized for putting national interest and political alliances ahead of the protection of the most vulnerable when repatriating North Korean refugees back to the DPRK, and ethnic Kachin refugees back to Myanmar, at a time when both groups face significant threat to their well-being and even lives upon their return. On the other hand, maintaining good relations with these two rogue regimes has allowed Beijing a degree of leverage over them conspicuously denied to Western actors. In 2011, at the time of the breakthrough in negotiations between the Government of Myanmar and the National League for democracy, most internal commentators attributed the mellowing of the government's position to three things: pressure from China, pressure from ASEAN, and awareness of the Arab Spring uprisings (NLD, 2011). China is often accused of supporting rogue regimes, but in recent years, as pointed out by Stephanie Kleine-Ahlbrandt and Andrew Small (2008, p. 38), Beijing has been quietly overhauling its policies toward pariah states, conditioning its diplomatic protection of them, forcing them to become more acceptable to the international community, and 'supporting – in some cases even helping to create – processes that chart a path to legitimacy for these states'.

The PRC has generally been perceived as hostile toward security and governance multilateralism and humanitarian intervention. Certainly in its role as a permanent member of the United Nations Security Council (UNSC), it has been viewed as standing in the way of purported humanitarian interventions in Kosovo, Darfur, and most recently, Syria. Likewise, when, in 1971, it assumed its UNSC seat, it rejected entirely the concept of international peacekeeping. China is not, however, the out-and-out opponent of humanitarian intervention or R2P it is sometimes portrayed. China has, in fact, twice endorsed R2P at the UN, first at the World Summit in 2005 and later in Security Council Resolution 1674, since which time, the PRC has 'clearly and consistently affirmed the R2P principle and issued corresponding statements in favor of bolstering the UN's capacity to avert mass atrocity' (Teitt, 2008, p. 2). As further pointed out in an International Crisis Group (ICG) report in 2009:

> [China] supported the resolutions authorizing IFOR and KFOR in Bosnia and peace enforcement operations in Somalia in the early 1990s. Although it opposed the first Gulf War, China abstained and allowed Resolution 678, authorising member states to use all necessary means to restore international peace and security after Iraq's invasion of Kuwait, to pass. Despite its opposition to intervention in Kosovo and damage to its embassy in Belgrade, China has supported every operation in Kosovo since, including peace enforcement operations. (ICG, 2009, p. 3)

As pointed out by Sarah Teitt's (2008, p. 2) detailed report on the subject, insofar as China's interpretation of R2P is representative of the views of similarly cautious, yet engaged states, these developments hold out hope for deepening the consensus on R2P and for translating the R2P from words to deeds. In terms of peacekeeping, China's attitudinal change is nothing short of revolutionary. In the last decade and a half, China has deployed over 10,000 peacekeepers serving in more than 20 UN peacekeeping operations worldwide, including Asia, balancing new motivations against its traditional adherence to non-intervention (ICG, 2009, p. 1). It regularly has more than 2,000 peacekeepers in the field at any one time, second to France among the five permanent members (P-5) of the Security Council and 14th among 119 troop contributing countries. 'In fact, China and France have alternated in occupying the position of top P-5 contributor' (ICG, 2009, p. 6). China's contribution to the peacekeeping budget while remaining small is also growing, from around 0.9 per cent throughout the 1990s, to 1.5 per cent by December 2000, to just above 3 per cent by 2008 (ICG, 2009, p. 8).

While China's support for problem regimes has fed suspicions that Chinese peacekeeping is primarily motivated by economic interests, in fact China's economic and peacekeeping decision-making tracks operate separately. Furthermore, again, as mentioned above with North Korea and Myanmar, China's relationships with difficult regimes may well benefit UN peacekeeping efforts, as the PRC 'can bring to the table valuable political capital and economic leverage, in some cases even encouraging host countries to consent to peacekeeping operations' (ICG, 2009, p. i). China has, in addition, provided economic and personnel assistance to countries suffering from natural disasters including the Southeast Asian countries ravaged by the 2004 Tsunami (Hu, 2011). Also in 2004, at the non-official meeting of the 12th APEC leaders in Santiago, Chili, President Hu Jintao called for the strengthening of human security – the first time the concept had been expounded by a Chinese head of state (*ibid.*).

More controversial has been the role of the PRC as an aid donor. China in fact remains a substantial recipient of foreign aid. What international assistance it does give is often criticized as motivated by strategic gain (competition with Taiwan for recognition or support for allies), or for economic gain, financed through the China Eximbank in the form of concessional loans that directly support Chinese companies or China's appetite for resources. Such accusations are, of course, similar to those leveled at the other East Asian donors, Japan and South Korea, detailed in Chapters 9 and 10, and in a like manner, we can hope for collateral development benefit for recipient countries, even if the prime motivation is not humanitarian. Indeed, Hideaki Asahi (2012, p. 1) has noted that in the case of Timor-Leste, 'China has already made inroads in the construction and maintenance of lifeline infrastructure, whereas for decades overseas development cooperation with a relative advantage had been Japan's turf'. He points to a threefold presence of Chinese aid: the demonstrative aid strategy of the Chinese government, such as donations of brand-new government and public buildings; vigorous investment and expansion of retail and commercial businesses with the support of overseas Chinese communities based in East Asia; and a prevailing competitive edge of China's public corporations in underbidding competitors' tenders for public construction project contracts (*ibid.*).

The PRC actually has a long history of international assistance beginning with material assistance to the DPRK and Vietnam in 1950, then following the Asian-African Conference in Bandung, Indonesia in 1955, the scope of China's aid extended from socialist countries to other developing countries. 'In 1964, the Chinese government declared the Eight Principles for Economic Aid and Technical Assistance to Other Countries, the core content of which featured equality, mutual benefit and no strings attached, hence the basic principle for China's foreign aid was formulated' (PRC, 2011, p. 3). It is this that purported 'no strings attached' principle which allows Chinese aid to reach places other aid cannot reach, such as detailed in Chapter 4 with regard to North Korea, thereby contributing to the promotion of human security in hard to access places. 'By the end of 2009, China had provided a total of 256.29 billion yuan in aid to foreign countries, including 106.2 billion yuan in grants, 76.54 billion yuan in interest-free loans, and 73.55 billion yuan in concessional loans' (*ibid.*, p. 5). The 2011 White Paper on China's Foreign Aid also seeks to challenge the criticisms leveled above, asserting, as shown in Figure 11.1, that the majority of Chinese concessional loans (61 per cent) support 'economic infrastructure' and only 8.9 per cent of its loans support 'energy and resources development'.

Since 1981, China has worked with the UNDP to host training courses for personnel from developing countries, and by the end of 2009, had run over 4,000 training sessions, attended by some 120,000 people, from over 20 fields, including economy, diplomacy, agriculture, medical and health care, and environmental protection. China has also funded clean energy initiatives and trained over 1,400 people in developing countries on how to develop and use renewable resources (*ibid.*, pp. 7 and 13). Although Africa receives the largest share of Chinese assistance, Asia still receives about a third, and, in accordance with international guidelines, the largest share (almost 40 per cent) goes to LDCs (*ibid.*, p. 10).

Thus, although emerging China poses governance challenges at the national, regional, and even global levels, nevertheless, there is hope that it can contribute significantly to the future protection and promotion of the human security of the most vulnerable. Importantly, the PRC offers something different, and potentially complimentary, to the policies and roles of traditional donors and actors. The same can also be said of ASEAN, and is dealt with in the next section.

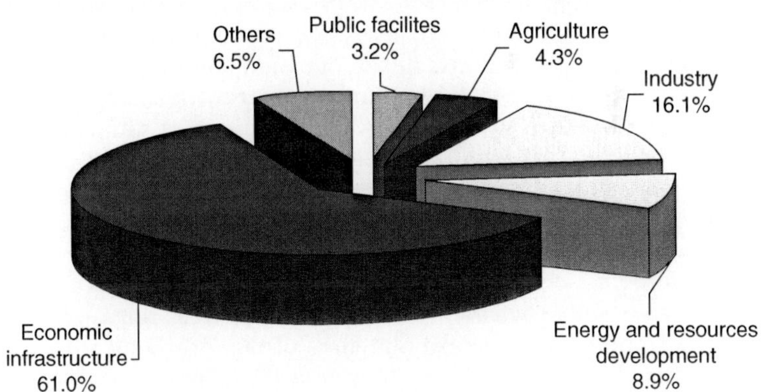

Figure 11.1 Sectoral distribution of concessional loans from China (by the end of 2009)

Note: Graphics shows the figures of sectoral distribution of concessional loans from China to other developing countries by the end of 2009, according to a white paper on China's foreign aid issued by China's Information Office of the State Council on April 21, 2011. (Xinhua/China's Information Office of the State Council).

ASEAN's good governance agenda

Chapter 3 developed the concept of state-centric governance in East Asia in considerable detail. Likewise, ASEAN's historical role, and particularly that of the 'ASEAN Way' in perpetuating such a world view, has been extensively documented. The ASEAN Way is recorded as: 'a. Mutual respect for the independence, sovereignty, equality, territorial integrity and national identity of all nations; b. The right of every State to lead its national existence free from external interference, subversion or coercion; c. Non-interference in the internal affairs of one another' (Bali Declaration, 1976). Consequently, not only did Southeast Asian states condemn the invasion of Cambodia by Vietnam, despite the collateral benefit of removing the Khmer Rouge from power, but ASEAN states were also very reluctant to take direct action in Timor-Leste despite calls for regional intervention in the face of the post-referendum violence in 1999 (Terada, 2011, p. 6).

While, as detailed in Chapter 8, the UN eventually dispatched the Australian-led International Force for East Timor (INTERFET), to address the humanitarian and security crises in the country, the participation of ASEAN was limited, with Thailand and Malaysia eventually deciding to join the peacekeeping force not out of genuine humanitarian concern for the people in East Timor, but out of unease at being seen as Indonesian supporters and to restrict Australia's dominant control over the operation (Terada, 2011, p. 7). Although ASEAN's silence could in part be attributed to Indonesia's dominant status in the organization, 'a main rationale was its adherence to the non-intervention principle', and the view that the occupation was a domestic matter of one member state (*ibid.*).

Similar concerns have also been expressed regarding ASEAN's failure to hold Myanmar to account for its sins of omission and commission regarding the protection and promotion of human security. Here, however, again as detailed in Chapter 3, we can see the beginning of a shift in ASEAN's anti-interventionary position. Catherine Drummond (2009, p. 8) feels that ASEAN's relations with Myanmar, in this regard, 'serve as the most pertinent illustration of the Association's gradual move towards a more flexible understanding and application of non-interference'. As noted in Chapter 3, much of the pressure for a change in ASEAN's stance toward non-intervention in Myanmar came from Thailand. It might be argued that this merely once again reflects the national security interests of one of the member states, given the instances of cross-border drug smuggling, conflict, flows of refugees and economic migrants, and terrorist style hijackings and the seizure of government buildings in Thailand (Drummond, 2009, p. 9). This case study highlights not only the spillover between human, national, and international insecurity but it also shows the evolution of the ASEAN way.

Although Pitsuwan's flexible engagement was rejected, in December 2003 member states launched the Forum on International Support for National

Reconciliation in Myanmar 'Bangkok Process'. The 11th ASEAN Summit in December 2005 saw open criticism and condemnation of the domestic situation in Burma and a resolution to send a delegation to investigate. By the 13th annual Summit in November 2007, ASEAN was accepting terms of interference in a member country that it was starkly opposed to nine years earlier, and a new ASEAN Charter which embodied a compromise between the traditional principle of non-interference and a more flexible perspective (Drummond, 2009, pp. 10–11). Ultimately the ASEAN Political-Security Community (APSC) Blueprint which was adopted by the ASEAN Leaders at the 14th ASEAN Summit on 1 March 2009, in Cha-am/Hua Hin, Thailand went much further than the initial proposal for flexible engagement. According to Article 7 of this document, the members were committed to the promotion of 'political development in adherence to the principles of democracy, the rule of law and good governance, respect for and promotion and protection of human rights'. Indeed, two of the main actions plans refer to the promotion of 'good governance' and 'human rights' (ASEAN, 2009, pp. 1–2; 8–9). Much more striking, however, than ASEAN's active promotion of human security norms, has been its creation of an operating environment conducive to the facilitation of human security protection through civil society.

The underlying premise of Thakur and Newman's (2004, p. 1) influential volume on *Broadening Asia's Security Discourse and Agenda: Political, Social, and Environmental Perspectives* is that 'traditional security has failed to deliver meaningful security to a significant proportion of the people of Asia'. Awareness of this failure has, however, stimulated alternative security approaches in the region. As noted in Chapter 9, comprehensive security was developed by Japan in recognition of the shortcoming of traditional security planning, but the concept was also influential in Southeast Asia as far back as the Cold War, with at least three ASEAN states, Indonesia, Malaysia, and Singapore, developing their own versions (Caballero-Anthony, 2004, p. 160). Likewise Article 9 of the APSC Blueprint 'subscribes to a comprehensive approach to security, which acknowledges the interwoven relationships of political, economic, social-cultural and environmental dimensions of development' (ASEAN, 2009, p. 2). Historically therefore, instead of conventional security approaches of deterrence, power-balancing, and alliance building, ASEAN has focused mainly on 'norm-building, building trust and confidence, and developing cooperative approaches with like-minded and non-like-minded states to address non-traditional threats to state security' (Caballero-Anthony, 2004, p. 162).

The major facilitating initiative in the field of NTS carried out under the auspices of good governance in ASEAN was actually not state-centric. Running alongside the official 'track 1' inter-governmental dialogues (officials acting in their official capacities), almost from its foundation ASEAN accepted and facilitated input from unofficial 'track 2' processes (officials and non-officials acting in unofficial but influential capacities) such as eminent persons groups (EPGs), the ASEAN-Institutes of Strategic and International Studies (ASEAN-ISIS), and the Council for Security Cooperation in the Asia Pacific (CSCAP). This process in turn stimulated and helped create a space for the participation of civil society groups in governance discourse. These groups were, on the whole, deeply critical of state-centric security and development models. To these NGOs, 'if issues of extreme poverty, diseases, food scarcity, and environmental disasters are the security issues of people in ASEAN, these should be the security concerns of their governments as well'; security thinking would have to be reexamined to allow for people-centered security and development, and to them, 'security was the other side of development' (Caballero-Anthony, 2004, pp. 167–8).

In recognition of the increasing role being played by 'track 3' representatives of civil society, the ASEAN People's Assembly (APA) was launched in 2000 with the support of the Japan International Cooperation Agency (JICA) and the impetus of ASEAN-ISIS in the hope of bridging the gap between track 1, track 2, and track 3. The APA championed the importance of a people-centered ASEAN with caring and sharing societies in ASEAN community-building. With the direct interface between the ASEAN Leaders and representatives of the merged ASEAN Civil Society Conference (ACSC, originating in 2005 in Kuala Lumpur) and the ASEAN People's Forum (APF, originating in 2008 in Thailand), however, the role of APA as a bridge between the tracks was no longer required (Hernandez, 2012, p. 2). With JICA's continued support, a further step toward placing human security at the center of the governance discourse of all the tracks, but in particular in promoting the work of track 3, was taken when the ASEAN-Japan Project on Mainstreaming Human Security was launched in Tokyo on March 30, 2009 (*ibid.*, p. 1).

Thus, ASEAN has not only shifted its own policy position to one reflecting more flexibility on the question of state sovereignty and non-interference but it has also opened up policy space to grass roots movements which are more inclined to support human security and development rather than state-centric macro and aggregate measurements. The consensus-based model of governance and interaction in Southeast Asia then serves to further facilitate civil society pressures. These track 3 approaches are likely to prove increasingly influential in the most 'wired' and connected region of the world, leading to a further diffusion of intra- and inter-regional norms and an overlapping consensus concerning the R2P and provide havens free from fear and want.

Conclusion

This chapter has examined two political entities which not only have reputations of prioritizing sovereign interests, but are also, currently involved in a traditional security standoff with each other in the South

China Sea. Although both pose certain challenges to the advancement of the human security paradigm, and are at a fairly early stage in their governance evolution, nevertheless, there are significant indications of progress. Despite the overwhelming impression of Westphalian state-centricity in terms of both security and development policy prioritizations, macro and aggregate measurements of governance success, and a remarkable econophoria, even the most unlikely candidates in East Asia hold promise for the future protection and promotion of human security.

While the PRC is at an early stage of development and humanitarian assistance, the signs are that its attempts at a peaceful rise and to be a responsible global citizen will bring collateral benefit to the most vulnerable, even if only as a result of the cynical calculation of national policy-makers. ASEAN, meanwhile, has transformed in policy terms almost beyond recognition, but more importantly, the long-term multi-track policy traditions of the organization have created a space within which civil society, with its greater sympathy toward human-centered security and development can be empowered.

These cases, therefore further advance the primary and tertiary unifying themes of this volume, not only that there is an overlapping consensus regarding the R2P and provide (or at least facilitate the production of conditions conducive to) human security and good governance, defined as safe havens, free from fear and want, but also that East Asian actors do things a little differently. The volume as a whole has identified ongoing human security challenges in the region and the complex relationships between the human security paradigm and its implementation, and the competing demands of traditional security, development, and human rights approaches. These tensions are also clear in Chinese and ASEAN policy-making. Nevertheless, despite the desperate challenges, and the inbuilt resistance to the human security paradigm in governance discourse and practice in East Asia, the overwhelming take-away from this project is one of cautious optimism.

References

Asahi, H. (2012) 'An Uneasy Future for East Timor', http://www2.jiia.or.jp/en/pdf/research/20120628e-An_Uneasy_Future_of_East_Timor.pdf.

ASEAN (2009) *ASEAN Political-Security Community Blueprint* (Hua Hin: ASEAN), http://www.asean.org/archive/5187-18.pdf.

Aung San Suu Kyi (2011) Interviewed by author, National League for Democracy Headquarters, Yangon, Myanmar, 26 July 2011.

Bali Declaration (1976) *Treaty of Amity and Cooperation in Southeast Asia* (Bali: ASEAN), http://www.aseansec.org/TAC-KnowledgeKit.pdf.

Botel, G. (2013) 'Fuelling Insecurity: Energy and Human Security in Sino-Myanmar Relations' in G. Wu (ed.), *China's Challenges to Human Security: Foreign Relations and Global Implications*, 215–244 (Oxford: Routledge).

Bron (2010) 'Insight in Security China's (own) Human Security' *Current Affairs*, http://www.insight-in-security.com/2010/10/04/chinas-own-human-security/.

Caballero-Anthony, M. (2004) 'Revisioning Human Security in Southeast Asia', *Asian Perspective*, 28(3), 155–189.

China Human Development Report (CHDR) (2010) *China and a Sustainable Future: Towards a Low Carbon Economy and Society* (Beijing: UNDP and Renmin University).

Christofferson, G. (2013) 'The Human Security Implications of China's Foreign Energy Relations' in G. Wu (ed.), *China's Challenges to Human Security: Foreign Relations and Global Implications*, 193–214 (Oxford: Routledge).

Chu, S. (2002) 'China and Human Security' *North Pacific Policy Papers No. 8* (Vancouver: University of British Columbia).

Drummond, C. (2009) 'Non-interference and the Responsibility to Protect: Canvassing the Relationship between Sovereignty and Humanity in Southeast Asia', *Dialogue* 7(1), 1–22, http://www.polsis.uq.edu.au/dialogue/articledrummond2.pdf.

The Economist (2010) 'The Millennium Development Goals Global Targets, Local Ingenuity', 23 September 2010, http://www.economist.com/node/17090934?story_id=17090934.

Hernandez, C. (2012) *Mainstreaming Human Security in ASEAN Integration Volume 1: Regional Public Goods and Human Security* (Quezon City: Institute for Strategic and Development Studies).

Hu, Y. (2011) 'Human Security: Concept, Disputes and Practice' *China Human Rights Magazine*, http://www.chinahumanrights.org/CSHRS/Magazine/Text/t20110525_748537_3.htm.

International Crisis Group (ICG) (2009) 'China's Growing Role in UN Peacekeeping', *Asia Report No166 – 17 April 2009*, http://www.unhcr.org/refworld/pdfid/49ec24ca2.pdf.

Jung, Y.J. (2012). 'Rising China and the Chinese Public's Security Perceptions', *EAI Asia Security Initiative Working Paper* (Seoul: East Asian Institute).

Kleine-Ahlbrandt, S. and Small, A. (2008) 'China's New Dictatorship Diplomacy; Is Beijing Parting With Pariahs?', *Foreign Affairs*, 87(1), 38–56.

Lauder, S. (2007) 'Climate Change a Huge Security Problem: Keelty', *ABC News*, 25 September 2007, http://www.abc.net.au/news/2007-09-25/climate-change-a-huge-security-problem-keelty/680208.

National League for Democracy Membership and others (NLD) (2011) Interviews with author. National League for Democracy Headquarters, Yangon, Myanmar, 21–28 July 2011.

People's Republic of China (PRC) (2011) *China's Foreign Aid* (Beijing: Information Office of the State Council).

Qing, D., Lansdowne, H. and Adams P. (2013) 'The Exploding Balloon: Environmental Costs of China's Participation in Global Capitalism' in G. Wu (ed.), *China's Challenges to Human Security: Foreign Relations and Global Implications*, 164–192 (Oxford: Routledge).

Teitt, S. (2008) *China and the Responsibility to Protect* (Brisbane: Asia-Pacific Center for the Responsibility to Protect).

Terada, T. (2011) 'ASEAN and Human Security: Crisis-Driven Explanation' *Global Institute for Asian Regional Integration (GIARI) Working Paper*, Vol. 2010-E-5.

Thakur, R.C. and Newman, E. (eds) (2004) *Broadening Asia's Security Discourse and Agenda: Political, Social, and Environmental Perspectives* (Tokyo: United Nations University Press).

United Nations Development Programme (UNDP) (2013) *National Human Development Reports for China*, http://hdrstats.undp.org/en/countries/profiles/CHN.html.

Wu, G. (2013) *China's Challenges to Human Security: Foreign Relations and Global Implications* (Oxford: Routledge).

Index

O

Printed and bound by CPI Group (UK) Ltd, Croydon, CR0 4YY